GET
IT
DONE

GET
IT
DONE

SURPRISING LESSONS FROM
THE SCIENCE OF MOTIVATION

Ayelet Fishbach

Little, Brown Spark
New York Boston London

Little, Brown Spark
Hachette Book Group
1290 Avenue of the Americas, New York, NY 10104
littlebrownspark.com

First Edition: January 2022

Little, Brown Spark is an imprint of Little, Brown and Company, a division of Hachette Book Group, Inc. The Little, Brown Spark name and logo are trademarks of Hachette Book Group, Inc.

The publisher is not responsible for websites (or their content) that are not owned by the publisher.

The Hachette Speakers Bureau provides a wide range of authors for speaking events. To find out more, go to hachettespeakersbureau.com or call (866) 376-6591.

ISBN 9780316538343 (hc) / 9780316435895 (international tpb)
Library of Congress Control Number: 2021941894

Printing 2, 2022

LSC-C

Printed in the United States of America

To Alon, Maya, Shira, and Tomer

CONTENTS

CONTENTS

GET
IT
DONE

INTRODUCTION

IN RUDOLF RASPE'S 1785 stories, *The Adventures of Baron Münch-hausen*, the fictional baron tells many imaginative tales of his extreme resourcefulness. In one story, he accidentally tosses his hatchet all the way to the moon and uses quick-growing beans to grow a stalk tall enough that he can climb to the moon and retrieve it. In another, he fights a crocodile and a lion, surviving because he ducks just in time for the lion to lunge into the crocodile's mouth. And in yet another tale, he sticks his arm down a wolf's throat, grabs onto the animal's tail, and turns it inside out like a glove.

In perhaps the best-known story, Baron Munchausen is riding his horse when he finds himself stuck in a large swamp. As the horse sinks deeper into the bog, the baron glances around, trying to figure out how to get out of this latest precarious situation. He comes up with a somewhat peculiar solution. The baron grabs himself by his pigtail, a long braid and a common hairstyle for men at the time, and pulls himself and the horse out of the swamp by his own hair.

Pulling yourself up by your own hair, even if only metaphorically, seems impossible. But, with exception to the laws of physics the baron breaks, we've all found ourselves in similar situations. You may have pulled yourself out of bed this morning or calmed yourself down during a heated debate. Maybe you pulled yourself out of a party when you knew you'd had one drink too many. You surely had to pull yourself through major life changes, as when you moved to a new town, when you launched your career, and when you started or ended a relationship. The baron's story about pulling himself out of the muck has become an allegory for many of the moments when we have to motivate ourselves.

Like yours, my life has involved a fair amount of pulling. I grew up in an Israeli kibbutz—a communal society where private property was frowned upon and money was considered dirty...and not only because it touched many hands. As part of the ideology, I shared my property, which included my room, toys, and clothes, with the other children my age, even though we weren't family. Now I'm a professor in the business school at the University of Chicago, which prides itself on embracing a capitalist ideology, including the fundamental value assigned to personal property. During my first week at the university, a colleague politely declined my request to borrow his book, kindly suggesting that professors should own books rather than borrow them. That was a shocking moment for me. I realized I'd need to do a good amount of pulling to switch so drastically from the mind-set I grew up with to the mind-set my new country and my new coworkers valued.

Yet I had already pulled myself to get there. My community cherished agriculture and manual work more than education. A college degree was considered the right move mainly if you were a bright man seeking to learn something useful. I'm not a man and didn't think I was particularly bright. I also wanted to study psychology, which wouldn't be considered useful to my kibbutz. People in my community encouraged me to learn to drive a tractor (which I stubbornly resisted) and suggested I study engineering or architecture. Usually, the kibbutz would pay for your education if you spent one year working in the community. I had no interest in the type of work they encouraged me to do, so I moved to the big city. I worked in a bakery, cleaned houses, and saved money to study psychology at Tel Aviv University. I had to pull myself to move out on my own, to work long and arduous hours, and to do well in school.

Fast forward, and here I am. My husband and I pulled ourselves when we moved to the US. We pulled ourselves when we applied to be citizens. We pulled ourselves through raising three wonderful children. And we continue to pull ourselves toward other, smaller goals every day: keeping the kitchen clean, walking our dog, helping our young son study, and so on.

Getting anywhere, as well as sustaining the things you cherish in life, requires a great deal of pulling. If you weren't pulling, you would barely be moving at all. I write this book in the midst of the 2020 pandemic. Like most people, I worry, get distracted, and struggle to stay motivated. Over the past several months, I've learned to take nothing for granted, be it my health, my job, my children's education, or meeting a friend for coffee. And even though I love my job, I find it harder to stay motivated. To write about self-motivation, I start by motivating myself to write.

So how do you motivate yourself? The short answer is by changing your circumstances.

If you ever put a psychologist, a sociologist, and an economist in one room, that basic principle—changing behavior by modifying the situation in which it occurs—might be the one truth they'll agree on (and you should expect heated arguments on just about everything else). This principle is fundamental to behavioral science. It also underlies many of the discoveries in the science of motivation.

Motivation science is relatively young. It was born just a few decades ago. But it has been growing exponentially, as has public interest in how circumstances enable personal growth. We most often use insights from motivation science to motivate others. Companies set organizational goals to motivate employees to work harder, teachers give students feedback on their progress to motivate them to keep going, health care workers send messages that motivate people to follow medical advice, and energy companies that care about the environment share information about others' low energy use to increase energy conservation. We've developed valuable insights into the processes of motivating others, be it our students, coworkers, clients, or fellow citizens.

But we can also use these insights to motivate ourselves.

You modify your own behavior by modifying the situation in which it occurs. You might, for example, know that you'll eat whatever is in sight when you're hungry. So if you want to start eating better, a good solution would be to fill up your fridge with fresh fruits and veggies. Another way would be to tell your family that you want to eat healthily so they hold you accountable next time you reach for a doughnut. You could also mentally change the meaning of a creamy doughnut from "delicious" to "detrimental." These very different strategies (more about them later) have one thing in common: they change your circumstances. Filling your fridge with veggies changes the options you have when you're reaching for a snack. Telling your family you want to eat better changes who you're accountable to. And telling yourself that doughnuts are "detrimental" changes your mental image of that fluffy fried dough.

In this book, I'll make the scientific case for how you can use insights from motivation science to guide and own your desires, rather than be subject to them. I'll share with you the four essential ingredients in successful behavior change.

First, you need to choose a goal. Whether you set your mind to finding romance or doing a handstand, and whether you're an expert or a novice, you start by marking a destination. Second, you need to sustain your motivation as you move from here to there. You monitor your progress by soliciting feedback on your performance, both positive and negative, and by looking back at what you've achieved as well as forward at what is still left to do. Third, you must learn to juggle multiple goals. Other goals and desires will pull you in opposite directions. You need to learn to manage these goals, set priorities, and find the right balance. Finally, you'll learn to leverage social support.

It's hard to reach your goals by yourself and even harder when certain people stand in your way. On the other hand, when you let others help you, pursuing your goal gets easier.

Knowing these ingredients is just one step. You also have to figure out which ingredient is missing from your recipe for success. You don't need to add salt to a dish that's missing pepper, so, for example, gathering social support (which I discuss in Part IV) when you already feel supported won't increase your motivation. Your problem might instead be that you're feeling unenthusiastic about your goal. You'll want to find a path to success that maximizes your intrinsic motivation (which we'll talk about in Chapter 4).

The four parts of this book each grapple with one ingredient in the recipe. Part I focuses on how to set a goal that's powerful and specific enough (but not too specific) to pull you toward the finish line. Part II will teach you how to keep your momentum going, through the right way to monitor your progress and avoiding the "middle problem." Part III explains how to best juggle multiple goals, describing which to prioritize and when. Finally, Part IV teaches you how to both use and help the people in your life as you all try to reach your goals.

Bearing in mind that our problems are diverse and can't be solved with a single strategy, this book invites you to design your own journey of behavior change and choose the strategies that are right for you under your unique circumstances. At the end of each chapter, I've listed questions to guide you as you create your own path to change. As you answer these questions for yourself, think about the goals you wish to achieve, but also keep in mind your specific circumstances, including both opportunities and obstacles.

This book is an invitation to apply the principles of motivation science to yourself. You'll learn about the goal systems we mentally create, about how different types of goals affect the way you approach them, and about where and when people commonly get stuck. But most critically, you'll learn how to pull yourself out of the muck by your own hair.

Part I

CHOOSE YOUR GOAL

On May 10, 1996, twenty-three climbers arrived at the summit of Mount Everest. They must have felt on top of the world, literally and figuratively, as they looked out and saw a hundred miles in any direction. Their elation, however, didn't last long. The guides running the expedition grew increasingly worried as their party took too long to get to the top. Though they knew they'd have to start climbing back down by 2 p.m. to ensure a safe return, by the time everyone made it to the summit and was able to enjoy the view, it was four o'clock. Still, the guides thought, maybe it'd be okay. But soon after they started their descent, the weather took a turn. The skies went dark, the wind picked up, and the snow began to fall. The climbers were now facing an extremely risky journey. Not only were they likely to be stuck on the mountain in subzero temperatures overnight, they were running out of supplemental oxygen. It's extremely difficult to breathe at the high altitude of Mount Everest's summit, nearly nine thousand meters above sea level.

As the blizzard became a whiteout, at 9 p.m. a group of climbers decided to stop for the night and huddle together to wait for a break in the storm. The wind chill registered 100 degrees below zero and the climbers felt as if their eyelids were frozen together. Many lost hope that they'd make it back to camp alive.

When the weather cleared and rescue missions were able to search, five of the group members were found either dead or so badly injured that they wouldn't make it back to the base of the mountain. Other expeditions also lost people—in total, eight climbers who were at or near Everest's summit when the storm started died. The night of May 10, 1996, continues to mark one of the biggest tragedies to happen on Everest. This night also illustrates the power, at times detrimental, of holding a goal.

Reaching Mount Everest's peak was these mountaineers' ultimate goal. Even when they felt so exhausted they could barely move, two of the 1996 climbers continued toward Everest's summit instead of turning around. What made the idea of summiting Mount Everest so powerful that they were willing to pay for it with their lives?

The goal to reach Everest's summit encapsulates all elements of setting a powerfully motivating goal. First, climbing Mount Everest is not a proxy or a means to another goal. Because mountain climbers want only to reach that summit, not to reach the summit to be qualified for another challenge, they frame their goal as an end and not a means to an end, thus making it feel less like a chore. Second, reaching the summit is a specific goal with uncertain success. That is, you know whether or not you've achieved it, just not whether or not you *will* achieve it. There's a decent chance you'll fail, and unless you try, you won't know. This makes the goal more attractive. Third, there are great incentives for making it to the top. If you live to tell the tale, it's a story just about anyone would want to hear. Fourth, it's an intrinsic goal—even if no one else cared that you'd topped Everest, you'd feel endlessly proud of yourself.

We can implement these principles in setting powerful goals for ourselves, while not neglecting the other lesson Mount Everest has taught us: we need to choose our goals wisely. Certain goals put our lives at risk. These goals are set without regard to our circumstances and abilities. They pull us in the wrong direction. Rather than advancing our emotional and physical well-being, such goals blind us to dangers in their path. Take extreme diets, injury-causing sport, or sticking with an unhealthy relationship. Goals are powerful tools and, as such, they should be handled with care. We want to set powerful goals, but only after carefully considering whether they're right for us.

Powerful goals have the ability to pull us toward our ultimate desires, energizing us to put in the work we need to do to get there. Part I of this book will unpack the features of a powerful goal: that it feels exciting and not like a chore (Chapter 1), that it's specific and quantifiable ("how much" or "how fast," Chapter 2), that it includes incentives that will keep you interested along the way (Chapter 3), and that it harnesses the power of intrinsic motivation (Chapter 4).

1

GOALS AREN'T CHORES

WHEN ALICE ASKED, "WOULD you tell me, please, which way I ought to go from here?" the Cheshire Cat replied, "That depends a good deal on where you want to get to."

This quote from Lewis Carroll's famous children's book *Alice's Adventures in Wonderland* reminds me of a popular exercise in my management class. Each year, I ask teams of business students to imagine that they're passengers on a floatplane that has just crashed. Each team must decide which items to salvage from the plane to ensure that they'll survive in the wild. There are two approaches my students could take: they could either choose items, like matches and an ax, that will allow them to set up camp and wait until help arrives; or they could choose items, like a compass and a navigation book, that would allow them to leave and search for help. Too often, teams jump into the task of sorting and selecting items without first deciding on their objective: take off or stay put. Not knowing their goal, they make decisions that contradict each other, resulting in an eclectic array of items that serve opposite purposes. In the end, they don't get anywhere.

While the missteps of Alice and my students may seem obvious from a distance, many of us make their same mistake. If you don't select a goal to point you in a specific direction, you're likely to move in circles. You'll do whatever is at the forefront of your mind, even if it contradicts other actions you might have taken just moments ago. You might decide to go on a diet the same day you sign up for a macaron-making class, or you'll open a savings account while also taking out a loan for a new car.

The goals we set are powerful motivational tools. A goal doesn't just point you in a specific direction, it also pulls you in that direction. Once you set a goal, it mobilizes your resources toward achieving it. You'll spend mental and physical effort, money, time, and your social capital. Consider deciding to become a parent or to change your career. These goals require continuous effort invested over a long period of time. Other goals, like trying to eat more healthily or exercise more, require willpower and self-control. Even goals that seem straightforward—wouldn't it be fun to adopt a puppy?—might over time prove to be costly. And yet, despite the cost, once a goal is set, you're willing to expend resources and pay the price.

Powerful goals feel worth the price tag—they pull you toward your greatest wish. And in order to pull you, a goal has to feel more like an aspiration and less like a chore. For example, reaching the summit of Mount Everest is an aspiration, but training for it seems like a chore. Similarly, studying law describes an aspiration, but studying for the bar exam might seem like a chore. And while becoming a parent is an aspiration, doing so because you fear regretting a decision to remain childless makes it seem more like a chore. These examples illustrate three traps in setting and framing a goal: framing it as a means to another goal instead of the end goal itself, setting a goal that is too specific or concrete instead of an abstract goal, and setting a goal in terms of something you wish to avoid rather than something you wish to approach. Falling into any of these three traps will diminish the power of your goals.

SET GOALS, NOT MEANS

When it comes to setting a goal that feels like an aspiration and not a chore, the old adage to "keep your eyes on the prize" holds true. A powerful goal defines a desirable state, not the means to get there.

Consider dining out. You might not hesitate to order a $12 cocktail at a restaurant, but you'd think twice, and even drive around the block a few times, before paying the same amount for valet parking. You don't like paying for parking because parking is, by definition, a means—it gets you into the restaurant and in front of the dinner plate you'd set your sights on. Similarly, shipping and gift-wrapping fees are a means to the goal of getting your friend the perfect birthday present and, indeed, we dislike paying these fees. Many of us would rather pay a little extra for the gift and earn free delivery than pay a shipping fee. In general, we want to invest our resources in the goal, not in the means. And because companies know we dislike paying for means, many online stores will include shipping costs in the product price, giving the impression that shipping is free.

This aversion to investing in means can have surprising effects, as Franklin Shaddy and I found. An experiment we conducted with our MBA students showed us that people are willing to spend more overall to avoid spending *anything* on a means (as many of us do to avoid shipping fees). In our experiment, we auctioned an autographed book by the prominent economist Richard Thaler, which is something our MBA students would treasure. The average bid for the book was $23. We next auctioned a tote bag, which contained the same autographed book, to another, similarly enthusiastic group of students. While these students were technically bidding on a bag, their deal was economically superior given that the highest bidder would win both a bag and a book. To our surprise, the average bidder was willing to pay only $12, significantly less than what bidders were willing to pay for the book alone. In economics terms, the value of the tote bag was negative, meaning that throwing it in decreased the value of the deal.

The reason for this surprising result? It didn't feel right to pay that much for a bag whose only function was to carry a free book. People don't want to invest in means.

When you're setting goals, remember this lesson and choose to define the goal in terms of benefits rather than costs. It's better to set your goal as "finding a job" rather than "applying for a job," or as "owning a house" instead of "saving for a down payment." Finding a job and owning a house are desirable outcomes. Filling out applications and saving for a down payment are the costly means needed to achieve these outcomes. Achieving a goal is exciting; completing the means is a chore.

SET ABSTRACT GOALS

Imagine you're trying to find a new job. You could describe this goal as "exploring career opportunities" or as "reading job postings and submitting applications." These are two different descriptions of the same goal. "Reading job postings" is a concrete description that explains how you explore career opportunities, and "exploring career opportunities" is an abstract description that explains why you read job postings. But while they describe the same goal, one description is more motivating than the other. The concrete description emphasizes actions, thus turning the goal into a chore. The abstract description, however, emphasizes the meaning behind those actions.

More abstract goals capture the purpose behind an action, describing what you're trying to achieve rather than the actions you'll take to achieve it. And while an abstract goal identifies the purpose of a goal, a concrete goal only identifies the path to get there; it's a means.

Cultivating an abstract mind-set while pursuing a goal can make any goal seem less like a chore. If you think about your day-to-day life in the abstract—that is, you focus on the purpose and meaning of your actions—your orientation toward specific goals will also be more abstract. To test this principle, psychologist Kentaro Fujita and his colleagues assigned people to an abstract or concrete mind-set by having them answer a series of "why" (abstract) or "how" (concrete) questions. For example, they answered "Why do you maintain good physical health?" or "How do you maintain good physical health?" After answering several such questions, the research participants started to think about their goals either more abstractly or more concretely, depending on the series of questions they'd answered. Those who answered a series of "why" questions were more motivated to channel resources to their goals. They worked harder. So, for instance, they exercised more physical effort when holding a handgrip.

There is, of course, a downside. When you make a goal *too* abstract, it becomes vague. It may not be linked to a specific set of actions and is therefore difficult to actively pursue. "Explore new career opportunities," for instance, is miles better than "be successful." Similarly, "start going to church" is better than "be morally pure." There are no clear or specific means by which we should pursue success or, if it's your thing, moral purity, rendering these goals ineffective. When there's no clear path to get from point A to point B, people revert to fantasizing about their goals instead of taking action toward achieving them.

When we fantasize, we imagine what our lives will look like once we achieve our goal. We envision how great it will feel to wear that graduation gown, medal, or wedding dress. But fantasizing doesn't generate action. Fantasizing about graduating with honors won't necessarily make you study harder; fantasizing about coming first in a 5K won't make you run more; and fantasizing about walking down the aisle won't make you set up more dates.

Indeed, in one study, the psychologists Gabriel Oettingen and Thomas Wadden had weight watchers rate their expectations (how likely they were to lose weight) and how much they fantasized about weight loss at the beginning of a weight loss program. A year later, those who had high expectations lost more weight than those with low expectations, but those who fantasized more didn't. Those who fantasized actually lost *less* weight.

Fantasies might feel good, but they're largely ineffective as a motivational tool. And when abstract goals become too abstract, they're at risk of turning into fantasies that substitute for action. Optimally abstract goals describe a purpose without losing sight of the actions you need to take to reach them ("improve my mental health" is better than "be happy"). You should immediately know what to do next (start therapy, for example). They allow you to contrast your current state with where you want to be so that you can connect the dots from here to there by making an action plan.

"DO" VERSUS "DO NOT" GOALS

When dining out, is it better to define your goal as eating healthily or as avoiding unhealthy food? When playing a sport, should you define your goal as winning or as not losing? "Do" goals, also known as "approach" goals because they identify a desirable state that we're approaching, pull us toward eating healthily or playing well to win the game. "Do not" goals, also known as avoidance goals, push us away from a state we wish to avoid. These are essentially "anti-goals."

When we define our goals as approach goals, we move toward those goals (decreasing the gap between us and our desires). When we define them as avoidance goals, we move away from anti-goals (widening the gap between us and the outcomes we want to avoid).

Just as framing your goal as a means or as too concrete is likely to make your goal feel like a chore, framing it as an anti-goal is likely to do the same. If you want to win your school's championship basketball game, the "approach" frame of winning the game is more enticing than the "avoidance" frame of not losing the game.

The strongest case against setting avoidance goals comes from research on thought suppression. Consider the goal to get something off your mind. You might try to repress an unpleasant argument at the office, stop obsessing about your ex, or get rid of an annoying tune that's stuck in your head. Recently, my son has been practicing his violin day and night. His teacher has him playing Suzuki, a Japanese composer and teacher whose music is exceedingly upbeat. As wonderful as it is to hear my son's musical skill grow, once the practice is over, I would be thrilled to get those happy songs out of my head.

My struggle reminds me of a classic experiment by Daniel Wegner. Wegner's experiment was quite simple: He gathered a group of participants and asked them "to not think about white bears." And, of course, once he'd put the idea of white bears in their heads, they couldn't not think about them. (Can you not think about those bears?) Whether it's your colleague, an ex, or a white bear you want to stop thinking about, your attempt to suppress your thoughts is an avoidance goal. You wish to move away from an anti-goal state of thinking about something unpleasant or forbidden.

Suppression is notoriously hard to do. The more you're determined to not think about something, the more you'll find yourself obsessing over it. A deliberate attempt to suppress certain thoughts makes them more likely to surface. Part of the reason for this is that, to determine whether you've successfully suppressed a thought, you need to ask yourself whether you're still thinking it. And each time you check, the mere act of checking brings the forbidden thought back to your mind. The irony of this phenomenon is why it came to be called "ironic mental control." Suppression is also a challenge simply because it's not much fun. Suppression is a chore.

While avoidance goals are more like chores, and therefore tend to be less powerful, they aren't always ineffective in motivating action. For certain people and in certain situations, avoidance goals are effective.

Some people—let's call them "approachers"—are particularly prone to responding more strongly to approach goals. When they play a game, they hope to win. In psychological terms, they have a strong Behavioral Approach System (BAS). Other people—let's call them "avoiders"—can tolerate and be responsive to avoidance goals. When they play a game, they hope not to lose. Therefore, in psychological terms, they have a strong Behavioral Inhibition (or avoidance) System (BIS). To figure out whether you're an approacher or an avoider, ask yourself whether you agree more with the statements "When I want something, I usually go all-out to get it" and "When I see an opportunity for something I like, I get excited right away" or the statements "I worry about making mistakes" and "Criticism or scolding hurts me quite a bit." If you go all-out, you're an approacher. If you fear mistakes and criticism, you're an avoider.

Sometimes, the situation determines whether people are focused on approach goals or avoidance goals. When people feel they're in power, they're more motivated by approach goals. So if you're the boss, you probably want people to like you. This is an approach goal. But when you're the intern, you want to make sure you're not disliked. This is an avoidance goal.

For avoiders, or for those in situations that predispose us to avoid, avoidance goals work just fine at motivating action. Behaviorists who study motivation using rodents and birds claim that "negative reinforcement" (not to be confused with punishment) accounts for the appeal of moving away from an anti-goal; that is, taking actions that remove negative outcomes. In the 1940s, psychologist B. F. Skinner created a "Skinner Box" for the rats he was using to study avoidance. The floor of the box was covered in an electric grid that would shock the rats no matter where they stood. As they moved about the box, trying to get away from the electricity, the rats would accidentally knock into a lever that would shut the grid down. Over time, the rats learned they could go directly to the lever to stop the shock.

And this kind of learning doesn't just happen with rats. After a painful sunburn, we humans learn to use sunscreen next time we're at the beach. The fear of injury has also taught us to buckle our seat belts in the car and wear a helmet when we ride our bikes, even if we were never involved in an accident. These activities are motivated by avoidance goals and are negatively reinforced. By pursuing them, you avoid negative outcomes.

Avoidance goals are particularly powerful in the context of preventing harm and escaping danger. When motivating yourself to apply sunscreen, it feels right to set your goal as avoiding sunburn more than as approaching healthy skin. When motivating wearing a helmet, it feels right to set your goal as avoiding injury more than as keeping your skull intact.

In determining how to frame your goals, you could think about the "fit" (a notion that suggests that certain goals match certain orientations). For instance, safety goals fit the orientation of moving away from danger. In contrast, when you decide to start dating, it's more fitting to set your goal as moving toward romance than as avoiding rejection.

The psychologist Tory Higgins made a distinction between "ought" and "ideal" goals to explain when avoidance versus approach framing provides a better fit. Ought goals include everything you need to do, like being safe by locking your door and being responsible by taking care of your family. Ideal goals include everything you hope or aspire to do but don't necessarily feel you must do. These include reading this book or getting a business degree. When pursuing an ought goal, it's fitting to avoid losses. When pursuing an ideal goal, it is more fitting to approach gains. For example, when your goal is to keep yourself safe (an ought), you can motivate yourself by defining your goal as avoiding damage to yourself or your property. When pursuing a goal to join a choir (an ideal, for many), you can motivate yourself by defining your goal as mastering a certain vocal range.

Also, while approach goals are generally more exciting, avoidance goals have the advantage of seeming more urgent. To illustrate, try completing these sentences:

A. "I must prevent [enter your response]."

B. "I want to achieve [enter your response]."

Now compare A to B. The upper, avoidance goal likely seems more urgent but less pleasant. The lower goal seems more pleasant and easier to stick with in the long run. So if you set your goal as "not losing," you might believe it's more urgent than if you set it as "winning." You'll respond more quickly to the not-losing goal, but you'd have more endurance in the long run to stick with your goal to win.

Finally, pursuing approach and avoidance goals feels different. Successfully pursuing an approach goal will make you feel happy, proud, and eager. Failing to pursue an approach goal will result in feeling sad and depressed. For example, when I got a promotion at work, I felt proud. In contrast, successfully pursuing an avoidance goal makes you feel relieved, calm, and relaxed. Failing to pursue an avoidance goal will result in anxiety, fear, and guilt. For example, when I went for my mammogram this year (an ought goal with avoidance framing to not get breast cancer), I was relieved to get my negative results.

Motivation science teaches us that our feelings and emotions are highly instrumental. They provide feedback on goals. They serve as the sensory system for motivation. When you feel good, you know you're making progress on your goal, and when you feel bad, you know you're falling behind. This feedback is immediate and easy to understand.

Feelings also serve as an extra motivator, or a mini-goal, in the process of achieving your overall goal. When we feel happy or relieved, those emotions act as a reward. Similarly, negative emotions like anxiety or guilt serve as punishment. So you're motivated to pursue a goal not only because you want to achieve it, but also because achieving it—or merely making progress—feels good and failing to do so feels bad. In this way, emotions are a powerful motivator. You even use your emotions to incentivize yourself. You decide to feel good only at the "right" time. If you learn you're about to land a job offer, you suppress your happiness until the offer is official. You say you don't want to jinx it, but in reality, you wait for the "right" time to feel good about it (more on incentives in Chapter 3).

Overall, a nuanced understanding of the approach/avoidance distinction implies that, once you realize which goal type is more effective for you and your situation, you can best set your goal. Absent such personalization, the general rule is that, for many of us under most circumstances, defining our goals as approaching a state of success and good health is more motivating than avoiding failure and sickness. You should therefore always consider setting goals in terms of approach ("do it") rather than avoidance ("don't do it") and adjust from there.

QUESTIONS TO ASK YOURSELF

Goals are powerful. Once they're set, you're eager to reach them. Your goals modify your behavior; they pull you. You should therefore not neglect to set your goals. But how you set your goals will determine their power. Your goals become less effective when, rather than feeling excited by them, you see them as chores. To set goals that aren't chores, you can start by asking yourself the following questions:

1. Have you set your goals and are these the right goals for you? Do your goals fit the person you are and are they the best for the person you hope to become? You want to get the content of your goals right.
2. How do you define your goals to yourself? Can you make them feel more exciting by focusing on what you're trying to achieve, rather than on the means you take to get there?
3. Are your goals optimally abstract so that you don't lose sight of where you're going as well as exactly how you'll get there?
4. Can you define your goals in terms of approaching a state of physical and mental comfort instead of avoiding an undesirable state of discomfort? You'll likely be more motivated with an approach goal, though you might feel it's more urgent to avoid an anti-goal.

2

PUT A NUMBER ON IT

EVERY TIME SOMEONE BOOTS up a Fitbit, the device loads a 10,000-step daily goal. At this point, it's commonly agreed that walking 10,000 steps per day is best for your health. But where did that number come from?

Though we may think that decades of rigorous study went into finding the exact number of steps that would keep us fit, the truth is less scientific. Our daily step target originally came from ads for a Japanese pedometer.

In the 1960s, Japan was preparing to host the 1964 Olympics. With excitement about athletes coming to Tokyo from all over the world, Japanese people started talking and thinking more about physical fitness. They realized that exercise was a good way to stave off diseases like hypertension, diabetes, and stroke, all of which were problems for the Japanese at that time. Given that walking was the easiest way to get exercise, since it required no special equipment and could easily be done with friends or family, the Japanese started forming popular walking groups.

Around the same time, a Japanese professor of health science decided that 10,000 steps per day would be ideal and invented a pedometer to help people track their steps. He named it Manpo-kei, which translates in English to "10,000-step meter." Ads for the pedometer happily exclaimed, "Let's walk 10,000 steps a day!"

More than fifty years later, Japan has one of the healthiest populations in the world, and we still use 10,000 steps as a guide for daily movement.

The goal to start walking was of course important, but perhaps most important both to Japan's health and the sale of pedometers was the professor's choice to put a number on that goal. As a rule, goals, like recipes, work best if you list the exact quantities. "Walk 10,000 steps a day" is better than "walk a lot." And while your goal might be to start running, a better goal would set a target such as running the Chicago Marathon in under five hours.

Numerical targets usually come in two forms: how much (save $10,000) and how soon (within one year). Not only do these targets have a long history in motivation science—we've been somewhat obsessed with studying their generally positive impact—but targets are also popular in everyday conversation about goals. You refer to them so often that you might not even realize when you're setting a goal versus a target. You might say, for example, that your goal is to save $10,000. But really, your goal is to save money and $10,000 is merely your target.

The reason targets are common is quite obvious: they work. Targets pull you toward a goal and make it easier to monitor progress. They even tell you when to quit or slow down. Targets motivate us because, once they're set, we care deeply about meeting these exact numbers. If you set your target at saving $10,000, you'll be disappointed if you "only" save $9,900. On the other hand, saving $10,100 won't make you much happier than saving exactly $10,000. A hundred dollars matters immensely if you haven't yet hit your target, and less so when you have. In general, once a target has been set, you see anything below it as a loss, which you care deeply to avoid. In contrast, anything above the set target is a gain, which is nice to have but not necessary for your peace of mind.

This is a principle psychologists Daniel Kahneman and Amos Tversky termed "loss-aversion." As humans, we're greatly disappointed and sometimes even angry when we feel we've missed out on something, but we care less when we've gained a bit more than we expected. By the loss-aversion principle, you'll work harder to meet your target than to exceed it.

Take marathon runners, for example. Ultimately, their goal is to finish the race as quickly as possible. Yet runners often like to set a specific time target—finishing the race in less than four hours is considered a real accomplishment. Analyzing data from about ten million runners, one study found that many more people finish the race just under their set target time than just over their target time (more people finish in 3:59 hours rather than 4:01 hours, for example). As they get closer and closer to the finish line, realizing they have a good chance of beating their target time, runners push harder and faster. So, many marathoners cross the line just under the time they've set for themselves, having run their hardest in the last minutes to ensure that they'll make it.

Understanding this psychology, clever marketers have devised awards programs to capitalize on our desire to hit a set target. A study examining how people behave when they've nearly earned elite status in a frequent flyer program, which awards points for each flight, found that people took more and more flights with the airline as they got closer to gaining the airline's top status. Yet once they hit the 100,000 miles per year they needed to reach the program's Tier 1 ranking, their frequency of flights slowed down. This happens because after we reach a target, we feel as if we've been partially "reset." Earning airline miles seems more important if it helps you reach your target status, but less important if you're only starting to accumulate miles toward achieving this status the following year. And once you've bested a four-hour marathon, you may relax your running regimen until your next marathon is in sight.

Beyond pulling us toward them, targets also motivate us by helping us evaluate our progress. The earliest models of goal pursuit, developed in the 1960s, described pursuing a goal as a process of closing a discrepancy toward a numerical target. George Miller, one of the founders of cognitive psychology, proposed a model he named "TOTE." This somewhat mechanistic model of motivation assumes that once a target has been set, the person "Tests," or evaluates, the distance to it. Next the person "Operates," that is, pursues the goal. Then another "Test" is performed to determine the distance to the target. This loop of Test-Operate-Test keeps going until the goal is achieved, and the person "Exits" pursuing it (hence "TOTE"). Years later, this model of goal pursuit is still popular (more about it in Chapter 5), and it makes a simple point: once we set a target, we have to determine how far we are from completing it and then mobilize efforts to eliminate the gap.

Now that you understand the power of targets, you'll want to set them wisely. Motivation science tells us that a good target is challenging, measurable, actionable, and self-set.

CHALLENGING TARGETS

The first ingredient in setting an effective target is to make it somewhat optimistic. And when left to our own devices, we naturally tend to set optimistic targets. If you're like most people, you're currently working on something you were planning to finish yesterday (or last month). Your optimism planned to accomplish more by now. That's not necessarily bad.

There are two main reasons we're optimistic, believing we'll accomplish more and sooner than what's realistically possible. One is that we're imperfect planners. The "planning fallacy" is the tendency to underestimate the time and resources it'll take to do just about anything. Whether you plan to file your tax return early this year or complete your home renovation within your budget, realistically, these plans probably won't become reality. Even large construction projects, which you'd assume involve careful planning, are frequently subject to the planning fallacy. When Danish architect Jørn Utzon started working on the now-famous Sydney Opera House in 1959, he expected it to take no more than four years and cost $7 million. Instead, Utzon resigned in frustration in 1966 with the building already years late and so over budget that he couldn't pay his workers. A new architect took charge, but still the opera house wasn't finished until 1973, more than ten years over deadline and at a cost of $102 million.

Interestingly, the planning fallacy persists even when people are reminded that they've made similar mistakes in the past. Despite telling yourself that you've learned your lesson, you'll likely still procrastinate on next year's taxes or underestimate the cost of future home renovations.

Optimism caused by the planning fallacy is a mistake you'd wish to correct. It happens because when budgeting time and money, people tend to focus on the task at hand while neglecting all other demands on their resources. Clearly, we'd all be able to file our taxes next February if that were the only thing we needed to do that month. But once we add up everything else that needs to happen—the birthday parties, soccer games, dance recitals, dinner parties, and doctors' appointments—all that seemingly free time is no longer free.

The second explanation for optimism points to the strategic reasons we set overly optimistic targets. You may set optimistic goal targets to impress someone, to land a contract with someone, or (most central to our discussion) to motivate yourself.

People set optimistic predictions to pre-commit themselves to act. To the extent that many of us intuitively realize the power of numerical targets, we intentionally set them a bit too optimistically to challenge ourselves. This happened when Dan Ariely, at the time a business professor at MIT, offered his students an unusual freedom. While business students typically expect their teacher to give strict deadlines for papers written during the semester, students in Ariely's course were offered the ability to set their own deadlines. To pass the class, they needed to write three short papers before the end of term. They could either set deadlines for each paper throughout the class or choose to have no deadlines and hand their papers in whenever they wanted. Most students chose to create deadlines, even though they knew that if they missed them they'd be penalized with grade deductions. But they were no fools. The early deadlines helped these students motivate themselves to start on their course work sooner for fear of missing the deadline, while students who didn't set deadlines had no such motivation. We can learn from these students that if the deadline is approaching soon, you'll immediately start working on your task (more on pre-commitment in Chapter 10).

That's also the reason we often choose to challenge ourselves. You might plan to run a marathon in under four hours, knowing that, at this point, you cannot meet this time. Yet the promise of one day running a four-hour marathon motivates you to train harder. When you challenge yourself, you recognize that you're overly optimistic, but you prefer to err on the side of expecting too much rather than too little. You choose to overshoot rather than undershoot to motivate yourself.

Even if you don't commit to a hard deadline, you may set optimistic expectations strategically to get yourself moving. Ying Zhang and I found that people do so in a study similar to that of the students who set their own deadlines. In our study, we asked students to set a soft deadline, merely estimating the time it would take them to complete an assignment rather than committing to finishing by that time. These deadlines were aspirational, as there was no penalty for failing to meet them. But we treated two groups of students differently. Some were told that they were getting a difficult assignment and others were told they were getting an easy one when, in fact, the assignments were the same. To test whether students set early deadlines to motivate themselves, we compared the deadlines set for the "difficult" home-work versus the "easy" homework. We found that those who expected the assignment to be difficult said they would finish it earlier than those expecting it to be easy. This might seem surprising—why would you plan to finish something that's harder sooner?—but it was just what we thought would happen. Those expecting a difficult assignment set early deadlines to motivate themselves to start working sooner.

We also measured the time it actually took students to complete the homework assignment so we could test how expecting something to be more difficult influences both predictions and performance. We found that those who expected a difficult assignment and therefore set earlier deadlines finished the assignment earlier than those who expected an easy assignment. Notably, the planning fallacy prevailed: the average person missed their deadline whether they had set it early or late. Yet merely expecting an assignment to be more difficult leads people to start and finish earlier. It's actually beneficial to expect greater difficulty when it incentivizes you to do your best and start doing so immediately.

Of course, there are times when meeting the deadline is more critical than doing your best, as when the consequences of failing to meet the deadline are worse than those of falling short in the quality of the work. In another study with students completing assignments, we emphasized that they *had* to be accurate in setting their deadline. These people set later deadlines when they expected the homework assignment to be more difficult. When we prioritize an accurate dead-line over a deadline meant to motivate us, we allow more time to complete a difficult task.

The conclusion is that, when setting deadlines and other targets, you have a better chance of motivating yourself to do your best if there are relatively minor consequences for failure to meet the targets. In this case, you set targets to challenge yourself and simply hope to make it.

These challenging targets motivate you because when facing a difficult task, you recruit resources, or energize yourself, to meet the upcoming challenge. The expectation that the task you're facing will be difficult—but not impossible—results in shifting more mental and physical energy to do it. At times, as you face a challenging task, you may feel slightly aroused or excited; you may even notice that your heart beats faster or louder. You feel ready to act. Other times, you get energized, preparing to act, yet all this is happening outside your awareness. Regardless of whether you're conscious of your mental preparation, you're mostly energized when expecting a difficult but not impossible task. Easy tasks don't require preparation, and for impossible ones, you don't bother. You give up.

But when people prepare to meet a medium challenge, their motivational system gets geared up. They're energized. That's a good reason to be optimistic when setting targets.

MEASURABLE TARGETS

The second ingredient in effective target setting is making sure your target is easy to measure. If a target is vague and missing a clear number, it becomes hard to measure and therefore less motivating. Consider the targets to excel at your new job, save enough for retirement, and get enough sleep. These targets are less motivating than completing a work project by the end of the week, saving $10,000 this year, or getting eight hours of sleep every night.

A measurable target provides a meaningful number that's easy to understand and monitor. You know if you've slept eight hours based on when you went to bed and when you woke up, but it's not nearly as easy to tell if you're getting enough sleep without any target number of sleeping hours per day.

Yet in order to be motivating, a target can't be just any number. Consider, for example, setting a daily reading goal. You could set your goal as reading twenty pages a day. Alternatively, you could set it at 6,000 words or 30,000 characters a day. These targets refer to a similar amount of reading, but while the page target is easy to measure, you'd have a difficult time counting 6,000 words to ensure you've read enough—counting would probably take more of your time and energy than reading would! Of course, you might still find it confusing to measure twenty pages, as it requires keeping track of exactly where you started. Consider using a twenty-minute daily reading target instead. When my eight-year-old's teachers set a twenty-minute reading goal, I was thrilled at the target's brilliance. Not only is a timed goal easy for children to understand, it's also easiest for parents to monitor. When creating your own targets, first think through what type of number would serve you best. Is it an amount or a time? And if it is an amount, what's the easiest unit of measurement to monitor?

ACTIONABLE TARGETS

The third ingredient in setting effective targets is making them actionable. Even specific, measurable targets are ineffective if they cannot be easily translated into action. Consider aiming to eat no more than 2,500 calories per day. For many, this is an optimistic goal with a precise measurement. Yet a calorie is hard to measure. When you look at a dessert, you may see chocolate, whipped cream, or caramel, but you don't see calories. You can only vaguely answer the questions: How much food equals 2,500 calories? How many steps does it take to burn 100 calories? How many calories does one need to burn to lose one pound?

As a side note for the curious, it takes on average 2,000 steps to lose 100 calories. You'll need to burn about 3,500 calories to lose one pound. So, in general, if you cut 500 to 1,000 calories a day from your typical diet, you'll lose one to two pounds a week.

Imagine a world in which, instead of calories, food is labeled in terms of daily allowance (similar to what Weight Watchers, now WW, does with SmartPoints—more on that later). Knowing that the Pasta Napoletana at the Cheesecake Factory, which is loaded with sausage, pepperoni, meatballs, bacon, and other rich ingredients, accounts for 99 percent of your daily caloric allowance (2,470 calories out of 2,500 calories per day) might encourage you to instead order Tuscan Chicken—grilled chicken with capers, artichokes, tomatoes, and basil—which is 590 calories and only 23 percent of your daily allowance. Percentage of daily allowance is an actionable target, which encourages healthy eating.

Or imagine a world in which, instead of calories, food is labeled by how much exercise would be needed to burn it off, another method of translating calories into an actionable target. Using this metric, foods are evaluated by the number of steps or other physical activity you'll need to take to burn those calories. For example, one study found a reduction in soda purchases when teenagers were told they would have to jog for fifty minutes to burn off 250 extra calories from a bottle of soda.

Instead, the metrics we currently use for foods provide ample examples of numbers that make less-than-ideal targets because they aren't actionable.

In most countries, food manufacturers are required by law to provide nutrition labels on packaged foods. These labels not only tell you how much fat, sodium, and fiber are in your food but also what percentage of the recommended daily consumption of these nutrients—aka, your target—you will consume with every serving you eat. In theory, you should know exactly what and how much to eat based on these labels. But in practice, nutrition labels don't work. They're too complicated for the average person to figure out how much of the food they should eat as part of a healthy diet. Nutrition labels miss the most critical piece of information: Is this food something you should eat or avoid to meet your healthy eating target? An actionable food label could tell you, instead, whether the food is healthy. In one study, cafeteria items were labeled green (healthy), yellow (less healthy), or red (unhealthy). After these labels were introduced, consumption of red items declined while consumption of green items increased. Indeed, it's easy to set your target as eating 90 percent "green" foods and 10 percent "red" foods.

Other actionable targets include brushing your teeth twice daily, walking 10,000 steps a day, calling your parents twice a week, and reading for twenty minutes every night before bed. These are intuitively meaningful targets. They offer numbers that aren't only easy to understand, but also easy to attain.

SELF-SET TARGETS

The last ingredient in setting effective targets is owning the target by setting it yourself. Most of the time, when trying to motivate ourselves, we default to setting our own targets. But sometimes we transfer target setting to our boss, teacher, physician, or gym instructor, to name a few. While getting the expert's advice is beneficial, the risk in letting others set your targets is that you'll be less committed to them. If your personal trainer asks for ten more push-ups, you might sneakily try to do one or two fewer when she isn't looking. But if you told yourself you'd do ten push-ups, it would be harder to hide.

Another risk with letting others set your goal targets is that you might feel the urge to rebel. Recall a time when you didn't want to do your homework only because your mother asked you to. You experienced what the psychologist Jack Brehm called "psychological reactance": the request, or the order, felt like a threat to your sense of freedom. You felt you had no choice. For avoidance goals, psychological reactance is especially likely because when you're asked *not* to do something (e.g., "Quit smoking, it kills you"), it becomes exactly what you want to do. The result of reactance is that you might act against your best interests because someone else is demanding that you do what's best for you. The goal is rejected only because it didn't come from within.

Reactance often feels like traveling back in time to your teenage years, when you hated doing anything an adult instructed you to do. Self-selecting your goals and setting your own targets means you aren't reverting to situations where others called the shots. Nowadays, I exercise regularly, but I hated high school gym class. The only difference is that, back then, someone else demanded that I exercise. Now that I'm an adult, exercising is my own choice and I'm excited to lace up my sneakers for my daily run.

When consulting the expert (be it your boss or your personal trainer), ask for a set of options to choose from. This will allow you to own your selected targets. Whether it benefits your physical, mental, or financial health, if you own your targets, you make the most of them.

RECOGNIZING MALICIOUS GOAL TARGETS

In the fall of 2016, federal regulators accused Wells Fargo of mass-scale illegal activity. Employees at the bank secretly created millions of unauthorized bank and credit card accounts between 2011 and 2015, allowing the bank to make more money in fees and meet internal sales targets. The federal investigation revealed that Wells Fargo set an extremely difficult internal goal, called the "Gr-eight initiative," to "sell at least eight financial products per customer." Under pressure to meet this ambitious target, employees found themselves behaving unethically.

This story is not uncommon. Despite the clever "Gr-eight" slogan, eight financial tools per customer is a malicious goal target, one that cannot be realistically achieved unless through unethical behavior. In this case, the bank would have been better off had it set a more modest "Awe-some" initiative, calling for employees to sell "some" financial products per customer. This story also demonstrates why it's important to recognize malicious targets in advance. If there's no right way, people will end up taking the wrong way—through unethical actions, unwarranted shortcuts, or unjustified risk. For example, if you believe the only way to get your dream job is by "fixing" your résumé, you should expect it will be hard to stay honest during your job interview. A better way would be to postpone applying until you've earned the skills needed to do well in that role.

Other ambitious goal targets cause you to stretch too thin or work too hard. Recall that the first marathon runner—the ancient Greek messenger who raced from the site of Marathon all the way to Athens to deliver the news of a Greek victory—collapsed and died. In our modern world, athletes are still often overworked and succumb to injuries.

Goal targets are also malicious when they are too narrow and can therefore make you forget about important aspects of the goal you're pursuing. If you reduce your goal to get regular exercise to "walk 10,000 steps a day," you might leave important muscle groups out of your fitness routine. If you reduce your goal to get a good education to "get good grades," you might miss out on important exploration and development of your own, unique expertise.

Further, goal targets with short-term horizons can lead you to neglect your long-term interests. If you stop too soon, you won't get very far. Take cab and rideshare drivers, like those who work for Uber or Lyft, for example. Their ultimate goal is to maximize their earnings by driving people around. Yet drivers often set a daily target for how much money they want to make, and once they hit the target, they quit for the day. That means that drivers finish too early when demand, and the potential income it generates, is high. Drivers who stop working as soon as they hit their daily target miss out on opportunities to make more money on rainy days, when demand temporarily increases. Yet drivers also tend to work too late when demand is low but they haven't yet hit their daily income target. In both cases, focus on the short-term horizon has the potential to harm the driver. Further, when your target is set too close, you might even undo your goal: after meeting your healthy-eating challenge, you'll revert to your old habits.

Other malicious goal targets are unrealistic. Here, the risk is that a failure to meet the impossible target will cause you to give up on the entire goal. In one study, Kosuke Uetake and Nathan Yang found that dieters, whose ultimate goal is to lose weight, often focus on meeting an ambitious daily caloric target. Those who miss their daily target by just a few calories are more likely to get discouraged and may give up on the goal completely. This is what Winona Cochran and Abraham Tesser once termed the "what the hell effect." After missing your target by a few calories, you think "what the hell" and keep eating so you end up missing it by a lot. In the study, dieters who missed their target by a little lost significantly less weight than those who met their daily goal by a similarly small number of calories (say, eating 1,995 calories instead of 2,005). Having just half a piece of avocado toast can sabotage your diet if it means you've missed your daily target and feel that you might as well eat everything in the fridge.

Similarly, the "false-hope syndrome" occurs whenever, due to over-confidence or extreme optimism, people set unrealistic expectations of success. In believing they can meet an impossible target, they set themselves up for failure and ultimately give up on the goal. Inspired by ads presenting before-and-after diet images, many weight watchers, for example, resolve to reach an unrealistic target weight. When they can't whittle their bodies down to their ideal size, they lose their confidence. Overly optimistic goal targets can further lead you to fantasize instead of work to achieve the goal. Fantasizing about being rich or famous won't make you either one. Making plans might.

QUESTIONS TO ASK YOURSELF

This chapter reviews the science of setting goal targets. But once you set a target, don't get discouraged if you fail to meet it. Realizing that the goal target is somewhat arbitrary is often the key to a healthy relationship with our goals. While missing the train by one minute is as bad (and feels worse) than missing it by an hour, missing your annual savings goal by a few dollars, your exercise goal by a few workouts, or your reading challenge by one book doesn't make a big difference in your life as long as you don't let these small discrepancies discourage you from sticking with your goal. Keeping this in mind, set targets by answering the following questions:

1. Can you put a number—how much or how soon—on your goals?
2. Are these goal targets challenging? Easy to measure? Actionable?
3. Have you set these targets yourself or did someone else set them for you?
4. Do these targets work for you? If you're concerned that a goal target might be malicious, you should revise it. You might even revert to the "doing your best" or the "be awe-some" vague target, until you have a better sense of what a realistic, challenging number to attach to your goal might be.

3

INCENTIVES MATTER

WHEN I'M NECK-DEEP in a stack of papers to grade or emails to send, I don't seek out the eerie quiet of my office. Instead, I'm drawn to the bustle of a crowded café. Though it may seem counterintuitive, the environment of a café helps me get more work done. It's crowded and noisy, yes, but it also allows me to reward every complete paper and evaluation with a sip of a warm, spicy chai latte.

While the exorbitant price of café coffee has long been touted as a reason people aren't saving enough money, I suspect that many of us keep coming back to these $5 drinks because they feel like a reward for finishing that report or for simply getting out of bed and going to work. When I need to motivate myself, I have my chai lattes, and when my daughter is studying for her medical school exams, she has bubble tea to keep her going.

No matter your long-term goal, whether it's growing emotionally and intellectually or becoming healthier or wealthier, incentives like an expensive coffee are tangible and immediate. Rewards for your efforts motivate you to stick to your goals in the short run. When we add incentives to our goal—both rewards and punishments—we motivate action by adding a mini, tangible goal of getting the reward or avoiding the punishment. If you want to start running, for example, and have set a target of joining a charity run next month, donations your friends make to the charity in your name incentivize you to lace up your sneakers and finish the run.

Yet, while we may want to use incentives to motivate ourselves, the study of incentives is often focused on how to motivate others to reach their goals. Parents and educators use both rewards and punishments to motivate children to study harder, clean their rooms, eat their vegetables, and do their chores. Governments set incentives to motivate adults to stay healthy and safe. Our fear of getting a speeding ticket, for instance, motivates us to follow the rules of the road, driving no faster than the speed limit.

And when we want people to achieve a goal that serves our own ends, the study of incentives informs us how to motivate others to act in a way that benefits us. When managers set bonuses for employees or sellers set discounts for customers, they intend to motivate them to work harder or to buy certain products. Society at large incentivizes behaviors that promote the welfare of its members. Those who cause harm are fined or jailed and those who do good are publicly recognized and praised. Tax-deductible donations, for example, incentivize giving.

Although most of the incentives studied are not set by the people being incentivized, setting incentives for yourself can be part of your self-motivation arsenal. You can strategically opt in to an existing incentive system that helps you meet your own goals. Alternatively, you can use what we've learned from the study of incentives to reward yourself for making progress toward a goal.

The study of incentives has a long history in psychology and economics. Understanding when and how rewards and punishments work originated in psychology by the behaviorism movement. It started with Pavlov's research with salivating dogs at the end of the nineteenth century and flourished in the mid-twentieth century when radical behaviorists led by B. F. Skinner claimed that external rewards could fully explain our behavior. According to radical behaviorists, if you fully understood the system of incentives within which someone operated in the present and had complete knowledge of their past systems of incentives, you could predict exactly how they would behave. Given that this calculation is awfully complicated, behaviorists studied animals. They asked, for example, what incentives would make a rat run through a maze and a pigeon peck at a colored disk. But make no mistake: they wanted to understand how incentives influence *human* behavior. And while most modern psychologists no longer subscribe to this view of motivation, much of what we know about incentives dates all the way back to behaviorism. More generally, we've learned from behaviorists that to modify behavior, we can start by modifying the situation in which it occurs; no need to change people's personalities (or "blame" their heredity). Incentives, accordingly, modify the situation.

In parallel to psychological research on incentives, the field of economics generated much of the empirical data on how and when monetary incentives work. Economists are far less interested than behaviorists in the impact of food at the end of a rat's maze, but they are curious about money and how it shapes human behavior. And while economic theory states that monetary incentives motivate behavior, the relatively new subfield of behavioral economics has found that this isn't always true. Sometimes, the offer of money doesn't motivate us and can even undermine our motivation. We've learned from behavioral economics research that understanding when incentives fail is key to understanding how incentives work.

REWARD THE RIGHT THING

In the early 1900s, just a few years after scientists discovered that flea-infected rats were responsible for the bubonic plague, Hanoi was facing a major rat problem. The fancy new sewer system that had recently been built in the French colony allowed rats to thrive. And now they were coming to the surface in droves, causing panic about a new wave of the plague. To fight the epidemic of rats, French colonists created a bounty program that paid one cent for each rat killed. At first, the program seemed to be going well. Within a month, tens of thousands of rats were killed every day. One day, just two months after the bounty was set, more than twenty thousand rats met their untimely end at the hands of Hanoi's rat hunters. But to the great surprise of health officials in the city, it seemed the hunters had barely made a dent in Hanoi's rodent problem.

Soon, tailless rats were spotted running around the city—curious given that hunters earned their bounty when they handed in a rat tail. Many hunters, it became clear, were catching rats, cutting off their tails, and setting them loose back into the sewers to breed. Health officials later discovered that more enterprising hunters, who were now making a living off rats, developed farming operations dedicated to breeding them. The bounty program was called off and rat farmers released the thousands of rodents they had bred into the city. In the end, the incentive program resulted in more, not fewer, rats wandering the streets of Hanoi.

This is a particularly salient history lesson on what happens when you reward the wrong thing. It was termed the "cobra effect" after a similar failed program instigated by British colonists to eliminate the cobra populations in India using bounties. As it would happen, in order to have a dead cobra, one needs to have a live cobra first.

Is the lesson here that rewards don't work? On the contrary. Rewards work well enough to get people to farm rats and breed cobras. Clearly, rewards can modify behavior. But if you reward the wrong thing, you'll get the wrong action.

Finding the right thing to reward is not always trivial. As a business professor, I want to promote teamwork. After all, my students' future success depends on their ability to work with others. Yet none of the incentives we typically use in higher education—good grades and letters of recommendation or the punishment of failing a class—

are designed to support excellence in teamwork. These incentives are given for individual, not group, performance. Even when I try to incentivize group work, as when a group of students in my class turns in a report on how to improve management performance, the incentive of a collective grade sometimes fails to ensure teamwork. Every former overachieving kid will remember taking on the brunt of the work in group projects, while pushing others aside, to ensure they'd get the A. The teamwork problem follows us into our professional lives, too. Knowing performance evaluations are given based on individual performance, we have no external incentives to excel as a team and lack the motivation to set such incentives for ourselves.

Other times, rewarding gets tricky because we aren't sure how to evaluate success. We might reward ourselves for something that's easy to measure but just misses the point of our goal. At work, you'd ideally set incentives for finding creative solutions or for taking a step toward long-term growth. But because these are hard to measure, you're more likely to reward yourself for finishing your work quickly or for finishing more projects than anyone else. You reward the quantity rather than the quality of your work. This system of rewards compromises your creativity and long-term vision.

Rewarding the right thing is even trickier when you're pursuing an avoidance goal. When your goal is to avoid danger or poor health, you need to reward warning signals. Yet we struggle to reward bad news. People don't usually raise a toast to congratulate themselves for spotting an irregular mole, even though spotting it on time leads them to get it removed and potentially avoid skin cancer. The phrase "shoot the messenger" captures our reluctance to congratulate those who deliver bad news, including ourselves. This phrase originated in ancient Greece, which goes to say that the tendency to punish bad news isn't a modern phenomenon. And yet rewarding bad news will help you achieve your goals. Perhaps you *should* raise a toast after a biopsy, do a little happy dance when you discover that your heating system needs fixing before the first snow, and buy a drink for the friend who warned you not to get cozy with your selfish neighbor. Discovering bad news in time to do something about it is worth celebrating.

To optimize the impact of your incentives, you want to reward the right thing, whether it's teamwork, creative solutions, successfully preventing harm, or a pest-free neighborhood (rather than lots of dead rats). Of course, recognizing that you've incentivized the right thing is easier said than done. To check that you're on the right track, ask yourself two questions.

First, does the incentive motivate progress toward a goal, or is it a meaningless target that's easier to measure? When you're trying to move up at work, for example, consider rewarding yourself for the amount of work you've completed rather than the amount of time you've spent in front of your computer (which includes daydreaming and checking social media). Taking it a step further, you could choose to reward the quality of your work, rather than its quantity.

Second, ask yourself: What would be the easiest route to achieve these incentives? What potential shortcuts exist? If the easiest route doesn't pull you toward making progress on your goals, you're using the wrong incentives.

TOO MANY INCENTIVES

In 1973 psychologist Mark Lepper walked onto the campus of Stanford University with a box of Magic Markers. He was there not to shower college students with colorful gifts, but to test a hunch at the university's nursery school. He brought his box of markers to the school every day for three weeks and gave them up for the class to use during their free playtime. Each day, he watched from behind a one-way mirror as the three-to-five-year-old artists drew colorful pictures. Some of these little students were told they'd get a "Good Player Award" with a big gold star and a bright red ribbon if they chose to draw during free time. Others were given no incentives, and still others were given the prize unexpectedly only after they'd drawn a picture.

After the kids drew their first pictures and, for those in the prize group, received their reward, they were told they wouldn't get a prize for any pictures they subsequently drew. The reward was a one-time deal. Although all of the kids were initially excited to draw, Lepper noted that kids who got the big gold star and bright red bow the first time drew for only 10 percent of their playtime after they were told there'd be no more prizes for their "commissioned" artwork. The other kids, those who either got no reward or got a surprise reward, used the Magic Markers for 20 percent of their free play.

As with many things in life, when it comes to rewarding a behavior, less is more. Having too many incentives can backfire, as Lepper's research on the "overjustification effect" discovered.

The overjustification effect happens when adding a justification (or an incentive) to an action and then removing it undermines motivation. For the kids in Lepper's study, adding the award shifted the purpose of drawing from self-expression only, to self-expression plus receiving a prize. Once self-expression was again the sole reason to draw, young artists were no longer interested in producing art.

One narrow interpretation of this classic effect is that external rewards like money and trophies undermine internal motivators such as the ability to self-express. But the problem doesn't lie with external motivation alone. In a study conducted twenty years after Lepper's original study, researchers handed second and third graders short stories that doubled as coloring books. Each book told a one-page fable and presented a picture of characters from the story, which children could color themselves. Each activity, reading and coloring, was an internal motivator—the opportunity to express oneself through coloring and the interest in reading. Given together, though, they undermined each other. Removing the option to color the pictures decreased children's motivation to keep reading, just as much as removing the reading option decreased their motivation to keep coloring. It turns out that any added incentive, whether external or internal, can undermine the original one. If, for example, we were rewarded with more independence at work until a new boss took it away from us, we should expect a decline in our motivation. So the idea that only external rewards undermine only internal motivators seems too simple to explain what happened in Lepper's study.

Moreover, even when incentives are not removed, we still sometimes see added incentives negatively affecting motivation. In Lepper's study, the incentive of a big, bright bow was first added and then taken away, allowing children to experience making art after the awards were gone. This seems like one obvious reason their motivation tanked—why keep drawing if you no longer get a prize for doing it? But studies conducted forty years after the original study found that adding incentives can decrease motivation even while these incentives are still in place.

In one such study, Michal Maimaran and I asked what would happen when young children learned that food is instrumental for something other than tasting good. We brought a picture book featuring a girl who ate crackers and carrots to a preschool in the suburbs of Chicago, and also brought along bags of these very snacks. But the version of the story we told differed across groups of children. In one version, the girl ate carrots and crackers to feel strong and healthy. In another, she ate them to learn how to read. In a third version, she ate them to learn to count to one hundred. Hearing these stories, the children learned that food featured in the book could help them grow stronger and smarter and were incentivized to eat it to gain these great benefits.

Although you might expect that learning about the amazing benefits of food—to make you strong or give you the energy to learn—would make the kids excited to eat these healthy snacks, we found the opposite. When the preschoolers heard that crackers would make them strong, they concluded the crackers were not very tasty and ate fewer of them. And when other children heard carrots could help them learn to read or to count, they ate fewer carrots. All in all, emphasizing benefits reduced food consumption by over 50 percent. Our young listeners inferred that a snack that serves multiple purposes—tastes good and helps you learn how to count—is probably not very good at the one purpose they really care about: being tasty. It's a big blow to parents who've long relied on the promise that carrots and broccoli would "help you grow up big and strong" to persuade kids to eat their vegetables.

Note that in these studies, the supposed external benefits were never removed. Children still expected that eating carrots would help them read and crackers would help them count. Nevertheless, they were less interested in eating the snack compared to those who weren't told that crackers and carrots would make them stronger and smarter.

Although we often tell ourselves that certain foods will make us look good, live longer, and feel better, research on food marketing finds that advertising food as healthy can also make adults lose their appetite. In one study conducted in campus cafeterias across several US colleges, food labels that emphasized health benefits (e.g., "Healthy Choice Turnips," "Nutritious Green Beans") decreased consumption by almost 30 percent compared with food labels that emphasized taste (e.g., "Herb 'n' Honey Balsamic Glazed Turnips," "Sizzlin' Szechuan Green Beans with Toasted Garlic"). Because your central goal when you eat (compared, for example, to taking medicine) is to enjoy taste, when consumption is framed as instrumental for other reasons, we expect the food to taste less good.

These newer studies teach us that the overjustification effect, which shows a decrease in motivation once more incentives are introduced, is not only a response to the disappointment you feel when an incentive you expected is taken away. Although it's upsetting to get less bang for your buck or fewer incentives for your efforts, and although disappointment decreases motivation, the overjustification effect also has another cause: the mere presence of additional incentives undermines—or dilutes—the central reason we pursue an activity.

THE DILUTION PRINCIPLE

When Lepper watched kids at the nursery school the first day, before he'd offered any reward, he saw fun. The kids enjoyed expressing themselves through art. But when the incentive of a prize was added, they lost some of the meaning they'd originally felt in drawing. So the Magic Markers no longer had the same pull.

What he saw was the "dilution principle" playing out before his eyes. According to the dilution principle, the more goals, including incentives (i.e., mini-goals), a single activity serves, the more weakly we associate the activity with our central goal and the less instrumental the activity seems for this goal. Therefore, our central goal is less likely to come to mind when we pursue the activity. And when a goal doesn't come to mind, the activity doesn't seem to serve the goal. The kids didn't want to draw after getting a prize because drawing was no longer so much about self-expression.

By the dilution principle, adding a new goal to a goal-directed activity weakens the mental association between the activity and the original goal. If you hear that eating carrots is good for lowering your blood pressure, you'll assume carrots are less beneficial for your vision. If I tell you that my friend is a good source for cooking advice, you'll assume she is less likely to be a good source for medical advice, though she might be a physician who loves to cook.

This dilution is especially potent when the added incentive is one you don't care much about. You should expect your motivation to dwindle, for instance, when you learn that the recycling program you're trying to start at work would provide tax breaks for your employer. When a goal or an incentive you don't care for is introduced to an activity that served an existing goal, the activity you were pursuing seems less beneficial for the original purpose. And if you don't care for the new purpose (like lining the pockets of your CEO), you're likely to let it overtake the original goal and shut your motivation down.

Let's use wine as an example. Often, two main incentives guide my selection when I buy wine: I want wine that's tasty and affordable. Yet these two incentives compete in my mind. By the dilution principle, when I learn that a bottle of wine is more affordable, I assume it's less tasty, and when I learn that it's tasty, I assume it's less affordable.

There are times, though, when one incentive becomes less pressing. Each year, my university hosts a holiday party with an open bar. At this party, I don't care much about how affordable the wine is—I'm not paying for it. So I choose the wine I believe is more expensive, because I assume I'll like it more. The cheaper wine's perceived taste is diluted (cognitively, not literally) by the financial incentive. I assume that wine that serves two goals—good taste and affordability— isn't great for either one.

The same can be said of the multipurpose tools advertised as great stocking stuffers each holiday season. Take laser pens as an example. In a study Ying Zhang, Arie Kruglanski, and I conducted, research participants completed a survey, which required half of them to try a pen that had a laser pointer. After completing the study, as everyone approached the sign-out desk, they faced a choice between two pens to sign their name: a regular pen and a laser pen identical to the one half of them had tested before. Those who had tested the laser-pointing function did not select the laser pen when signing their name. They instead chose the regular pen. In contrast, those who didn't test the laser function were equally likely to choose the laser pen as the regular pen. They made their selection at random. This study explains why multipurpose items often end up serving no purpose at all—we'd rather a pen just be a pen.

The principle of dilution helps us determine when it's better to set fewer incentives. Adding incentives and then removing them is disappointing, as the drawing children in Lepper's study discovered. It further weakens the association between the activity and its original purpose. For that latter reason, adding incentives that you don't care for will also reduce your motivation, even when the incentives remain in place.

When you're tempted to add an incentive to an existing goal, take a moment to ponder whether that incentive will serve you well. Is it going to pull you even further toward the goal, or is it going to obscure the purpose of your action and move you away from it?

HOW INCENTIVES BACKFIRE

If the idea that incentives can undermine motivation leaves you a little puzzled, there's good reason. After all, we've seen incentives work in our own lives. Very few of my MBA students feel they've lost their motivation to study because of the chance they'll earn a degree. And I have yet to meet employees who complain they've lost their passion for work because the paycheck is too high. Monetary rewards and other incentives seem to do their job, at least some of the time.

You might even worry that the idea that incentives, especially monetary ones, decrease motivation is popular only because it lets people off the hook financially. If you consume art for free—for example, illegally downloading music or streaming TV shows using your ex's account—you may want to believe that creativity, not money, motivates artists. And if you've just landed a managerial position at a struggling company during a recession, you may want to believe that raises make employees feel less motivated to do a good job. The idea that paying people undermines their motivation is a convenient one if you're on the "paying" side of the deal. It's sometimes used to justify underpaying people for their work.

But paid artists produce more, not less, art. And raises boost employees' morale—a good thing for management. In these examples, people expect to get paid; the monetary incentive is part of the reason they engage in the activity. Because you expect to get paid for your work, getting your paycheck doesn't cloud your understanding of why you do the work in the first place, just as selling art doesn't cloud artists' understanding of their motivation.

Yet there are activities we pursue without really knowing why. When we ask ourselves why we do something, the presence of incentives gives us a clue. But sometimes, those clues can lead us astray.

There's a reason so many of the studies that found that incentives undermine motivation were conducted with children. Children are busy figuring out their likes and dislikes. When I ask my eight-year-old if he likes a subject at school, he needs to think about it; he doesn't intuitively know the answer the way you might. Children are relatively new to a world that's largely controlled by adults, so many of the activities that occupy their days need explanation. They might ask themselves, "Am I drawing because I like to draw or because my teacher made me draw?" or "Does this food taste good to me or am I eating it because otherwise I won't get dessert?" Incentives give them the clues to start piecing together their likes and dislikes. And if you're a child, and an adult is willing to pay you to do something, that's a clue that you wouldn't otherwise enjoy doing it.

Adults, in contrast, figured out many of their likes and dislikes long ago, so incentives have less impact on our understanding of why we do what we do. Every day, you go to work. If you've been in the same job or the same field for many years, you know exactly how you feel about your work, and incentives won't do much to change those feelings. An increase to your paycheck will not undermine your work motivation; it might even make you more motivated because it signals success. But if you're trying something new, maybe something you're a bit uncertain about, you're more likely to rely on incentives to figure out why you're doing it. And most of the time, you'll conclude that the main reason you're doing whatever you're doing is to get the incentives. I learned this lesson when I started teaching overseas. When I signed up to teach a course in Singapore the first time, I assumed I was doing it because my university offers extra teaching credit for teaching outside Chicago. But after a couple of trips to Singapore I realized that I cared less about the teaching credit and more about the great teaching experience and the opportunity to explore an exciting country.

The clues incentives give you about why you're invested in a new activity can lead you astray whenever they obscure the central reason for pursuing this activity, making you think you're less invested in a certain goal than you actually are. Incentives are even more harmful for motivation when the incentive is a poor match to the activity. It would feel strange, for example, if someone paid you to call your grandmother. Financial incentives that don't feel right interfere with your motivation. But when they're a central feature of the activity—like when you're doing a job or earning an allowance—financial incentives increase motivation. In one study, paying kids to play with blocks made them enjoy the game less. But kids playing a coin-toss game were more excited and motivated by payment because coin-toss games are associated with winning cash. Many people find gambling exciting, and they're motivated to gamble because of, not in spite of, the financial rewards. When we expect to get paid, payments increase rather than undermine our motivation.

To make sure your incentives don't backfire, ask yourself what a stranger would infer about your reasons for performing the activity. If the incentives lead this stranger astray, and if the reason you perform the activity isn't crystal clear in your mind at all times, consider revising these incentives.

INCENTIVES OBSCURE THE IMPACT OF ACTIONS

Imagine you could be totally invisible for twenty-four hours. No one would see you, hear you, or feel you, so you could easily get away with anything. What would you do? I've asked this question of hundreds of students in my classes over the years. An overwhelming majority contemplate robbing a bank, trespassing, spying, and eavesdropping (on their boss, friends, other students, family members, romantic partners, and celebrities). A few contemplate killing someone they strongly dislike (usually by poisoning). They're joking, of course (or so I hope). The uniting theme behind these answers? When negative incentives are removed, and you know your actions will go unpunished, bad ideas come to mind.

My students' answers suggest that fear of punishment is the only reason people who normally care about others adhere to basic moral principles. But shouldn't people care about doing good even when no one is watching? I would like to believe that most people, or at least most of my students, don't rob, trespass, spy, or murder because they care about other people, not just because they might get arrested.

This leads me to another unintended consequence of incentives: they might obscure the impact of an action. Crime still causes harm, even if no one is watching. And yet, because our society establishes negative incentives for committing crimes, we might feel that it's okay to commit one if we can't get caught. Society may further relax drug laws, but the health consequences of drug use will not change. And while speed limits vary from place to place, speeding remains just as dangerous no matter where you are.

This effect is also true for positive incentives. Giving to charity will do good in the world, but if you give mainly to receive the tax benefits, that tax incentive obscures the purpose of your action. So while incentives are set to encourage people to adhere to their goals, they might prevent people from realizing why they pursue or avoid certain actions in the first place.

When setting incentives, be mindful of how those incentives shape the way you think about your goals, and what would happen if they were taken away. When you turned twenty-one, drinking lots of alcohol became legal, not healthy. Just because the negative incentive of breaking the law was lifted doesn't mean you should allow yourself to drink to excess, undermining your goal to be a healthy person. Just as we should resist letting incentives modify our goals, so we should resist letting them obscure the impact of our actions on our goals. Ask yourself: If the awards and/or punishments were taken away, would you still want to do what you're doing?

THE CASE FOR UNCERTAIN INCENTIVES

When I immigrated to the US in the early 2000s with my husband and two little girls, I felt overwhelmed. I was a fish out of water, suffering from cultural shock. I was especially worried about money, since I had only a vague idea of how much life would cost in this new country.

But while my expenses were unknown, my income was surprisingly predictable. I had come from Israel, where employees are paid on a month-to-month basis, unlike the annual salary we get in the US. In Israel, my pay stubs changed every month, so I had no idea how much I'd make for the year. In the US, my income was fixed.

While I value predictability in my personal life, I wondered how fixed payments influence motivation. Would you work harder for a fixed reward or a variable one? Consider the following two hypothetical jobs: job A pays you $100,000, and job B pays you a 50 percent chance of getting $85,000 and a 50 percent chance of getting $115,000. Most people appreciate certainty and would therefore choose job A. Yet most people would work harder when the amount of pay is uncertain.

Why do uncertain incentives increase motivation? The first answer comes from behaviorism. As you may recall from a distant introductory psychology class, behaviorists identified two basic schedules of rewards, aka "reinforcement schedules": 1. a continuous schedule, where the animal gets the reward after every correct response, and 2. an intermittent schedule, where the animal gets the reward only in some instances of performing the behavior. Surprisingly, intermittent schedules work better. Whether you're teaching your dog a new trick or training your pigeon to play Ping-Pong (as Skinner once did), it's best to give them food on some successful instances but not others. This way, their behavior will persist when rewards become sparse. When animals can't figure out when the reward will come, they remain hopeful and continue to do what you tell them—sit, stay, be quiet, or come—even when there are no longer treats to be handed out.

Since humans are animals, too, the same trick can be used to train ourselves or others. On a fixed schedule, for example, each time a student in my class answered a question correctly, I would say, "What a great answer!" On an intermittent schedule, I would only sometimes compliment a student's brilliant answer. As with animals, the intermittent reinforcement is almost always better than a fixed schedule in motivating action. When incentives are uncertain, like when they vary in magnitude or frequency, receiving a smaller-than-expected incentive or no incentive is less discouraging. You realize that you don't always win a reward for good behavior and hope that maybe you will next time.

Other times, uncertain incentives are motivating because they're harder to get. You need to get lucky or work hard to win. Just as moderately difficult goal targets increase motivation, so do uncertain incentives that pose a challenge. Athletes stay motivated because of, rather than in spite of, the fact that victory is never a sure thing.

Uncertain incentives are also exciting. Take, for example, a visit to the arcade. My kids loved them; I, less so. In my experience, the typical arcade offers you a bad deal: you put some money into machines that light up and make funny noises and then you win some cheap plastic toys that are worth significantly less than the money you put into the machines. Why is this deal so popular? Likely because it's a game of luck and only a little bit of skill. You don't know how much you're going to win, and resolving the uncertainty is exciting. You'll pull or push a lever, or throw a ball, and if you're lucky, you'll get more bang for your buck.

Not knowing whether your efforts will pay off makes you curious to find out. Uncertainty by itself is no fun; no one likes staying in the dark. But resolving the uncertainty, learning the payoff for your efforts and thereby moving from the dark to the light, is psychologically rewarding.

Because uncertain incentives are exciting, they encourage most people to work harder. Luxi Shen, Chris Hsee, and I tested this phenomenon in a somewhat unusual study. We gathered participants to play a little game. If they could drink 1.4 liters (about 1.48 quarts) of water in two minutes or less, we'd pay them. Drinking this much water is challenging but possible for most people (and poses no health risks, don't worry!). Unbeknownst to our players, we offered some people a $2 fixed reward and others an uncertain reward of either $2 or $1, to be determined by a coin toss. The certain reward was overall a better deal—players who drank enough water were guaranteed $2, while the others only had a 50 percent chance at that amount. Yet many more people drank the water within the time limit when assigned an uncertain reward. We learned that resolving the uncertainty—whether they would win $1 or $2—was significantly more motivating than winning $2 for sure.

Still, people don't usually choose uncertainty. Most of us would take the guarantee of a million dollars over playing a lottery that might pay $2 million or might get you nothing. Uncertainty is not always fun, but it motivates action.

Luckily for us, uncertain incentives are common. When applying for jobs or schools, you don't know whether your application will be successful, so you're motivated to work hard. When you propose, you don't know if your sweetheart will accept. Not knowing keeps you motivated to make the best case for yourself. In the future, embrace uncertainty. It keeps you motivated.

QUESTIONS TO ASK YOURSELF

The study of incentives advises us to take caution when adding extra reasons to pursue a goal. While incentives motivate action, too many incentives can backfire. They change or dilute the central reason we've aspired to a goal and therefore make it seem less pressing or exciting. In addition, incentives might prevent us from realizing the impact of our behavior on our goal in the first place. And while certain incentives might seem more powerful than uncertain ones, the opposite is true. Certainty results in habituation such that people stop caring about receiving the incentives. Keeping these risks in mind, you should ask yourself the following questions about your incentive system:

1. What incentives can you add to your goals so you have extra reasons to follow through? Consider, for example, rewarding yourself with a movie night or a long bubble bath after

getting your annual flu shot or finishing an important project at work.

2. Consider the incentives that exist for pursuing your goals. Do they modify the meaning of pursuing your goals? If so, these incentives need to be revised. If, for example, external rewards reduce your enjoyment of reading books, get rid of these rewards.

3. Have you added incentives to new activities that you're still exploring? If you're still figuring out your preferences, incentives might lead you to believe you're only doing something for the incentive it provides. Remove these incentives.

4. Do your incentives fit the activity? Financial rewards, for example, are a poor fit for pursuing relationship goals. Many of us would feel less motivated to keep in touch with people if we were paid to do so. Remove these incentives.

4

INTRINSIC MOTIVATION (AND WHY YOU SHOULD HAVE MORE FUN)

IN THE ADVENTURES OF *Tom Sawyer*, Mark Twain's titular character comes home one night covered in dirt, to the fury of his aunt Polly. As punishment, Polly sentences Tom to a Saturday of work, painting the fence in the front yard. Tom languishes at first, thinking of all the fun he's missing out on and the ridicule the neighborhood boys will put him through. But just as the first boy comes toward him, Tom gets an idea.

As he expects, Ben Rogers—whose ridicule Tom has been dreading most—immediately starts to heckle him. "I'm going in a-swimming, I am," he says. "Don't you wish you could?" Tom, looking at the fence as if it were the most fascinating art project, tells Ben that no, he wouldn't rather be swimming. He's perfectly happy where he is. "Does a boy get a chance to whitewash a fence every day?" he says.

Soon, Ben not only asks but begs to paint the fence himself. He sells Tom the rest of his juicy apple for the opportunity. More boys come along and Tom swindles them, too, selling the privilege of painting the fence for such treasures as a kite, marbles, chalk, tadpoles, and a one-eyed kitten. By the end of the afternoon, the fence has three coats of paint and Tom has barely lifted a finger.

In this famous scene, when Tom gets his friends to paint the fence for him by pretending it's a rare and pleasurable opportunity, Mark Twain offers an insight into the psychology of intrinsic motivation. He observes that "work consists of whatever a body is obliged to do, and that play consists of whatever a body is not obliged to do."

Despite this early insight, to this date intrinsic motivation is the least-understood concept in motivation science. People have used the term to mean doing something without getting paid, or just because you're curious. But the definition of intrinsic motivation is "pursuing an activity that feels like an end in itself." When you're intrinsically motivated, you do something for the sake of doing it.

Intrinsic motivation is the best predictor of engagement in just about everything. As Adam Grant found, intrinsic motivation increases the number of hours firefighters work and the creativity security officers display at work. When we set goals that are intrinsically motivating or apply strategies that increase intrinsic motivation, we have a better chance at success. We're excited both about short-term goals, like attending our first aerial yoga class, and long-term goals, like learning to speak Chinese, because we want to, not because we feel we have to.

Take New Year's resolutions. Every year as December turns into January, hundreds of thousands of people in the US make New Year's resolutions. But if you set a resolution, I can confidently guess that you're not too excited to follow through with that goal. If you were 100 percent intrinsically motivated to do whatever you set your mind to on January 1, there would be no need to set a resolution. Still, New Year's resolutions—like whitewashing a fence—vary by the degree to which they are intrinsically motivating, and these variations matter.

In a study I ran with Kaitlin Woolley, we followed up in March with people who had shared their resolutions with us back in January. As we expected, the degree to which these goals were intrinsically motivated predicted engagement. As you might guess, many of the people we talked to made resolutions to exercise more in the new year. But who succeeded and who didn't depended heavily on how each person felt about exercising. People who enjoyed exercising, and were therefore more intrinsically motivated to do it, exercised more than people who enjoyed exercising less. The same was true for all other resolutions. Interestingly, though, how important people thought their resolutions were didn't correlate with how frequently they adhered to them. Just because someone said exercising was incredibly important for their health, that didn't mean they'd actually do it more than people who felt it was less critical for them. If you want to predict how much a person— including yourself—will stick to a resolution, ask how excited they are to engage in it rather than how important the resolution seems to be.

The implications for goal setting should be clear. If you can find a way to make the path to your goal enjoyable or exciting, you'll be intrinsically motivated, which means you'll stick to it longer. This idea won't help much if your goal is to do something you already love doing. Fans of classical music can listen to Mozart every day, sports fans can watch an hourslong game, and ice cream lovers could eat gallons of ice cream. But we can harness intrinsic motivation even toward goals we don't find inherently fun or exciting. When we find ways to make exercise or work or even organizing a messy closet more enjoyable, we make it easier for ourselves to follow through on these important goals.

WHAT IS INTRINSIC MOTIVATION?

What does it mean to pursue an activity as an end in itself? You're intrinsically motivated whenever you cannot separate pursuing an activity from receiving its benefits. If you love your work, you do your job because it feels right. Similarly, if you're someone who enjoys working up a sweat, you have no trouble getting yourself to the gym. You would find it strange to question what you're getting out of pursuing your job or completing a workout, because the main purpose for doing it is to be able to do it. In your mind, there is a perceptual fusion between the intrinsic activity and its purpose.

The moment you achieve a goal is intrinsically motivated by definition. The activity that got you to the goal and the goal itself converge at that moment; they are completely fused. A nice meal, a stroll in the park on a spring day, watching fireworks, solving a riddle, sex: these are all activities that you're intrinsically motivated to do. Pursuing them usually immediately achieves the goals they serve. If I asked what you accomplish by watching fireworks, you'd say that you get to watch them. Yet most activities vary by intrinsicality, or the degree to which they're experienced as goal attainment. A self-fulfilling job and an energizing workout would still serve some ulterior goals: getting paid and living a long, healthy life. To most of us, work and exercise are only partially intrinsically motivating. To determine the degree to which a given activity is intrinsically motivating, we should therefore ask: To what extent does pursuing the activity feel like achieving a goal rather than a *step* toward achieving a goal?

The answer depends on the person, the activity, and the circumstances in which it occurs. Take the activities presented above. A nice meal is usually intrinsically motivating, but if it's part of a job interview, your ulterior goal is getting a job offer rather than enjoying the meal. As you avoid the pasta Bolognese that might stain your suit, watch your manners, and drink no more than a few sips of your wine, you focus on the long-term goal of getting the job, not on the immediate goal of having a nice meal. A stroll in the park or watching fireworks can similarly serve some ulterior motives, such as supporting your partner during her office's annual retreat. And sex serves a different motive if you're desperately trying to conceive. When an ulterior motive is introduced, the activity and the goal are separated in your mind, making you less intrinsically motivated.

To determine the extent to which you're intrinsically motivated to do something, estimate the degree of fusion between the activity (the means) and its goal (the end). Does the activity feel as if it's accomplishing the goal? If not, how far from your end goal do you feel once you've finished? If you're exercising purely for long-term health, for instance, the activity and the goal are separated by decades. Activities that are low on intrinsic motivation might still be important for you. These important activities are "extrinsically" motivated; they help you achieve external benefits. Consider, for example, completing your annual physical checkup. Hardly fun but highly important.

To maximize your intrinsic motivation, you also need to understand what it's not. For one, intrinsic motivation is not limited to resolving curiosity. The misconception that it is dates back to the middle of the twentieth century, when researchers discovered that animals would explore their environment simply because they were curious, without any external rewards for doing so. Their conclusion was that satisfying curiosity (by means of exploration for the animals) is intrinsically motivated—it is its own end. In the years that followed, the valid conclusion that exploration could be intrinsically motivated was taken to mean something else: that intrinsic motivation *is* satisfying curiosity through exploration.

Yet while exploration is often intrinsically motivated, not all exploration is. If your curiosity has ever led you to sit on a long flight, squeezed between other airline travelers, on your way to a distant part of the world that you haven't yet seen, you've likely felt extrinsically rather than intrinsically motivated. Flying somewhere, unlike hiking the Rocky Mountains, is experienced as a means to an end. Flying tends to be low on intrinsic motivation, even if the purpose of the trip is to satisfy your curiosity. And, as with watching fireworks or taking a nice walk, some intrinsically motivated activities have nothing to do with curiosity. We know what fireworks look like—we see them every year on the Fourth of July—but we still want to watch them.

Intrinsic motivation is also not limited to innate motives. Motivation scientists distinguish between innate and learned motives. Innate motives are those that every human is programmed with at birth. We're born with the motivation to form social relationships, as well as to express our autonomy and competence. We see this in babies, who are born with a reflex to smile (to keep parents attached for the few weeks until they learn to smile voluntarily), and toddlers, who seek to demonstrate their independence (those "terrible twos" every parent is warned about) and to be challenged physically and cognitively. In contrast, other motives like gaining power, status, and money are learned through the culture and society in which you grow up. This important distinction in the origins of motives is sometimes taken to imply that only innate motives are intrinsic. You might assume that the pursuit of wealth, for example, can never be intrinsically motivated.

But this is not the case. If you've ever been to Las Vegas, you've seen that people can be intrinsically motivated to win money. Gambling doesn't feel like a job you're required to do; the activity (gambling) and the end (winning) strongly overlap in the gambler's mind, making gambling feel more like an end. When you're playing games for the chance to win money, the pursuit of wealth (a learned motive) becomes intrinsic. But the same goal can be extrinsic when a boring day job is your path to making money.

With a broad understanding of what intrinsic motivation is (and isn't), watch for the following signs to determine whether someone (including yourself) is intrinsically motivated. First, when you're intrinsically motivated, you feel eager to stay on task. You don't want to quit. Ask yourself, for example, how you feel at the end of the workday. Are you eager to have a few more minutes to finish what you've been working on or are you relieved it's finally time to pack up your stuff and go home? Motivation scientists use the "free-choice paradigm" to capture this aspect of intrinsic motivation. In this paradigm, research participants are told they can continue their task after the experimental session is over or they can go home. If they stay on task after completing their duties, as when you hang out in the office a few minutes after you could go home, we conclude they're intrinsically motivated.

To learn if someone is intrinsically motivated, we also ask about their experience and feelings while doing the activity. Are you eager, curious, enjoying yourself? Does pursuing this activity feel more like play than work? Does pursuing the activity feel like achieving your goal? If the answer is yes, you're likely intrinsically motivated.

CAUSES OF INTRINSIC MOTIVATION

While some activities, like exercising or working for a paycheck, will never be purely intrinsically motivating, we could nonetheless ask what would bring these activities closer to a goal.

An activity feels more intrinsically motivated when it immediately achieves a goal, even if it's not the goal you originally set out to achieve. Maybe you started exercising because you want to stay healthy. But if each workout makes you feel energized, working out and feeling energized become a single entity in your mind and you'll be more intrinsically motivated to exercise.

This may remind you of the conditioning techniques used in experimental psychology and behavioral therapy. In "operant conditioning" training, people and other animals learn through repetition that a behavior leads to a reward. Think of Pavlov's dogs salivating at the sound of a bell they'd been conditioned to associate with food. Over time, people and animals who've been conditioned to connect a certain behavior (exercise) with a certain reward (feeling energized) tend to both do the behavior more often and feel more positive about it. The excitement about the reward transfers to the behavior that leads to it. Animal research finds, for example, that a pigeon that learned to press a lever in order to receive food is already visibly excited while pressing the lever and before receiving any food. And intrinsically motivated gym users, like pigeons, already feel excited before they've finished exercising and experienced the benefits.

An activity also feels intrinsically motivating whenever achieving a goal is solely reliant on doing the activity. If only one activity helps you achieve a goal and only that specific goal is achieved by the activity, you strongly associate the activity with the goal. For example, if you meditate in order to reach a state of calmness and you only feel calm through meditation, you will be intrinsically motivated to meditate. This one-on-one relationship may remind you of the dilution effect we talked about in Chapter 3, whereby an activity that serves several goals appears less instrumental to achieving any of these goals (your mind tells you that wine can't be both cheap and tasty). Another outcome of diluting the activity-goal association is that the activity will feel less intrinsically motivating. If you stroll through the park for the sole purpose of spending time outdoors, you'll be more intrinsically motivated than if this walk is also part of your commute to work. But note that more unique associations might come with a cost. If you only feel calm through meditation, you might struggle to keep your cool when you can't fit meditation into your busy schedule. Flexibility, such as having more than one way to feel calm, can be important in reaching your goals.

Another factor that increases the intrinsic motivation of an activity is the extent to which the activity and its associated goal appear similar. When the activity and goal appear to fit together, they're more closely connected in your mind. You're more intrinsically motivated to learn how to play the piano, play basketball, or speak Spanish if your goal is to grow as a person than if you want to feel more relaxed. We learned in the last chapter that ill-fitting activity-goal associations can tank our motivation—when someone pays you to call your grandmother, you question why you're doing it in the first place. When framing your goals, make sure your incentives and your internal motivations match the goal.

Finally, *when* you reach your goal matters for intrinsic motivation. The shorter the time between doing the activity and reaching your goal, the more intrinsically motivated it will feel. When the activity and the goal occur simultaneously, you experience even stronger intrinsic motivation. Think of a romantic dinner, a vacation in Paris, an intellectual or emotional breakthrough, or walking your dog in the park on a sunny day. All of these activities immediately achieve the goal we connect with them—to feel close to our partner, to explore a new city, to grow as a person, or to relax. Immediate gratification creates the strongest pull on our intrinsic motivation.

Consider the more mundane, daily routine of getting caught up on the news. These days, more people are turning to late-night shows as their source of world news. It's easier to tolerate everything that's happening in the world when it's served with a joke. With this in mind, Kaitlin Woolley and I invited people to watch a news clip about the Dalai Lama and the political situation in Tibet, presented by John Oliver on the late-night show *Last Week Tonight*. We asked half of them to consider what the immediate benefits of watching the show might be. How could it inform them while they watched? The others considered the delayed benefits of watching the show. How could it make them more informed in the weeks that followed? This brief exercise influenced people's experience while watching the show. Those who thought of immediate benefits felt more intrinsically motivated.

Temporal associations are powerful tools for increasing intrinsic motivation. Even external rewards increase intrinsic motivation when they're delivered sooner rather than later. It's more enjoyable to work when you're getting paid immediately rather than after a few weeks. And while paying people for work they didn't expect to get paid for may undermine motivation—recall the overjustification effect—delivering expected payment for paid work sooner will increase intrinsic motivation. On the other hand, if the time between when you do an activity and when you see the benefits is drawn out, intrinsic motivation dwindles.

HOW TO INCREASE INTRINSIC MOTIVATION

An acquaintance recently wrote to me about her daughter, Olivia. Olivia is a twenty-nine-year-old diabetic woman on the autism spectrum. These days, she regularly walks a two-mile trek through her small, rural community in the western US. But only a few years ago, she hardly walked at all. She doesn't drive, so she would walk to the grocery store or to restaurants near her house if no one was around to drive her, but otherwise she found walking boring and preferred to stay home. Then she downloaded Pokémon GO.

Growing up in the late 1990s, Olivia was a big Pokémon fan. So when Pokémon GO came out in 2016, she was excited to start playing again. The game uses your phone's GPS and clock to detect where and when you're in the game and make Pokémon characters "appear" around you so you can go and catch them. Soon after downloading the game, Olivia started taking her two-mile walks. That route was the best for catching Pokémon. The game gave her a reason to go out and walk—this was the Pokémon journey she'd dreamed of going on since she was ten years old.

Olivia's isn't the only story I've heard about Pokémon GO motivating more exercise. In fact, the game was a big reason my eight-year-old son and I started taking walks around our neighborhood, and it was so wildly popular when it first came out that researchers estimate the game added 144 billion steps across the US at its peak in the summer of 2016. It was so successful that people blamed Pokémon GO for getting too many distracted walkers out on the streets.

Pokémon GO motivated so much exercise—more than other exercise apps—because it relied on people's intrinsic motivation. It turned walking into a game. There are three ways to make a boring or difficult activity more intrinsically motivating. First, we have the aptly named "make-it-fun" strategy, which as you might guess involves making an activity fun. The make-it-fun strategy actively associates immediate incentives (i.e., mini-goals) with pursuing the activity. These incentives harness our need for instant gratification to make a previously dull activity more exciting and therefore let us experience it as its own end. For example, when Woolley and I (to the chagrin of some teachers) encouraged high school math students to listen to music, eat snacks, and use brightly colored pens while doing their math assignment, we found that students worked longer. Doing math was fun because it delivered immediate auditory, taste, and visual benefits. Catching a Pokémon is also an immediate incentive for Pokémon GO players.

People frequently apply this principle to make it fun when they bundle goals with temptations. Associating a workout with watching TV or working on a school assignment with listening to music are examples of "temptation bundling." This strategy is particularly effective if you limit yourself to engaging in the tempting activity only while pursuing the goal. So, for example, you only let yourself eat a square of chocolate while answering your many work emails. These temptations increase intrinsic motivation to pursue the goal. It's critical, however, that the reward is immediate. Adding delayed rewards, like five squares of chocolate by the end of the workweek, won't work.

The second strategy in the motivation science tool kit is to find a fun path. When you set a goal and have to think about the path you'll take to get there, factor in immediate enjoyment. For example, people who want to exercise more should consider finding workouts that sound fun. Rather than slogging away on a bike at the gym, try a spin class that uses upbeat music to keep you engaged. For people who like metal, some New York City spin studios offer "Death Cycle" classes in which instructors blast metal music while everyone works out. This is an effective strategy. As Woolley and I found in a study, gymgoers who chose a weight-lifting exercise they enjoyed completed around 50 percent more repetitions than those who chose an exercise they thought would be most effective. Of course, you do still have to choose an activity that will ultimately help you accomplish your goal. If you're exercising to get fit, low-impact yoga probably won't help much. But when you have a set of activities that will accomplish the same goal, try to choose the one you'll find most fun.

The third strategy is to notice the fun that already exists. If you focus on the immediate rather than delayed benefits for pursuing an activity, you'll likely feel more intrinsically motivated and therefore be more likely to keep at it. Imagine you want to eat more carrots. If you focus on what you like about eating carrots—they're crunchy, sweet, and a little earthy—rather than the fact that carrots are a healthy snack or the idea that they might improve your eyesight, you'll be more likely to eat them. This is just what Woolley and I found in a study when we had people choose between two identical bags of baby carrots. We asked some people to choose the tastier-looking bag and some the healthier-looking bag. People ate almost 50 percent more when asked to choose the bag of carrots that looked tastier. Simply directing your attention to the immediate positive experience—to the extent that it exists—when making a choice will help you stick to your goals.

But make no mistake. If you're older than twelve, you know life isn't always a party. Not everything we do can be made intrinsically motivating. When I was pregnant for the first time, I expected that delivering my firstborn would be an amazing experience. After all, everyone talks about the beautiful miracle of childbirth. But I quickly realized that giving birth is a long stretch of pain with an impressive finale. Luckily, you don't need to be intrinsically motivated to get the job done. When going through a painful but relatively short experience, worry less about increasing your intrinsic motivation and more about getting it done and moving on.

Further, while intrinsic motivation helps us excel, it isn't required if we only plan to do the bare minimum. As a business professor, I speak with many employees who tell me they persist in jobs they hate, feeling they're "wage slaves." And yet people don't usually quit a job unless they have a better alternative. The fear of unemployment keeps many employees sufficiently motivated to show up to work. They don't do their best, but they don't quit either.

CORRECTING MYTHS AND MISCONCEPTIONS

Despite strong evidence, there are persistent myths and misconceptions about the power of intrinsic motivation. People believe that others don't care about intrinsic motivation as much as they do, and they predict they won't care about intrinsic motivation in the future as much as they do now. When we're aware that these myths and misconceptions exist, however, we can better connect to others as well as set goals that we can follow through on.

When we compare ourselves to others, almost everyone acts the same way. We all believe we're above average on positive qualities. This is a bias (the "better-than-average" effect). For any given positive quality—let's say generosity—about half of the population should be below average, while the other half should be above average. We can't all be more generous than the average person. But have you met anyone who thinks they're less generous than average? (As a side note, statistically, it's possible that most people are above the average, though not above the median. It would be more accurate to call this phenomenon the "better-than-median" effect).

This better-than-average effect is robust: even convicted prisoners rated themselves as more moral, trustworthy, honest, and self-controlled than the average person who's not in prison. We all like to see ourselves in a positive light.

When it comes to our goals and motivation, we similarly see ourselves as having stronger motivation and more pressing goals. In the workplace, while we realize that everyone wants to get a raise, most of us erroneously feel that getting a raise is more important to us than to most of our peers. And while we realize that others want to work on interesting projects, we also assume that we care about feeling interested in our work more than they do.

Knowing that people fall prey to this better-than-average effect, motivation researchers ask whether people's tendency to perceive their motivation as stronger than others' is particularly likely when it comes to intrinsic motivation. Do you think you care about how interesting your work is much more than the average person, but that you care about how much you're paid only somewhat more than the average person? Turns out, that's generally the case. The tendency for almost everyone to see themselves as above average is more pronounced for intrinsic than extrinsic motivation.

Every year, I ask my students to rate how much they care about different motivations at work relative to their classmates. They rate how much they care about extrinsic motivators like pay and job security, as well as how much they care for intrinsic motivators such as learning something new or doing something that makes them feel good about themselves. Most of my students believe everything is more important for them than their average classmate. Yet this bias is more pronounced for intrinsic motivation. While my students recognize that other classmates care about pay and job security, they fail to realize that others care about learning something new or feeling good about a job as much as they do.

Not realizing that others want to be intrinsically motivated—that they want to do something interesting and meaningful with people they enjoy—can stand in the way of our relationships with family, friends, and colleagues. When a parent undervalues a child's quest for intrinsic motivation in school, assuming she cares for high grades rather than having a meaningful, life-changing experience, it can undermine their relationship. And at work, when employers underestimate employees' intrinsic motivation while employees underestimate employers' intrinsic motivation, the interaction across the organizational hierarchy suffers. One study found that job candidates underemphasize intrinsic motivation in job interviews. The reason: although candidates want to be intrinsically motivated, they underestimate how much recruiters care about, and therefore are impressed by, expressions of intrinsic motivation. Thinking that employers are looking for someone who wants to climb the ladder, candidates don't mention how meaningful the job might feel.

To overcome the intrinsic bias, we need to put ourselves in others' shoes and ask what our priorities would be if we were them. While at times we fail to appreciate that other people are different from us—for example, that their tastes in food and their politics differ from ours—when it gets to intrinsic motivation, the challenge is to remember that most people think like we do. Imagining their perspective can help.

Not only do we underestimate others' intrinsic motivation, we also fail to predict our own. Most of us know that intrinsic motivation is important to us in the present, but we fail to realize that it will also be important in the future.

Most people realize that doing something moderately interesting with colleagues they like is critical to getting them out of bed and into the office. If you hate your job, no matter how much you like the pay and the perks, getting out of bed is hard. But how much do you prioritize doing something interesting with people you like when thinking about applying for a future job? If you're like most people, not enough. When thinking about applying for a future job, people tend to give lower priority to intrinsic motivators like their personal enjoyment and choose a position based on economic benefits like pay.

Underpredicting how much doing something that's intrinsically motivating will matter to you can result in choosing activities you'll later regret. In an experiment that explored this possibility, we asked people to choose between listening to the song "Hey Jude" by the Beatles and listening to a loud alarm for one minute. Seems like an obvious choice, right? But the people in our study were extrinsically motivated to pick the alarm because we would pay them 10 percent more if they did. The majority of people chose to listen to the loud alarm. They wanted to maximize their earnings in the experiment. But those who listened to this terrible noise were also more likely to regret their decision than those who chose to listen to the lower-paying song. While our research participants predicted they would care more about money than sound, they ultimately cared more about sound than money.

Regret isn't the only downside to picking extrinsically motivating activities over those that are intrinsically motivated. When we opt in to tasks that we think will be better for us, rather than tasks we'll enjoy, we're less likely to follow through. In another experiment, we asked research participants to choose between reading and rating jokes and reading a computer manual. Our participants predicted they would persist longer on whichever task paid more regardless of whether it was the fun task of evaluating jokes or the boring task of reading a computer manual. Yet the pay had no influence on their actual persistence. Almost everyone spent more time and therefore made more money on the fun task than the boring one.

This failure to appreciate how much your future self will care to be intrinsically motivated is related to the "empathy gap," the tendency to underestimate the strength of an experience that you're not currently having. While you're hot, it's hard to imagine how cold you'll feel on your next ski trip to Aspen, and so you might forgo packing your warmest sweater. And when you get behind the wheel first thing in the morning for a long drive, you can't imagine how miserable you'll be once the fatigue sets in, so you plan to drive for too many hours. We also fail to perceive our emotional experiences as temporary. If anyone ever broke your heart, you probably expected to feel devastated forever. You didn't imagine, at least not right away, that you'd move on and fall in love again.

This lack of empathy for your future self means you underestimate how much you'll care to be intrinsically motivated in the future, especially if you're fine right now. The result is a vision of your future self, as well as of other people, as "cold" individuals who are mainly focused on collecting external benefits and don't care as much about having fun or being interested. If you adopt a more realistic view of your future self, reminding yourself that you'll struggle to adhere to any goal that's low on intrinsic motivation, you'll make wiser choices when setting goals and choosing actions. One way to increase your empathy for your future self is to set goals while you're in a state similar to the state you'll be in when executing them. Plan career transitions while you're at work and your diet when you're not completely full. Keeping in mind that intrinsic motivation enables persistence and excellence will help you make wiser choices.

QUESTIONS TO ASK YOURSELF

Intrinsic motivation, defined as the experience of an activity as its own end, is an important ingredient in sticking to our goals. When setting a goal, we want it to be exciting and provide some immediate gratification. Yet we often underestimate how much intrinsic motivation will be the driving force of our actions, and so we fail to set goals in a way that capitalizes on intrinsic motivation. To increase your chances of following through on a goal, you can start by answering the following questions:

1. How can you make pursuing a goal more immediately rewarding? You could, for example, introduce music, podcasts, or audiobooks to your exercise routine.

2. What is the most fun path to pursuing your goals? You could, for example, choose to join a water aerobics class rather than buying a treadmill.

3. Are there immediate benefits you can focus on while pursuing your goal? You could, for example, direct your attention to certain parts of your workout, like that euphoria you feel when you exercise.

4. Can you remind yourself that other people, including your future self, care to be intrinsically motivated just as your present self does? Such a reminder will help you set achievable goals for yourself and others and can further improve your relationships.

Part II

KEEP PULLING

IN 1949, MONTHS AFTER Israel was established as a state, the Defense Service Law gave the state's defense forces the right to enlist any Israeli citizen, regardless of gender. That's how, many years later, I found myself, at age eighteen, after a two-week basic training, working at the Israeli equivalent of the NSA.

If you're imagining me as a fabulous covert spy, with a gun holstered at my hip, jet-setting around the world, don't. My military assignment was no more than an office job (though I did learn how to operate a gun). I moved intelligence reports from my inbox to my outbox (and hence into someone else's inbox). This was before there was widespread internet, so these were actually boxes on my desk. I was literally a paper pusher.

I was assigned to this unit based solely on a few tests I took. While the army kept people's preferences in mind when assigning jobs, I had no preferences to offer, as I found every job equally irrelevant to what I wanted to do with my life. I didn't want to serve in the first place. I did it because it was the law. Like most military jobs in the Israel Defense

Forces (and possibly elsewhere), my assignment was mainly extremely boring. I worked long hours and had little to do. My biggest challenge was figuring out how to pass the time.

As an Israeli woman, I was required to serve in the IDF for two years. No matter how dull my days were, I couldn't quit. To stay motivated, I counted down the days until my next vacation on a calendar I called the "Calendar of Despair." As depressing as it sounds, this turned out to be a good idea.

Whether you've set a life-altering goal like becoming a doctor or a mundane one like answering your unread emails, you'll need to get from point A (premed course work or 100 unanswered emails) to point B (an MD or an uncluttered inbox). How can you sustain your motivation along the way? For me, to get through my mandatory military service and move on with my life, I focused on monitoring progress — specifically, looking ahead at the days I had left until each vacation.

Monitoring progress is an important part of staying motivated. When we feel like we've made a dent in our goals, we're motivated to keep moving. But sometimes it's more difficult to see how much you've progressed. Let's use the metaphor of an analog clock. When you look at the watch's second hand, you can easily see time passing. It would be much more difficult to see time moving if you instead watched the subtler movements of the hour hand. Much like breaking an hour into seconds, breaking a goal into smaller units or subgoals helps us more easily recognize our progress. Setting a numerical target for a goal, as we talked about in Chapter 2, also helps, as it's easier to monitor progress when the target is clearly defined. When reading a book, you can say that you've read 25 percent or that you have 75 percent to go. Either way, this conveys a better sense of progress than saying you've read "the beginning." And when I spent my military service looking ahead from vacation to vacation, I was essentially breaking my two-year service into the six-month periods between my breaks. In Chapter 5, we'll investigate how making and recognizing progress help sustain our motivation.

While making progress is important on its own, how you monitor progress also matters. Whether you record progress in terms of how much you've done or how much you have left to do influences your ability to sustain your motivation. So whether you tell yourself you've read 25 percent of the book or have 75 percent to go actually matters. And, in fact, many electronic reading apps make one of these percentages really clear, telling you that you've currently read 28 percent of the book, for example. In Chapter 6, we'll learn whether I was using the right strategy when I focused on the shrinking days to my next vacation instead of the time that had elapsed since my previous vacation. Is a glass-half-full or a glass-half-empty mentality best? We'll find out.

Regardless of how you monitor progress, sustaining motivation is easier at the start of your journey and, then again, at the finish line. Chapter 7 addresses the "middle problem"; that is, how to avoid getting stuck in the middle of the road.

Finally, to keep moving, we rely on feedback from successful and unsuccessful actions. As we've heard before, we must not forget the past, but instead learn from it. And yet humans generally have a hard time learning from their mistakes. We suppress and ignore negative feedback and pay more attention to positive feedback. In Chapter 8 we'll discusses this asymmetry in learning and responding to positive versus negative feedback. You'll gain strategies to maximize what you learn from failures and setbacks so you do better in the future.

5

PROGRESS INCREASES MOTIVATION

ABOUT ONCE A WEEK, I look up from the computer in my office at the University of Chicago and head to the cafeteria for a smoothie. The thing is, I don't really like smoothies. They're *fine*, and I know they can be a great way to get extra servings of healthy fruits and vegetables, but they don't excite my taste buds. So why do I buy them so reliably?

Well, the cafeteria at my school has an effective rewards program. Last year, they handed me a little card that promised a free smoothie after I'd bought ten. At first, I gave little thought to the card. I don't like smoothies that much anyway, I told myself. But after I got a few stamps, I found myself heading to the smoothie stand more often. The closer I got to the free smoothie, the more I wanted it.

In motivation science, we call this the "goal gradient effect": the more progress you've made, the more eager you will be to keep going. We see this not just in humans, but also in animals. Rats in a maze will run faster as they get closer to the cheese at the end, as Clark Hull discovered. And when my dog spots me from a distance, she runs faster and faster as the space between us shrinks.

Where you are on the timeline of your goal, how much progress you have or haven't made, also affects how likely you are to quit. Consider college dropouts. Almost half of the students who matriculate in America don't graduate. These people are losing out twice: they both paid some tuition and failed to collect the economic benefits that come with a college degree. Economically, they're worse off after completing just part of a degree than they would have been had they never gone to college at all. Though people leave school for many reasons, sometimes because they can't afford to be there, a main reason people drop out is that getting a college degree is a bit like climbing a steep hill for four years straight. It's easy to get discouraged by a lack of progress. Accordingly, a disproportionally large number of students drop out before they complete their first year, at the point when they've made the least progress toward their goal. At the bottom of the hill, the climb looks too steep. But if you've finished the first leg of your hike, like college students who complete their freshman year, you're more likely to keep moving.

Why does progress encourage us to work harder and make it less likely that we'll quit? One reason is that, as we progress, every action we take toward our goal appears to have a larger impact toward achieving it. Another reason is that pursuing a goal increases our commitment to that goal.

PROGRESS INCREASES IMPACT

The potential to make an impact on a goal is a powerful motivator. When we're trying to reach our goals, each action that moves us closer to the finish line feels like it has a bigger impact than the one before. When I bought my first smoothie after getting my reward card, it earned me 10 percent of the free beverage (one out of ten). When I bought my seventh drink, it earned me 25 percent of the free smoothie (one out of the remaining four). And, of course, the tenth and final drink earned me 100 percent. Many have had the same experience with loyalty cards at a local café or from an airline that offers a free flight after you've gained a certain number of frequent flyer miles. Each consecutive drink or flight has a bigger impact on earning your reward.

The college students we talked about earlier, too, feel the surging impact of passing each class. Every semester completes a larger proportion of the remaining distance to their goal of getting a degree. Finishing your freshman year earns you a quarter of a four-year college degree, while completing the last year earns you a full degree. By the time you start your senior year, you expect to get a college degree in return for one year of academic work, which is significantly more than what completing your first year earned you. Whether you aspire to a free coffee or a diploma, the more progress you've made, the more bang you get for your buck. Your efforts pay off and pay more.

Even the illusion of progress increases motivation. It can make you feel closer to completing the goal than you actually are. If by the end of your freshman year you measured your progress toward earning a college degree from the point of applying to college, which often happens a full year before a student starts their first class, you would be 40 percent of the way to your goal; essentially two years into a college degree that takes (in this case) five years to complete. Instead, measuring your progress from the beginning of freshman year would give you only 25 percent. The lesson here: carefully choose how you measure your progress. If you exaggerate what proportion of the distance to a goal you've already covered, you'll feel closer to the finish line.

Let's go back to the example of café loyalty cards. Ran Kivetz, Oleg Urminsky, and Yuhuang Zheng partnered with a New York café to test the motivating effect of illusory progress in an experiment. Café customers received a reward card that offered one free coffee after they'd bought ten. While half of the customers received a card with ten open slots, the other half got a card with twelve open slots. Yet the twelve-slot card had two preexisting "bonus" stamps, so, strictly speaking, these were identical reward programs. Every customer who got a card needed to make ten coffee purchases at the café (and collect ten stamps) to get their free coffee. But the allure of the free stamps was high. People who thought they'd gotten a head start came back to the café more often, filling in their reward card more quickly than the others. When the card came with two out of twelve slots already filled, it felt to customers like they were already 16 percent finished with the goal before they'd even started. Believing they were closer to the reward, they were more motivated to reach the finish line.

The above examples all have one thing in common: they describe "all-or-nothing" goals. Whether you get the final punch in a reward card, graduate from college, or, in the case of your (or my) dog, reunite with an owner at the end of a long day, the structure of the goal is such that you only get your prize upon achieving the goal. These goals are categorically different from "accumulative" goals like working out five times a week or reading twenty books this year.

For all-or-nothing goals, the benefits are conditional on reaching the goal. If you collect *almost* all the points required for a reward, you get nothing, and you're not graduating with a diploma until you pass every required class. As the distance to the goal shrinks, the payoff for your remaining efforts increases. This makes all-or-nothing goals powerfully more motivating as you make progress.

In contrast, accumulative goals allow you to collect the benefits as you go. If you exercise for your health, you accumulate those benefits slowly over every workout. And if you want to read twenty books this year because you want to be well-read, each book is like a mini-goal of its own. Because the benefits gained from an accumulative goal add up over time, the "marginal value"—the added value or benefit of each action (reading a book or working out)—often declines. Economists call this "diminishing marginal value." Your first workout this week makes a bigger impact on your health than the fifth workout. The difference in your physical health between finishing one workout and zero workouts is bigger than the difference between finishing four and five workouts. And if you set your goal as reading twenty books this year, the difference between reading zero books and one book for your intellectual growth is larger than the difference between reading book nineteen and book twenty. You'd correctly assume that the person who read one book this year is significantly more well-read than the person who read no books, but that the person who read twenty books is only marginally more well-read than the one who read nineteen books (although missing the target by just one book would be disappointing; recall our discussion of barely undershooting a target in Chapter 2). You might further assume that reading thirty books this year, if your goal was to read twenty, would be overkill.

For accumulative goals, even if we fall just short of our target, we still collect most of the benefits of goal pursuit. With these goals, you wouldn't necessarily expect progress to increase motivation. Indeed, if we think of going to college as acquiring education, which is a cumulative goal, rather than getting a degree, which is an all-or-nothing goal, the last required course will have the least impact on our intellectual growth. We might as well skip that very last class. Yet even for accumulative goals, making progress often increases motivation. Only the reason is different.

PROGRESS INCREASES COMMITMENT

What if, so far, you'd achieved no progress whatsoever while pursuing your goal, not even illusory progress? Maybe you took a wrong turn at the beginning of a drive and by the time you realized your mistake, you were no closer to your destination than you were when you left. Maybe you were trying to sign up for an online class but were using the wrong link. Maybe you ordered a new sweater, but it got lost in the mail, so the seller canceled the order and asked if you wanted a replacement. Would the mere act of pursuing the goal motivate you to keep trying even before you've seen any progress? Turns out, it would.

Humans have a tendency to keep working on something simply because we've already invested in it. If you've paid upfront for an online knitting course, you want to keep taking classes even if you've learned that you hate knitting. We call this the "sunk-cost fallacy." It's the sense that you've come too far to stop now, or that because you've made an investment you need to keep going regardless of whether you're getting any closer to your goal or whether it's even the best choice for you.

As you can tell by the word "fallacy," an increase in motivation just because you're already doing something is often not in your best interest. You've fallen prey to the sunk-cost fallacy every time you do something just because you've already invested in it, ignoring better alternatives. It could be something as mundane as wearing uncomfortable shoes just because they were expensive or finishing the food on your plate when you're already full just because it won't reheat well. It could also be something as significant as sticking with an unprofitable investment because you've already lost money and are hoping to break even or staying in an unhealthy relationship because you've invested in a person you never should have dated in the first place.

Economic theory suggests that resources invested in the past that cannot be recovered (sunk costs) should not influence your motivation to persist in the present. But they do. And once again, we see this behavior in animals as well as humans. In one experiment, researchers gathered three groups of subjects—humans, rats, and mice (fortunately, in separate labs)—and set them up to gain some reward (food for the rodents and interesting video clips for the humans). Then, while the subjects were waiting, the researchers offered them a chance to switch to an even better reward, which was immediately available. Although it would have made more sense for all subjects to switch to a better reward as soon as it became available, most tended to continue waiting for the first reward, at least for a while. And the longer they'd been waiting, the less likely they were to switch. So the longer a rat had been waiting for plain-flavored pellets, the less likely it was to move to an area in the maze where it could eat chocolate-flavored pellets (like most humans, rats like chocolate more than plain food). And for the human participants, the longer they waited to watch a clip they were only mildly interested in (for example, of a bike accident), the less likely they were to switch to videos they were excited about (for example, of kittens).

I'd tell you to just ignore sunk costs when they're not in your best interests, but that's hard to do. Even when quitting is rationally your best option, you kick yourself for giving up. Why? Because engagement signals commitment. We can find comfort in the idea that our inability to let go of something we've already invested in stems from what is often an adaptive motivational principle: mere engagement increases motivation, and that can be a good thing. When we look back and see the effort we invested in a goal, even if we haven't made much progress, the mere pursuit of a goal signals us to keep going. We can use this knowledge to increase our commitment to goals we want to achieve.

Goal commitment is a two-ingredient recipe: it requires a goal that is both valuable and within reach. The committed person cares deeply about pursuing the goal. It's personally relevant for her, so she assigns a high value to it. She also feels confident that it's within her power to reach the goal. She expects to be able to do it. If the goal is sufficiently valuable and the likelihood of success is sufficiently high, the goal seems worthy of her effort.

To know whether a goal is valuable, you often look at your past actions. If you didn't value it, how else would you explain the effort you've put into the goal so far? By increasing value, past actions might sometimes make you act against your current interests (you might find yourself committed to win an election you've already lost, for example). Yet often, they help you maintain a healthy commitment to your goals (so you can stick to your relationship or to your career on certain days). What you've done in the past also shows you that the goal is within reach; after all, you're already partially successful. Each of these inferences—that the goal is valuable and that you can do it—contributes to your sense of commitment. Further, even if your engagement only makes the goal appear to be more valuable or only makes it appear more feasible, you'll have greater commitment, which in turn helps sustain your motivation.

So, for example, getting rejected after a first date would hardly build your confidence that finding a romantic partner is within reach, but it suggests to you that you care about finding a match. You've engaged in a goal-directed action but haven't made any progress, so your actions suggest to you that the goal is not more feasible, but that it is more valuable. To the extent that your actions are successful, your commitment will increase even more. You learn not only that you care about the goal, but also that, yes, you can achieve it. A first date and then a second tell you that maybe you can find a relationship.

Two classic theories in social psychology make a similar point about how engagement generates commitment. First, Leon Festinger's cognitive dissonance theory. This theory posits that when our behavior doesn't coincide with our beliefs, we change our beliefs to match the behavior. As humans, we don't like saying one thing and doing another. So we try to avoid the dissonance, or mismatch, between our cognition and our actions. Consider, for example, people's views on abortion. If someone has had an abortion, they're more likely to be pro-choice. Given that cisgender men don't personally undergo abortions, the principle of cognitive dissonance can explain why they're less likely to support abortion rights (and correspondingly, why more men than women oppose abortion rights). Applied to motivation, cognitive dissonance theory suggests that we tend to adopt goals that match our past actions and abandon goals that are a mismatch.

A second classic theory known as Daryl Bem's self-perception theory makes a similar point about how your behavior informs your goals. The basic tenet of self-perception theory is that we learn about ourselves in the same way that we learn about others: by observing and explaining our own actions to ourselves. If you saw me walking my dog, you would conclude that I'm a dog lover. By the same logic, if you find yourself walking a dog (and having a good time), you would conclude that you're a dog lover, even if your original motivation was to make money as a dog walker. Often, we aren't fully aware of the original reason for our actions (or we simply forget). The dog walker who deems herself a dog lover forgets that she started walking dogs for the money. And someone who attends a political rally to impress a date might later forget that motivation and conclude that they simply support the cause, meaning they'll support this cause again in the future, even if they've started dating someone else.

The idea that actions create commitment is a fundamental principle in persuasion. Whether you wish to persuade a friend, a team at work, or society at large to adopt a goal, start by getting them to pursue a single goal-congruent action. This single action will increase their commitment to the congruent goal. In a classic experiment that Jonathan Freedman and Scott Fraser conducted about half a century ago, people who were first asked to put a small sign in their front window reading BE A SAFE DRIVER were subsequently more likely to agree to put a giant sign in their front yard reading DRIVE CAREFULLY compared to people who were only asked to put up the big yard sign. While safe driving has long been a concern for society, it's probably not a goal you list high on your priorities. And yet, according to this experiment, safe driving could become heavy on your mind once you say yes to a small request to bring awareness to this cause. Scientists call this the "foot-in-the-door" persuasion technique.

Charities similarly rely on our tendency to act consistently when they solicit small, symbolic donations or collect signatures on a petition. Although a charity might only be interested in demonstrating widespread public support through symbolic donations, often the intention or hope is that the person who provided symbolic help today will adopt the goal of the charity and provide more substantial help tomorrow. As a general principle, you cherish the causes you've helped in the past. If you planted a tree, you're a fan of the forest; if you rescued a pet, you advocate for its entire species.

Even pursuing avoidance goals can increase commitment. The longer you've avoided an undesirable state, the more committed you are to continuing to avoid it. Because applying sunscreen helped you success-fully avoid getting sunburned in the past, you're hopefully committed to never leaving the house on a sunny day unprotected. Negative re-inforcement is effective—we get a sunburn, it's painful, so next time we avoid it by putting on sunblock. But even if your house has never been broken into (so you've never felt the pain of coming home to find your stuff stolen), each time you lock your door, you become more commit-ted to continuing this habit to protect your home. We learn it's within our power to avoid certain states, and when avoiding an undesirable state is possible, our commitment to keep avoiding it increases.

When trying to boost your commitment, and therefore your motiva-tion, regardless of your actual progress, consider reflecting on the effort you've already put into the goal to increase your sense of progress. In a study that explored the effect of attention to progress, Minjung Koo and I asked a group of University of Chicago undergraduates to tell us how motivated they were to study for an upcoming exam. Those who realized they had already covered half of their study materials said they were more motivated to keep studying than the undergraduates who realized they still had half of their materials to cover. Looking behind, rather than ahead, can make you feel more committed.

WHEN LACK OF PROGRESS INCREASES MOTIVATION

We've talked about how progress, or the illusion of it, increases motivation. But what if you haven't made progress? It turns out that sometimes the sense that you're falling behind can also motivate action. Think about a time you looked at the floor and saw a big dust bunny. Maybe that one pile of dust and hair made you look more closely at your home and realize it'd been a while since you'd cleaned. You saw scum on the bathroom sink and coffee stains on your desk and suddenly reached into your closet for the broom.

There are some goals you pursue because you're doing well, but then there are those, like cleaning the house, that you pursue because you're falling behind. The discrepancy between the ideal (clean) state and the present (dirty) state signals to you that you need to take action. Yet when your house is mostly clean, you don't feel the same need to reach for the bleach.

Cybernetic models in psychology portray a motivational system that spurs into action by detecting a discrepancy between the present state and a goal target, or lack of progress. Recall the TOTE (Test, Operate, Test, Exit) model mentioned in Chapter 2. The psychology underlying this model is like a thermostat controlling the temperature in your office or home. A thermostat signals the heating system to go into action when there's a discrepancy between the present temperature and how warm or cold you would like your room to be. To the extent that the room temperature is comfortable, the thermostat doesn't detect an error and the system stays at rest mode. The same process happens in your brain when you evaluate the gap between where you are and where you want to be and find your progress lacking.

Lack of progress can sometimes also be motivating for avoidance goals. Avoidance goals require increasing the distance between a present state and an undesirable state, such as being sick, lonely, or poor. In this case, you might be motivated by getting too close to the state you wish to avoid. When you feel sick, you're motivated to go to a doctor to get healthier. When you feel lonely, you're motivated to call a friend. And when you feel poor, you're motivated to find a higher-paying job.

And, like focusing your attention on how much progress you've made, focusing attention on how much progress you *haven't* made can sometimes help sustain your motivation. Recall the study that found that undergraduates were more motivated to study for an upcoming exam if they paid attention to how much they'd already covered versus the materials they hadn't. The thing I didn't tell you was that we were asking about an exam that wasn't very important for them (it was a pass/fail exam, which meant there was no incentive to work for an A).

When we measured undergraduates' motivation to study for a highly important exam (one that offered a letter grade and would influence their GPA), we found the opposite pattern. Those who paid attention to how much they hadn't yet covered were more motivated to study than those who considered what they had already studied. Lack of progress was more motivating.

When you find yourself facing a goal that's highly important, framing your progress based on what you haven't yet accomplished may be more motivating than thinking about what you've already done.

EMOTIONS CUE GOAL PROGRESS

We've learned that while progress generally helps sustain motivation, there are times when lack of progress is even more effective. In the next chapter we'll talk in depth about how to monitor progress and decide whether progress or the lack of it will be more motivating in any given situation. But first, let's look at how emotions play a role in monitoring progress.

Our emotions serve as a sensory system. When we feel good, we know that something is going right. It could be the weather or the presence of a loved one; it could also be that we're making progress on our goal. When we feel bad, we know something is wrong. And if we feel bad about our goal progress, we know we're falling behind on that goal.

This is not to say that pursuing a goal feels bad until the goal is reached. If that were true, we would rarely feel good. Feeling happy, excited, relieved, or proud throughout the journey is common and critical. In fact, the positive feelings on the road to reaching a goal can exceed the experience of reaching the destination. This tells us that the positive or negative feelings we have about our goal aren't evoked by the absolute distance to the target. Instead, our feelings are evoked by the difference between the actual rate of progress and the expected rate of progress. When you feel good about your progress toward a goal, it's because you're ahead of where you thought you would be at that point. When you feel bad, it's because you expected you'd be further along by now.

Many of our goals require long-term planning and continuous effort. We might pursue them over months or years. Yet at any point in time, we can compare our actual rate of progress to where we expected to be. If you decided to learn Russian and expected to be able to carry on a simple conversation after a few months, you'd likely be disappointed if you were only able to count to ten and name a few colors. But if you could name numbers and colors after just one week, you'd probably feel proud of your progress.

Further, as you recall from Chapter 1, the type of goal toward which you're making or failing to make progress will inform the specific feelings you experience. Faster-than-expected progress on approach goals makes you feel happy, proud, eager, and excited, while slower-than-expected progress on approach goals makes you feel sad, depressed, frustrated, and angry. Faster-than-expected progress on avoidance goals makes you feel relief, calmness, relaxation, and contentment, while slower-than-expected progress on avoidance goals makes you feel anxiety, fear, and guilt.

By providing feedback on our rate of progress, our feelings inform our motivational system. Positive emotions encourage us to work harder. You might exercise harder or cook a more elaborate meal because you're proud of or happy about the progress you've made at the gym or in developing your cooking skills. Or you might relax your effort because you feel bad. We get discouraged by feeling depressed or frustrated. In extreme cases, we might even give up on the goal.

Other times, lack of progress increases motivation, and the effects of our emotions reverse. We work harder when we feel bad about our slow progress and disengage with a goal when we feel too good about our progress. You might quit a diet after shedding just a couple of pounds, forget your debit card in the ATM machine, or leave the nozzle in the gas tank. With cash in your hands, it's easy to skip the final step of collecting the debit card. And with a full tank, it's easy to neglect the final but critical step of returning the nozzle to the pump. Our satisfaction signals to us that we've exceeded our expectations. We feel we're "overdoing it," so we slow down our efforts (often, too soon).

So while emotions help us gauge the progress we've made on a goal, the implications of emotions for motivation are a bit more complex. For example, in a study conducted with college students who were on a diet, Maria Louro, Rik Pieters, and Marcel Zeelenberg found that when these dieters felt good about their diet on one day, they paid less attention to their diet the following day. When they were less worried about losing weight, they could focus more on their schoolwork. But only dieters who had already made a lot of progress displayed this pattern. Among beginners, the pattern reversed: when they felt good about their diet on one day, they increased their dieting efforts on the following day.

A similar pattern happens when we tell people how well they're doing, rather than letting them rely solely on emotions for feedback. Szu-Chi Huang and Ying Zhang had research participants memorize details such as the place of origin and the vintage of the wine from several wine labels. When some learned that their progress was faster than average, they spent less time trying to memorize the labels. Yet, once again, this pattern only emerged among those who had experience (i.e., had already made a lot of progress). When beginners learned they were making faster progress than others, they increased their effort, spending more time reading and remembering facts about wine. Their behavior was consistent with what you'd expect if you assumed that progress, rather than lack of progress, motivates.

So while emotions help us recognize whether or not we're making progress fast enough, this feedback can have opposite effects on our motivation. At times, feeling good about our progress increases our motivation; at other times, feeling bad about lack of progress pushes us to work harder.

QUESTIONS TO ASK YOURSELF

Progress helps sustain your motivation by increasing your commitment, including building confidence in your ability and affirming the value of the goal you pursue. It is, therefore, useful to monitor your progress. Once you've achieved some, it's usually easier to keep going. Yet, interestingly, lack of progress can also help sustain your motivation. It's often useful to look ahead at what you have yet to achieve in order to stay on track. To motivate yourself by monitoring progress, ask yourself the following questions:

1. Look back at what you have accomplished. Does that mental exercise help you regain your goal commitment? Does it remind you why you've chosen to pursue this goal in the first place?

2. Look ahead at what you still need to do to accomplish your goals. Does that mental exercise make you eager to start moving? Looking forward is a reminder to stay on track and monitor the pace of progress to meet your goal.

3. Tune in to your emotions. How do you feel about your goals? If you feel good about holding your goal but not as good about your progress, your feelings will guide your actions and help you sustain your motivation.

6

THE GLASS HALF FULL
AND HALF EMPTY

NINE YEARS AGO, MY husband and I were sitting in a big, open room at a federal building in Chicago, waiting to be called in for our naturalization tests. For about a month, we'd been studying a list of one hundred US civics questions, preparing for this exam. If we passed, we'd become US citizens. We'd moved to the States eleven years before to pursue research careers in Maryland and found a home in Chicago with our two young daughters two years later, when I was offered a faculty position at the University of Chicago.

When the interviewer called my name, I squeezed my husband's hand goodbye, grabbed my application forms, and walked into a small room with a desk and two chairs. My interviewer motioned for me to sit in the chair in front of the desk. She sat on the other side of the desk and we got started.

As nervous as I was, I felt confident because I knew the answers to most of the questions. In the weeks leading up to the test, my husband and I had focused first on the easy questions: Who was the first president of the United States? Later, we encouraged ourselves to keep studying by reminding ourselves that many of the test questions were difficult, especially since we didn't grow up in the US: What did Susan B. Anthony do? Name one American Indian tribe.

In the end, our studying paid off. The interviewer asks only ten of the hundred possible questions, and you need to get six right to pass the test. Although my husband stumbled on the name of "The Star-Spangled Banner" (though he could sing every lyric), we both passed easily.

Monitoring progress is critical for sustaining motivation. But how should we monitor it? Different schools of motivation science offer different answers. Think of these solutions in terms of the proverbial question: Is the glass half full or half empty? Typically, seeing a glass as half full points toward someone being an optimist and seeing it as half empty indicates pessimism. But in motivation science, the terms have a slightly different meaning. Some suggest that keeping track of everything you've already done—the glass half full—will help you stay motivated because progress increases motivation. Others suggest that keeping track of what you plan to do—the glass half empty—will increase your motivation because lack of progress increases motivation. As we learned in the last chapter, they're both right. Sometimes progress is better at motivating action and sometimes the lack of progress is better. It depends on the person and the circumstances. As we were studying for our civics test, my husband and I switched between the two views. First, we focused on the easy questions, building up our confidence through easy progress. When we had those questions down, we focused on the more difficult questions. Knowing that much of the test would be difficult motivated us to study through a lack of progress. We knew we'd need to memorize the answers to those hard questions if we wanted to pass.

In this chapter, I'll explain how to tell if and when looking at the glass half empty or the glass half full will push you to keep going. To do so, I must first introduce you to the two dynamics of goal motivation (aka dynamics of self-regulation).

DYNAMICS OF GOAL MOTIVATION

Imagine you're out to dinner with friends. As you peruse the menu, you remind yourself that you want to start eating more healthily. So you skip over the burgers and the heavier pastas and land on a rice bowl with roasted cauliflower, kale, carrots, and spiced lentils. It's a flavorful, healthy choice. You feel good about keeping your promise to yourself. As the evening wears on and everyone finishes their plates, the table starts talking about dessert.

Now you're faced with another choice. Do you choose a healthy dessert like fruit or a small dish of sorbet, forgo dessert altogether, or allow yourself to indulge in something more decadent like a silky piece of cheesecake? Do you make a second healthy choice or does the first give you some leeway this time?

These two possibilities illustrate the two basic dynamics humans typically follow when pursuing their goals. I call the first "commitment promotes consistency." When we feel committed to our goals, each action we take toward a goal heightens our commitment and reinforces similar actions. Remember, people don't like cognitive dissonance, so we tend to do things that support what we've done before. Following this dynamic, after ordering a healthy entrée, you're more likely to choose a healthy dessert or skip dessert altogether. On the other hand, failure to pursue a goal signals lack of commitment and undermines our motivation.

In the other dynamic, which I call "progress promotes balancing," the motivation for pursuing a goal stems from a lack of progress. When you haven't yet made much progress, you're motivated to keep trying. But when you look back and see that you've made a good amount of progress, you feel that you can loosen the reins. You balance the progress on that goal by attending to something else that you've been neglecting or by deciding to take a break. After ordering a healthy entrée, you may balance it with a decadent dessert. In this dynamic, we often feel motivated again after having slacked off.

Some schools in motivation science assume that people follow commitment-promotes-consistency and others assume that people follow progress-promotes-balancing (or, in simpler terms, consistency versus balancing). These differing schools will offer you different recommendations for increasing your motivation. Social organizations also vary by the dynamic they advise you to follow. Alcoholics Anonymous advocates for complete sobriety; that is, a dynamic of consistency. Alcoholics are encouraged to interpret times of sobriety as a sign of personal commitment. They celebrate the time they've been sober and win rewards for getting to certain milestones. With each day of sobriety, the commitment to stay sober on the following day increases. At no point are alcoholics encouraged to relax their motivation to stay sober or balance it out by drinking on special occasions. In contrast, dieting programs traditionally advocate for a dynamic of balancing. Within this dynamic, dieters are encouraged to stay within a daily caloric budget, which means that eating fewer calories in the morning justifies a bit more splurging in the evening. What is considered a relapse for alcoholics is merely going over budget for dieters, as they're encouraged to balance low- and high-calorie foods.

Even religious ideologies vary by the dynamic they ascribe to their followers. Catholicism allows for balance. Sins are setbacks; they're viewed as lack of progress or even backward progress that can be overcome with extra religious work. On the other hand, Calvinism advocates for consistency. Calvinists are expected to follow a life of good work that offers no forgiveness for sins.

The two dynamics of goal motivation tell us that when progress (completed actions) increases our motivation, it does so in a very different way than lack of progress (missing actions). Completed actions increase motivation by signaling to us that we're committed to the goal. Missing actions increase motivation by signaling to us that we need to make progress.

To get a sense of these distinct routes to goal motivation, consider waiting in line. Whether it's the line in your coffee shop, the doctor's office, or the DMV, you can increase your motivation to wait and, ultimately, your patience, by either looking back and monitoring the progress you've made thus far or looking ahead and monitoring the remaining progress you need to make to reach the start of the line (more on patience in Chapter 11). Monitoring how far you've come would make you feel more committed to stay in line. Looking back increases your belief that whatever you're waiting for is valuable and worth your wait, so you'll stay motivated to keep waiting. Monitoring how far you still need to go will also increase your motivation, albeit in a different way. Looking ahead, you'll be able to calculate how quickly the line is moving (the rate of progress) and recruit patience to help you sustain your motivation as you wait. Indeed, when Minjung Koo and I surveyed people waiting in various lines in the US and South Korea, we found that making progress or merely looking back motivated people differently than lack of progress or merely looking ahead.

Around lunchtime in Chicago, the line for Einstein Bros. Bagels usually stretches through the shop and out the door. People flood the popular bagel place for quick and tasty sandwiches built on flavorful bagels like the asiago cheese, garlic, and cranberry. Knowing that this line builds every day, Koo and I surveyed customers standing in lines anywhere from four to fourteen people deep. We counted how many people were standing in line behind them (a proxy for how much progress that person had made) and how many people were standing in front of them (a proxy for lack of progress). We found that when more people were standing behind them, these customers expected their bagel sandwich to taste better than when only a few were standing behind. Seeing how far they'd come increased how much people looked forward to their meal. We also found that when more people were standing ahead of them, customers were preparing themselves to wait longer.

We concluded that while standing in line, just looking back (and considering progress) motivates people differently than looking ahead (and considering lack of progress). We observed this pattern when we surveyed people standing around the middle of a line for an amusement park ride in South Korea. One of the most popular rides at Lotte World, a theme park in Seoul, is an Indiana Jones–style adventure ride called Pharaoh's Fury. Passengers are loaded into a car that looks like a beat-up old jeep. They then plummet into a dark underground tunnel with creepy critters—snakes, bats, spiders, crocodiles, and, of course, lots of mummies—coming out of the walls. The ride winds around, in and out of these dark tunnels, eventually going through the titular pharaoh's mouth and plunging into a golden room. Most people coming to Lotte World know about, and are excited for, this signature ride. We chose to survey those in the middle of the line so that the objective progress was similar for all. When we asked people to look back, they expected the ride to be more fun than those we asked to look ahead. Though we didn't estimate remaining wait time, I'd expect that those who were looking at the number of people ahead of them were preparing themselves to wait longer.

LEVEL OF ASPIRATION

How ambitious are you? Do you reach for the sky or are you happy with where you are? As it turns out, which goal-motivation dynamic you follow influences your ambition.

We define ambition by your level of aspiration. You've heard the phrase "climbing the ladder" when it comes to your work. People who climb the ladder quickly are considered ambitious. And those who are stuck on one rung of the ladder aren't thought very ambitious at all. People's actions often follow a goal ladder in which each goal is a step toward another, more challenging goal. In your career, an entry-level position is a step toward a more advanced position in the organization.

This imagery of a ladder works for other goals as well. Your ambition further varies across goals, as you obviously care about some more than others. You may aspire to advance in your career but have little desire to advance as a tennis player. When I was counting down the days on my Calendar of Despair in the Israeli military, I had very little ambition. I was just trying to serve my two years and get out. I retired as a sergeant, low on the organizational rung of the army. But when I started as an assistant professor at the University of Chicago in 2002, I was always aiming higher. Now I'm a tenured professor.

Some goal ladders are highly structured, as when moving up the military ranks from private to corporal or the karate ranks from red to black belt. Others are less defined, as when you aspire to deepen your yoga practice. But beyond how much you care about the goal and how structured the goal ladder is, the way you monitor your actions and your dynamic of goal motivation influence your level of aspiration.

Paying attention to progress you've made makes you value your current position more; you might be more satisfied with where you are and less likely to desire change than if you considered what might be ahead. By looking back, you increase your commitment to where you are and feel less motivation to change. Paying attention to what you haven't yet accomplished, in contrast, will more likely encourage you to seek change and move forward. You're eager to either move up or move out.

I've heard many stories from friends and students looking for career advice that reinforce this idea. One story came from a former student who was questioning whether she should go for a promotion. A computer engineer who loves programming, she had two ways to look at her possible promotion to a management position. Engineering managers do little actual coding, instead organizing projects and delegating coding to other engineers on their teams. So my student could pay attention to what she'd already achieved as an engineer or she could look at what she hadn't yet achieved in her current role. If she looked back and saw what she had achieved, her commitment to coding would shoot up and she might forgo the management promotion, wanting to continue the work she loves. If, however, she focused her attention on what she hadn't yet achieved in her current role, she'd be more likely to want to move her career in a new direction. Directing her attention to the glass half empty, my student decided to take the promotion and move up the ladder.

When Minjung Koo and I asked half of the employees at an advertising agency to reflect on what they'd achieved at work and the other half to reflect on what they would like to achieve, we found that reflecting on what they would like to achieve in the future made people more ambitious. Those who considered what they had yet to achieve were more interested in moving up the ladder. Those who considered past achievements, however, felt they enjoyed their role more and were more likely to want to keep it. They were committed to their present level.

So what happens when a scientist isn't standing next to you, asking you to either look ahead or look back? Well, many of us unconsciously do one or the other. People who are intrinsically more ambitious and aspire to move up the ladder tend to spontaneously direct their attention to missing actions. If I asked you about your progress at work and you reported it in terms of missing actions, I'd suspect you're already preparing to move up to the next level. If you said, for example, "I have three more projects I need to complete this quarter," I'd assume you have a high level of aspiration because you're thinking of what you'll be doing once you've completed these tasks. But if you reported your progress in terms of completed actions, saying, for example, "I've already finished two projects this quarter," I'd assume you're committed to your current level and have a low desire to move up. Because you're thinking about your progress in terms of what you've completed rather than what is left for you to do, I could infer that you feel comfortable where you are.

THE REPRESENTATION OF ACTIONS

Whether focusing on completed actions, which increase commitment, or focusing on missing actions, which increase motivation by signaling lack of progress, is the best choice depends on the situation. Our emphasis should be on when to use one strategy over the other, not whether one strategy is better.

So when thinking which dynamic of goal motivation will work best for you, examine your current commitment. If you already feel firmly committed to your goal, completed actions won't change this. Focusing on the progress you've already made might even make you feel you've done enough and encourage you to take a break. Similarly, if you're very uncertain about your commitment and are contemplating the point of doing something, missing actions won't motivate you to move forward. Focusing on a lack of progress might even signal lack of commitment, which will lead you to quit.

Take your job, for example. If you're very certain about your commitment to your job—you either love or hate your work—completing work tasks won't move the needle on your commitment. While other employees feel more committed when they're achieving more, you take these completed tasks as a sign of progress and, once you've done enough, you relax your efforts; you might even go home early. Alternatively, if you're not sure about your job commitment—maybe wondering if the job is right for you—falling behind on work that's piling up faster than you anticipated won't make you eager to work harder or inspire you to move up the ladder. While other employees work harder when they fall behind, you take your slow progress as a signal that you aren't cut out for the job. You might think about quitting.

The dynamic of goal motivation that people follow may therefore depend on their action "representation": whether they interpret their actions as a signal of their commitment or as a signal of their progress.

For people who adopt a "commitment representation" of actions, their actions discern their commitment. They ask: "Does my behavior suggest I care for this goal?" They evaluate their confidence in their success as well as their personal attraction to the goal based on what they've achieved. In contrast, people who adopt a "progress representation" look at their actions to discern their progress. They ask: "Does my behavior indicate I've made enough progress?"

These action representations have direct motivational consequences. After success, people who adopt a commitment representation tend to select consistent actions that further help their goal. After falling short on pursuing a goal, they feel less motivated. These people are therefore more motivated by the half of the glass that's full. They're the employees for whom successes boost work motivation.

In contrast, people who adopt a progress representation tend to balance their success by relaxing their effort. When they've racked up achievements, they conclude they've made enough progress, and that this is a good enough reason to slow down. Yet after failing to take action, they increase their effort to catch up. These people are therefore motivated by the half of the glass that's empty. They're the employees for whom success at work will justify slowing down.

These categories aren't rigid. Adopting a commitment representation in one context doesn't mean you'll only ever be motivated by past achievements. In fact, many people in your life (including you) attempt to influence how you interpret your actions to persuade you to stick with a goal. Bosses, teachers, politicians, and salespeople are all trying to influence you by influencing how you see your actions. When a brand congratulates you on your loyalty, it frames your past purchase as an act of expressing commitment. You should come back to the store because you're a loyal customer who values the brand, not because you already bought a lot of stuff there. Alternatively, if you haven't been spending your money on this brand lately, you might get an email that says, "We miss you…" This email frames your lack of action as lack of progress. Rather than calling you disloyal, the sales pitch will emphasize that you haven't checked out the brand in a while and rely on your desire to catch up to motivate another purchase.

WHAT DETERMINES ACTION REPRESENTATION?

Let's go back, for a moment, to my time in the military. Was I using the right strategy when I looked ahead, focusing on the days left until my next vacation? Knowing what I now know about motivation, I realize I likely would have been better off looking back. My commitment was low to begin with, and by looking back, I would've had a chance of appreciating the work I'd done well and maybe have become more enthusiastic about my job.

Throughout your life, you might sometimes be the type of person who thinks about pursuing goals in terms of expressing commitment and other times be the type who thinks in terms of making progress. Which person you are and, hence, what you find more motivating, depend, as is often the case, on the goal and your circumstances.

When someone is new to something or unsure how much they like or value it, they take their actions as evidence of their commitment. When you've just started something new and want to figure out if you're good at it, your completed actions increase your commitment and your missing actions decrease your commitment. The result is that novices are more motivated by the glass half full. Experts and people who are working on something that's very important to them don't question their commitment; they already know they care. If you've been doing something for a long time, you don't have to ask yourself if you enjoy it or if it's valuable to you. You're better able to sustain your motivation if you focus on what you didn't do—you look at the glass half empty.

Take gym attendance, for example. If you're a new member at the gym, thinking about the days you've worked out so far will help you sustain your motivation more than thinking about how many days you've skipped the gym. But if the weight room feels like your second home, thinking about how many days you've recently skipped the gym will help you sustain your motivation.

Over time, you might go from being a gym novice to a gym rat. And as your identity shifts, so will the way you sustain your motivation. For many goals, you start by evaluating your commitment and, over time and with experience, shift to monitoring progress. When you open a new savings account, for example, you might evaluate your commitment, wondering whether meeting your saving goal is even feasible. But once you've spent some time building up your savings account, you'll feel more certain that saving is possible and switch to monitoring progress. You're moving from assessing the goal to pushing forward, or from deliberating to implementing action plans.

Yet the transition from asking about commitment to asking about progress is rarely complete; you might never stop evaluating or even doubting your commitment. Even people who feel secure in their commitment doubt themselves at times. This happens in part because our status as expert versus novice depends on the context. In the presence of a personal trainer, your workout routine might feel like a novice's, yet the same routine may make you feel like an expert when you compare yourself to a friend who rarely leaves the couch.

How important your goal is also determines whether you're more likely to be motivated by progress or the lack of it. Most people are more committed to saving for retirement than to saving for their next vacation. Therefore, when they consider retirement savings they don't yet have, they increase their monthly contributions more than when they consider how much they've already saved. But when it comes to saving for their vacation, they're more motivated to keep saving if they think about how much they already have in the vacation fund.

To determine which half of the glass will motivate you, you need to consider both the context and the importance of your goal. Do you feel like an expert or a novice? Is this goal one you *have* to achieve or one that would just be nice to reach? Based on your circumstances, you can flexibly switch between monitoring completed versus missing actions, looking back or looking forward.

QUESTIONS TO ASK YOURSELF

At times, you will need to think of the glass as half full; at others, you should consider it half empty. To effectively monitor your progress, you should flexibly and strategically switch between looking back and looking ahead. Ask yourself:

1. For a given goal you're pursuing, are you balancing your efforts, working hard when you're falling behind; or consistent in your efforts, highlighting the goal by consistently striving toward it? Does your pattern fit the goal? It might be more appropriate to balance if you wish to maintain your current state, but you'll need to highlight it if you're seeking change.

2. How confident are you about your goal commitment? When you're uncertain about your commitment, you can sustain your motivation by looking at the glass half full. What have you already achieved? When you're committed to a goal, the glass half empty will keep you going. Ask yourself what is left to be done.

3. How much experience do you have with your goal? If you're a novice, watch the glass as it's filling up; if you're an expert, check the glass as it starts to empty.

7

THE MIDDLE PROBLEM

WHEN NEW STUDENTS ARRIVE on campus, we celebrate the beginning of their academic studies with a weeklong party. Incoming freshmen come to school days before older students start arriving. We do this in part to give them time to say goodbye to their old lives and acclimate to their new ones. In a touching ceremony, parents dropping their kids at my college stay outside the gate at the center of the old campus as their children walk through it. Volunteers hold boxes of tissues for parents to wipe their tears as their kids cross over. After the tearful goodbye, incoming freshmen are ushered into college with convocation, trips to explore the city, dinners out, school-sponsored parties, and a ton of swag from organizations and clubs on campus. They get very little sleep during this transitory week.

Roughly four years later, we celebrate their leaving. Again, the college hosts multiple events and parents throw fancy dinner parties for their graduates, all leading up to the main event of graduation. Even when the COVID-19 pandemic forced us to move our operations online, we still had a virtual celebration to usher new freshmen into the university and virtual parties to usher graduating seniors out.

The only time we don't throw a party is in the middle. While beginnings and endings are special, middles are ordinary; they don't call for celebration. It's during these ordinary times that our enthusiasm and motivation are the hardest to maintain. We're highly motivated at the beginning. We want to reach our goal and we want to do it right. Over time, our motivation declines as we lose steam. To the extent that our goal has a clear end point, as in the case of all-or-nothing goals (such as graduating with a diploma), our motivation will pick up again toward the end.

Long middles are therefore dangerous. They should come with a warning sign: FRAGILE MOTIVATION. HANDLE WITH CARE. While most people are enthusiastic and conscientious at the beginning and at the end of goal pursuit, in the middle, both the motivation to get it done and the motivation to do it right (with high standards) tend to suffer. So how can we keep on track, even in the middle, when motivation is naturally low?

DOING IT RIGHT

A person who's willing to lie in a job interview to get a job is clearly highly motivated to land a job offer. He's willing to risk a lot, including how he feels when he looks in the mirror. But while his motivation to reach a desired outcome is high, his motivation to use the appropriate means in doing so is low. He lets the end justify the means.

When we think about people's motivation, we often focus on their motivation to get things done, giving less attention to their motivation to do it right. We may refer to people's eagerness to finish a task, including how much mental and physical effort they're willing to invest to finish quickly or to get a lot done. At times, doing something right overlaps with doing it quickly or doing a lot of it. If you're running a hundred-meter race, running quickly is, by definition, doing it right. The runner who finishes the race first wins the gold medal.

But eagerness to finish the task doesn't always correspond to, and may even conflict with, the motivation to do it well. Consider a contractor renovating your home. Finishing the work quickly doesn't necessarily correspond with doing it right. Taking more time to plan the budget, getting the right materials and the correct amount of them, checking and double-checking the work of the plumber, electrician, cabinet person, and others, and ensuring a high-quality finish mean better performance. Doing it right often takes time.

We can think of the motivation to do something right as wanting to pursue a task methodically and carefully as opposed to cutting corners, letting our attention drift away, or, more generally, compromising our standards. The motivation to do it right often gets priority. Whether you're at work, at the gym, or cooking a meal, you usually hope to get it right, not just get it done. The end should not justify the means.

Doing it right also means you follow ethical standards. You might care about fairness, in which case you aren't just concerned about getting what you want; you want to get it fair and square. Maybe you were appalled when I painted a picture of a person who lies on a job interview. The idea of pretending to have more skill or experience than you do is abhorrent because you can't imagine taking the opportunity from someone who rightfully earned it. And if you're playing a friendly game of basketball with coworkers, you want to win because your team is the best. It's much less fun to win if you suspect someone on your team is cheating.

For most goals, the motivation to do it right coexists with the motivation to get it done, and they both fluctuate over the course of the journey. At times, these motivations overlap, as they do for the competitive runner. At other times, these motivations can be in direct opposition to each other. You might relax your standards so you can get the job done, as in the case of a contractor who chooses to skip important steps, like ensuring that the electrical work looks sound, in order to finish faster. Yet, to a large extent, these are independent motivations.

We're motivated to do something right—to win the job or the game based on our skill and knowledge—largely because we're concerned with what our actions reveal about the kind of person we are. We want to make a good impression on people. So we choose to do things through the proper means, with both high standards and ethics. We also care about self-impressions. When no one is looking, we still have to make an impression on ourselves.

Recall that we learn about ourselves similarly to the way we learn about others: by drawing conclusions from our behaviors (if your date took you to a political rally, you'll later infer that you support the cause). When we relax our standards, we signal to ourselves that we have low standards. In this way, following high standards helps us maintain high self-esteem on top of receiving esteem from others. In contrast, relaxing ethical and performance standards undermines what others think of us as well as how we see ourselves.

To illustrate this point, consider how you would feel about getting money that isn't yours. When I find a dollar on the ground, I happily pick it up and put it in my pocket. But once, when buying tickets to an art museum in Zurich, I spotted a Swiss hundred-franc bill (about $110 in US money) on the ground. Assuming someone had dropped it when they were getting their tickets, I waited in the lobby for a long time hoping they'd come back to claim their fortune. It's no fun taking such a large sum from another person. In the end, to protect my self-esteem (I'm not a thief), I donated the money to an animal welfare group.

Most people would feel the same. If a cashier at the grocery store undercharged you by a dollar, there's a good chance you wouldn't correct the mistake. Getting an extra dollar is a small win that doesn't hurt whoever lost it. But what if you were undercharged $20 or $30? Many of us would likely point out the mistake so we could leave the store feeling good, not guilty.

But not all actions carry an equally weighted signal. Some, like when I picked up that Swiss bill, are repeatedly and thoroughly analyzed, while others fly under the radar, getting less attention and scrutiny. If you suspect that no one, including yourself, will pay attention to your behavior, you can behave in suboptimal ways without worrying too much about the consequences for how others, or even you, see you. Think back to my students, who openly admitted they'd consider robbing a bank if they wouldn't get caught. In that scenario, they'd still have their own sense of right and wrong to stop them. But if you've ever eaten a delicious dessert very quickly over the sink before your self-awareness kicked in, you know what it means to hide your actions from yourself.

So how does the motivation to do it right fluctuate over the course of pursuing a goal? The answer is in the tendency for some actions to appear more hidden. And, generally, it's easier to hide things from others and from ourselves in the middle. We see a literal example of this in an experiment Maya Bar-Hillel did with test questions. People who signed up for the study were asked to write one four-choice question. They could make up anything they wanted to. If I had been in the study, I might have written: "What is the capital of Illinois? A. Chicago, B. Springfield, C. Schaumburg, or D. Detroit." The researchers didn't care about the content of the question; they just wanted to know where participants put the correct answer. If people were to present the correct answers in truly random locations, around 25 percent of the correct answers would be in positions A, B, C, and D. But this wasn't the case. Around 80 percent of participants chose to place the correct answer in one of the two middle positions: B, just as I did, or C. Naïve test makers hide the correct answer in the middle because middles appear hidden.

The same goes for hiding our actions from ourselves. People follow ethical standards more closely at the beginning and end of a goal and relax their standards in the middle, even if only they will know. Beginning and end positions are more memorable than middle ones. When you try to remember everything you did during a weeklong vacation, what you did on the first and last days likely pops to mind more quickly than what you did on any day in the middle. And if you've had the luxury of enjoying a fancy, multicourse meal, the first and last dishes set the tone for the entire experience. We have a tendency as humans to remember the first few items in a sequence (we call this the "primacy effect") and the last few items (the "recency effect") better than the items in the middle. When you think about your actions, you similarly expect to remember what you did first and last on the path to your goal more than everything that happened in the middle. Knowing that we'll forget what we've done in the middle, we subconsciously realize that cheating won't undermine our self-esteem, and it's easier to hide from ourselves.

"Cutting corners" is a common phrase used when someone gives up quality in favor of finishing something quickly or cheaply. But Maferima Touré-Tillery and I found that in the middle of pursuing a goal, people literally cut corners. We handed our participants a pair of scissors and asked them to cut out five identical shapes (a square with arrows coming out all four sides). At first, the people in our study neatly cut their shape, but by the time they got to the third shape, they started cutting through more corners. Then, toward the fifth shape, their shapes became neat again.

While that experiment showed us that people literally cut corners in the middle of a project, another experiment revealed that the same is true in a more figurative sense. People lower their ethical standards in the middle. We had participants proofread ten passages, looking for spelling, grammar, and other types of mistakes. For each task, they had to assign themselves to a short version (a passage that had just two errors) or a long version (a passage that had ten errors). They did so by flipping a coin, presumably to ensure random allocation. We weren't interested in how they did on the tasks, but instead in how the coin toss came out. If the percentage of participants assigning themselves to the short task was greater than chance (50 percent), you could suspect that some were cheating. While we couldn't tell whether any specific person was cheating, if 70 percent of the participants ended up completing the short task, it's likely that 50 percent got it by chance and another 20 percent cheated on the coin toss. And we did find that some of the people in our study cheated. But once again, participants were relaxing their standard in the middle: they were more likely to cheat and assign themselves to the short task halfway through the experiment than at the beginning and at the end.

Outside the lab, we found that even in religious traditions, people tend to relax their goal in the middle. The Jewish holiday Hanukkah requires lighting the menorah every night for eight consecutive nights. As the story goes, when the Maccabees were driven out of the temple, they discovered they had only enough oil to light the menorah for a single day. Yet, miraculously, the oil burned for eight days, enough time for new oil to be pressed and made ready. To celebrate, Jewish people eat oil-rich foods and light the eight candles on the menorah one at a time (first one, then two, then three...) over the eight nights. When we surveyed people who celebrate Hanukkah, we found that more people adhere to the ritual on the first and last nights than on all the nights in the middle. Keeping with our expectations about the effect of the middle, people also tended to judge others more harshly, considering them less religious, if they didn't light the menorah on the first and last nights than if they skipped the ritual on any of the nights in between.

Adherence to standards—doing things the right way—is stronger at the beginning and end of pursuing a goal. To use this tendency to your advantage, you may want to keep middles short. A weekly healthy-eating goal is better than a monthly healthy-eating goal, as it offers fewer days to cheat on your diet. And when it comes to a large project with a faraway deadline at work, start by breaking it into weekly assignments so that you don't lose steam in the middle. You can also frame the present as a beginning or an end, just not as the middle. Think of your lunch choice as happening at the end of the morning or the beginning of the afternoon rather than in the middle of the day, and you'll choose healthier food.

GETTING IT DONE

In Chapter 5 we talked about all-or-nothing goals. These are goals for which you only get your reward at the end, and therefore you feel you're getting more bang for your buck the further along you are. With progress, each action covers a larger proportion of the remaining distance to complete your goal. While the first year of a four-year college gets you 25 percent of an academic degree, the last year gets you 100 percent. For these goals, progress is motivating.

Recall also that for accumulative goals, you collect the benefits as you go. And because you get little rewards along the way, typically, the more you do, the less additional value you get for extra work. The first book you read about astronomy teaches you more than the fifth book. Your motivation to read about astronomy should therefore be high at the beginning and decrease with each book you read.

Yet, like many things in life, your goals aren't always one or the other. Many goals combine elements from both goal structures. You'll be motivated to reach the end even if, technically, the marginal value of each additional action diminishes. Take the goal to reach a certain number of steps per day. The marginal value of walking 100 steps is lower after you've already walked 9,900 steps. But if your goal is to walk 10,000 steps a day, the last 100 steps are more important to you than the 100 steps before them. These last steps help you achieve your goal target, which feels good.

A goal might also offer benefits that are both accumulative and all-or-nothing. Although the marginal impact of pulling a pie out of the oven may decrease after you've already served the appetizer and entrée at a dinner party, plating dessert covers 100 percent to finishing dinner, while appetizers only finished 30 percent of your responsibilities as a dinner host. While the marginal value of each complete course decreases (satisfying hunger is an accumulative goal), a successful dinner party is an all-or-nothing goal, which means the motivation to serve dessert is high.

It follows that people have good reason to feel motivated when they're starting on a goal as well as when they approach the finish line. At the beginning, you accumulate benefits rapidly. With the last few actions, you rapidly approach the end. The problem, again, is with the middle. In the middle, you're at risk of feeling stuck.

Further, in the middle, whether you compare your next action to the distance you've traveled thus far or to the remaining distance needed to meet the goal, that action will seem to have a negligible impact. This problem results from what I refer to as the "small-area principle."

According to the small-area principle, to sustain motivation, we need to compare our next action to whichever is smaller: the progress we've already made, or the progress we still need to make to meet the goal. At the beginning of pursuing a goal, we should look back at our completed actions. Beyond the midpoint, we should look ahead at what's still missing. For example, if you're trying to read all seven Harry Potter books, you should monitor progress from the books you've already read up until you finish *The Goblet of Fire* (the fourth book). Afterward, monitor progress from how many books you have left, which will now be the small area. The reason is that at the beginning of a goal, the proportional impact of your next action will appear larger if you pay attention to what you've done so far (the small area) than if you focus on what you still have to do (the large area). Beyond the midpoint of goal pursuit, the proportional impact of your next action will appear larger when you look at remaining progress (the small area) than when you look at completed progress (the large area).

The underlying principle is straightforward: the proportional contribution of an action appears larger if you compare this action to few versus many other actions. This is true regardless of whether the actions are completed (counting from the beginning) or remaining (counting from the end). The small-area principle is a tested technique to motivate action. In one study, Minjung Koo and I used it to motivate diners to come back to a restaurant. We collected data from diners enrolled in a frequent buyer program at a South Korean sushi restaurant famous for serving a prix fixe New York–style sushi lunch. Like the cafeteria card that persuades me to buy more smoothies, the sushi restaurant's frequent buyer program gave diners a loyalty card that offered a free lunch after they'd bought ten. Half of the diners got a card that visually emphasized accumulated progress: every time they bought lunch at the restaurant, they got a sushi-shaped stamp. The other half got a card that visually emphasized remaining progress: a single sushi-shaped image in a line of ten was removed with each meal purchased. The question was: Which frequent buyer card would be more effective?

As the small-area principle would suggest, it depended on the customer's level of progress toward winning a free lunch. Those who initially made fast progress, buying several lunches soon after enrolling in the program, came back sooner if their card directed their visual attention to how few punches they had left. For them, the remaining progress was the small area. But those who made little progress soon after enrollment came back sooner if they received a card that directed their visual attention to their few existing purchases, which was their small area. So at the beginning of goal pursuit, attention to completed actions increased the rate of return, while toward the finish line, attention to missing actions got customers to return to the restaurant more quickly. Applied to self-motivation, this study teaches us to look back until the midpoint and then switch to looking forward.

But what about when you're at the midpoint? In the middle, you're far from both the beginning and the end, and since no area is small, motivation declines. You should therefore keep middles short. Frame your goals so that you won't stay in the middle for too long. A monthly savings goal is better than an annual savings goal. Although in the end you want to accomplish a long-term goal, setting boundaries that keep middles short can help you get there. If you set a weekly exercise goal, I can confidently guess that you also hope to exercise the following week and the one after that. But a weekly exercise goal has a short middle, unlike a monthly, yearly, or lifetime exercise goal.

Another strategy to combat the middle problem is to use temporal landmarks to celebrate a new beginning, even if only metaphorically. Hengchen Dai, Katherine Milkman, and Jason Riis named this the "fresh start effect." People have a tendency to work harder immediately after a special date like New Year's Day or their birthday. In an analysis of thousands of households' food purchases over several years, on average, people ate the healthiest food in January and then ate fewer healthy foods with each month that passed until the end of the year.

A new year, a birthday, and a Monday are all beginnings you can use to celebrate a fresh start. Interestingly, many people do so intuitively. Online searches for the term "diet," for example, are most frequent at the start of each new calendar cycle: the beginning of the week, month, and year. Taking advantage of this strategy, and fighting the middle problem, is as simple as reminding yourself that today is the first day of the rest of your life. If you can think of the present moment as a beginning, you'll feel more motivated to keep working on your goals.

QUESTIONS TO ASK YOURSELF

While beginnings and ends are clearly marked, middles can be long and ill-defined. You can't tell exactly when your middle started and when it will end. How can you sustain your motivation to work on a goal and do it right during that long and undefined period? When planning your strategy, ask yourself these questions:

1. How does being in the middle affect your motivation to get something done? How does it affect your motivation to do it right? For any given goal, which one is more important for you: getting it done or doing it right?
2. We sometimes slack off in the middle because middle actions don't seem to matter as much. Can you pay attention to your actions in the middle, make them memorable so they will matter?
3. To shorten middles, can you set monthly, weekly, or even shorter subgoals? By setting subgoals, you can minimize the tendency to cut corners in the middle by minimizing the middle itself.
4. Can you identify arbitrary temporal landmarks to mark a fresh start? A Monday, the first day of the month, or a birthday can all mark a new beginning for pursuing important goals.

8

"YOU'RE WRONG!": LEARNING FROM NEGATIVE FEEDBACK

SERENA WILLIAMS, ARGUABLY THE world's best tennis player, famously said, "I've grown most not from victories, but setbacks." Leadership expert John Maxwell implores us to "fail forward." And in one of his most famous stories, fiction writer and playwright Samuel Beckett wrote, "Try again. Fail again. Fail better."

Our society celebrates failure as a teachable moment. Again and again we've heard that in the wake of failure, we gain valuable lessons. And yet it's possible that the reason so many of these famous leaders emphasize learning from failure is because people aren't naturally inclined to do so. I remind my eight-year-old son to brush his teeth every night because I know he won't do it without the reminder. Similarly, leaders like Williams and Maxwell remind us to learn from failure, suspecting we don't already; that we often fail to learn from failure.

But if you allow yourself to learn from your failure, it can be a powerful force. Humans often care to prevent negative events more than they care to experience positive ones. So "bad" can be a stronger teacher than "good," as long as you bother to learn.

The idea that people deeply care to avoid negative events has been examined by fifty years of research on "prospect theory" and the study of loss aversion. As we talked about in Chapter 2, losses loom larger than gains. You care more, for example, to *not* lose $100 than to win $100.

There are many everyday examples of loss aversion. A few years ago, when cities all over the US introduced a bag tax, shoppers switched to reusable bags almost overnight. The threat that they'd be charged to use plastic bags powerfully changed their behavior. Interestingly, by that time, many stores were already giving a credit to those who brought reusable bags to the store. Yet the bag credit was ineffective compared to the bag tax. Shoppers who would happily forgo a ten-cent credit in the old system switched their shopping habits to avoid paying a ten-cent tax in the new system. Loss aversion teaches us that we hate losses even more than we dislike the absence of gains, even though these two are often very similar. But while we care so much to avoid losses, it's hard to extract the correct lessons from a loss we've experienced or, more generally, from negative feedback.

Consider learning the answer to a trivial question: Does *yaad* mean "hand" or "foot" in Hebrew? If you were to guess the answer and I told you your guess was wrong, you would still be able to learn the correct answer. In the case of a binary question like this one, learning that your guess was wrong is just as informative as learning it was right. If *yaad* is not a foot (it's not), it has to be a hand (which it is). Still, it's easier to learn the answer if your guess was correct. This is exactly what Lauren Eskreis-Winkler and I found when we ran an experiment in which people learned by guessing answers to binary questions. Fewer people learned from the negative feedback. But why?

One reason is that negative feedback undermines our motivation to learn. In the wake of negative feedback, you feel bad, give up, and stop paying attention, so you might not learn valuable information. Indeed, in our studies, instead of inferring the correct answer when they got a question wrong, our research participants tuned out and stopped paying attention. A second reason people have a hard time drawing lessons from failure is that it's objectively more difficult. If you got something right the first time, you've learned what to do. If you got it wrong, you only learned what not to do.

Negative feedback has a tendency to undermine our motivation and ability to learn. Yet learning from error is imperative to our growth. As Williams said, she grew more as a tennis player from setbacks than from success. When we're monitoring our progress, both positive and negative feedback indicate to us whether or not we're on track to reaching our goals or if we're taking the best route to get there. We need feedback of both kinds. This chapter is about how to get over the barriers to learning from your mistakes.

LEARNING FROM NEGATIVE FEEDBACK

Political theorist Antonio Gramsci once wrote, "History teaches, but it has no pupils." The same can be said of learning from negative feedback. So how do we learn from failure? First, we have to get over the two barriers I've mentioned: our tendency to tune out when our ego has been bruised (motivational barrier) and the objective difficulty of learning from our mistakes (cognitive barrier).

Barrier 1: Tuning out

In one of my experiments with Eskreis-Winkler, we invited a group of telemarketers to learn by guessing the answers to questions like "How much money, annually, do US companies lose due to poor customer service? A. Approximately $90 billion, or B. Approximately $60 billion." In another experiment, we invited research participants to learn by guessing the meaning of unfamiliar symbols in an "ancient language" (one we actually made up), asking, for example: "Is this symbol A. an animal, or B. a nonliving object?" After people submitted their guesses, we told them whether or not they were right. A few minutes later, we tested them on the same questions again to see if they'd learned from the feedback.

Because, in this paradigm, each question had only two possible answers, participants could easily learn the right answer to every question — either because they got it right the first time or because they got it wrong. Despite this, our learners learned more if they guessed the right answer and received positive feedback ("Correct!") than if they guessed the wrong answer and received negative feedback ("You're wrong!"). Often, those who guessed incorrectly were subsequently paying so little attention that they performed no better than chance on the follow-up test; they were guessing the answers, just as they did the first time. After getting negative feedback, people tuned out and failed to learn from their mistakes. In another experiment, learners who received negative feedback couldn't even remember which answers they originally chose, let alone what the correct answer was. We concluded that when failure threatens the ego, people disengage from the failed experience and stop paying attention.

A failure to learn from failure both is ironic and has grave consequences. If you only learn from the tennis matches you win, your rate of improvement is only half of what it could've been. You cannot learn from something you've chosen to ignore. Further, you might develop an unrealistic view of your abilities. Consider an investor who learns from her successful investments that she can sometimes predict the stock market but fails to learn from failed investments that her predictions are just as likely to fail. This investor might build up false confidence. If she's successful in her investments just as often as she's unsuccessful, which is far from a stellar performance, she'll feel more successful and become more confident in her (objectively poor) abilities the more she invests. Because she only pays attention to her successes, successful investments will lead to a positive view of her ability more than failed investments will lead to a negative view.

We often fail to learn from failure because it stings and we don't want to dwell on those negative emotions. And when we suspect that incoming information will be negative or indicative of failure, we often choose to avoid it in the first place. By a cold, economic analysis, information is valuable if it has the potential to influence a decision. It shouldn't matter how it makes us feel; it only matters whether knowing it will change what we decide to do. Yet it's a human tendency to seek or avoid information based on how we suspect it would make us feel, regardless of how helpful that information might be in making a good decision. If, for example, you ever avoided the doctor's office because you worried you'd get bad news, you avoided feedback that you expected to be negative in order to feel good, even though knowing could help you become healthier. Maybe you're nervous that an atypical mole indicates cancer, so you postpone getting it checked and prolong your ignorance (after all, ignorance is bliss).

Our tendency to intentionally avoid unpleasant information, even information that would help us monitor our goal progress, is called the "ostrich effect." The name comes from the (false) belief that ostriches bury their heads in the sand to avoid danger. Although it's untrue for the giant birds, we do tend to stick our heads in the sand (figuratively speaking) to hide from a coming threat—our threat being emotional. So, for example, some diabetics avoid monitoring their blood sugar, and many people strategically fail to monitor their household energy consumption or check their bank balances. Further, one study documented that investors avoid checking their accounts after market declines. We do this because we realize that what we don't know can't hurt our mood, so we avoid the information even though not knowing can hurt our health or wealth.

Negative feedback also undermines learning because it lowers your self-esteem. You're better able to learn from failure in situations when your self-esteem isn't involved. If you don't think the feedback reflects on who you are as a person as much as it provides an opportunity to learn something new, you'll have a better chance at learning from negative feedback. In the same vein, you might be better able to learn from others' failures than from your own. After all, when someone else slips and falls, you remain unbruised. Generally speaking, learning through others' experience—"vicarious learning"—is harder than learning from your own experience because you don't pay as close attention to what other people are doing. This is why hands-on experience is often emphasized in education—it's easier to learn if you're doing it yourself than if you're watching a teacher do it. But others' experiences of failure don't threaten our egos.

So in the case of learning from negative feedback, we're more likely to learn from watching than doing. Indeed, using the same types of binary questions as in our other experiments, Eskreis-Winkler and I found that learners did better on our test when they first saw someone else guessing the wrong answers than when they themselves made the wrong guesses. When you're just starting something new—whether it's learning to knit or beginning a new job—try to watch others fail first. Perhaps you can join a knitting class so you can watch other new knitters struggle along with you as you all try to learn the stitches.

Another way to protect your ego when you fail is to remind yourself that you're always learning and improving. When you recognize that your skills and knowledge are always a work in progress, you'll tune in and learn more.

Barrier 2: Mental gymnastics

If you've ever tried to train a puppy, you likely learned quickly that rewards worked better and faster than punishments. Your punished dog may understand that you're upset but likely has no clue how to make you feel better—he knows that peeing on the floor is what caused you to yell but not that peeing on the grass will make you stop yelling. Figuring out the desired behavior by eliminating the punished one requires sophisticated reasoning that your dog likely can't perform.

We call this kind of logic a "mental flip." To learn from successes, all you need to do is repeat whatever you did to be successful the first time. Learning from failure requires a mental inversion: you learn what *not* to think, say, or do. Through failure, you learn by eliminating possible solutions; if one isn't the answer, it must be the other. So if a product or a person has failed you, you need to choose another product or person—one that hasn't (yet) failed.

Such mental flips can be confusing. When your dog earns a treat immediately after sitting down, he can easily track that sitting down was the right thing to do. As we've pointed out, learning *not* to pee on the floor is more difficult. Though humans' brains are significantly more developed than our pets', mental flips are difficult for us, too.

Take the following thought experiment. Assume you're selecting one of three boxes, each containing some unknown amount of money. The three rewards are $100, $20, and $–20. You would owe $20 to the game if you chose that last box. Before you choose a box, I offer to tell you the location of either the small win ($20) or the loss ($–20). Once you know where one of these boxes is, you can choose which of the three boxes you would like to open. Which location do you want me to reveal to you?

You might feel tempted to ask which box contains the $20 reward, but the correct answer is that you should ask which one contains the $–20. If you know the location of the losing box, you'll randomly choose between two winning boxes and make money no matter what. If you make your choices based on expected value (as you should), once you know to avoid the revealed $–20 box, your expected value is $60 (the average of the potential $100 or $20 wins). This is a much better deal than revealing the $20, in which case you'll choose that box and end up with $20. By knowing the location of the losing box, you can avoid losses and stand a chance to win big. In an environment in which failures are rare, knowing how to avoid failure is the key to success.

This might seem obvious to you, but figuring it out can be confusing. A large proportion of people who played this game asked to reveal the location of the small win instead of the loss. It's easier for people to ask to reveal the amount they would choose to get than the amount they would choose to avoid. Similarly, learning from failure requires that you learn the solution by eliminating the solutions that don't work.

Whether you should pay attention to failure (find the $–20 box) or success (find the $+20 box) in a game, or whether failure or success contains objectively better information in life, depends on the environment you're in. If you're in an environment in which failures are rarer than successes, failures contain more information. If a restaurant menu includes many delicious entrées and only one that will make you sick, you want to know which dish to avoid. Alternatively, if success is rarer—for example, if there's only one profession that fits your skills or only one romantic partner who will make you happy—there's little information in learning about professions or potential partners you should avoid.

The absolute magnitude of the positive and negative choices also matters. If all options are okay except one that's terrible (you'll be fine working with any boss except that one manager who'll make your life miserable), you need to know about this bad option in order to avoid it. But if all options are okay except one that's amazing (all managers are fine but there's one who will make you truly happy and successful), you need to know about the good option.

Another reason learning from failure is difficult is that, despite our having failed in the past, failures catch us by surprise. We don't expect to fail because we don't pursue our goals intending to fail. We never actively seek information on how to fail, just how to succeed. So when we fail, it's easy to ignore the information we never sought in the first place. The phrase "confirmation bias" refers to the tendency to selectively search for and attend to information that supports, rather than rejects, our expectations. If you expect success, you look for evidence of success. If, for example, I think I'll do great in my cooking class, I'll be waiting for evidence that confirms my belief. When I make one decent dish, I take it as proof that I'm a great cook. But I ignore evidence that disconfirms my belief, such as the ten dishes I've burned. Similarly, if you believe you're the type of person who would only be in healthy relationships, you take note of supportive evidence, like the fact that you spend a lot of time together, and ignore warning signals, for instance, that your partner seems unhappy with you.

The Wason Selection Task, a popular logic puzzle created in 1966, nicely demonstrates this point (see Figure 1). In this task, you're shown only one side of a set of four cards placed on a table, each of which has a letter on one side and a number on the other. The visible sides of these four cards show: 1. the letter "A," 2. the letter "D," 3. the number "3," and 4. the number "7." Your goal is to test the following rule: "Every card with an 'A' on one side has a '3' on the other side." Which cards will you turn over to test the rule?

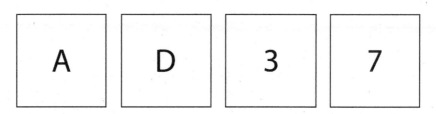

Figure 1: Wason Selection Task. You are a quality control technician working for a card games manufacturer. You have to ensure that cards have been produced in accordance with the following rule: If a card has an "A" on one side, then it has "3" on the other side.

You already know for certain that every card has a capital letter on one side and a single digit on the other side. Please indicate which card or cards you definitely need to turn over in order to verify that the four cards above follow this rule.

If you're like most people, you find it intuitive to flip over the card with the letter "A" to make sure it has the number "3" on the back. It's often less intuitive to try to falsify the rule by flipping over the number 7 card to make sure there's no letter "A" on the other side. (Note that no other card should be flipped. You don't need to check the number "3" card, because the rule doesn't state that it should have a letter "A" on the other side. Only that letter "A" cards have the number "3" on their other side.)

This exercise tells us that we tend to look for confirmatory information and neglect to search for information that disproves our beliefs. To the extent that people expect their actions to be successful, they don't look for failures. It is, in turn, hard to learn from them.

LESSONS LEARNED FROM NEGATIVE FEEDBACK

In the late 1960s, the psychologist Martin Seligman ran an experiment that today most people would probably consider cruel. Nonetheless, these experiments taught us something important about human (and animal) nature.

Seligman and his collaborator Steven Maier gathered three groups of dogs and strapped them into harnesses. The first group simply sat in their harness. The second group was placed in front of a panel and then given electric shocks. These dogs could shut off the electricity if they pressed the panel with their noses. The third (and most unlucky) group was also given electric shocks, but they had no panel to press, no way to escape the pain.

After these dogs learned either that they could do something to get out of the shocks (the second group) or that they had no chance of avoiding them (the third group), each dog was placed, one by one, inside a box with two chambers separated by a barrier. The floor of one side of the box—the side the dogs were put into—was electrified. No matter where they stood on that side of the box, the dogs would get shocked. But the other side of the box was not electrified. If they jumped over the barrier, the dogs could avoid getting shocked.

Only dogs in groups one and two in the first phase of the experiment bothered to try jumping over the barrier. Most of the dogs in the third group—the group that had to endure the shocks with no escape the first time—didn't even try to avoid them. They simply lay down on the electric floor and whined.

Later, Seligman ran similar experiments with humans (though not with electric shocks—that, even he knew, was too cruel). His human subjects were instead subjected to loud, distracting noises as they tried to solve puzzles like rearranging the letters in a scrambled word (BIATH = HABIT). Just as with the dogs, people were first put into one of three groups: one in which they had no noise to deal with, one in which the noise was avoidable if they pressed a button four times, and one in which the noise was unavoidable. Everyone was then put into a new situation in which they heard noise that they could turn off if they wanted. Just as with the dogs, groups one and two, who either had no noise or could avoid it before, chose to turn the noise off. But most people in the third group didn't press the button that would get rid of the noise, even though they could.

Seligman called this tendency for both animals and humans to passively accept punishment after repeated exposure "learned helplessness." It captures the least-adaptive lesson one can learn from negative feedback: bad stuff happens and there's absolutely nothing you can do about it. When all negative feedback teaches us is that the world is unkind, we passively accept negative outcomes, believing it's beyond our control to make things better.

In the case of learned helplessness, people do learn from negative feedback, but they learn the wrong lesson, a lesson that doesn't reflect the amount of control we have over our outcomes. As you now know, goal commitment results from the perception that a goal is both valuable and within reach. With learned helplessness, a goal no longer feels within reach. We feel that what happens to us is out of our control, and so we have extremely low commitment. This is one reason abused women struggle to leave their abusers. Often, people who've never been in an abusive relationship can't fathom why someone wouldn't just leave. But Seligman showed us that after suffering abuse that seems inescapable, people believe they have no power to avoid further punishment. Less tragically, learned helplessness also explains why people who've failed to quit smoking in the past believe they'll never be able to kick their habit, and why some people choose not to vote. After voting before and seeing no change (maybe because the person they voted for wasn't elected), they feel the election process is futile.

Luckily, the lessons we learn from negative feedback aren't always about a lack of commitment. When we face setbacks, negative feedback can also signal low progress, in which case feedback motivates us to act. The lesson we learn from negative feedback—whether it's that we have low commitment or a lack of progress—will therefore determine its effect on motivation. When people interpret negative feedback as a sign of low commitment, they give up. When they interpret it as a sign of lack of progress, they're motivated to work harder.

Consider stepping on your bathroom scale. If you've been trying to lose weight but haven't yet seen the numbers go down, you can interpret this negative feedback in one of two ways. If you take it to mean that you lack the ability or desire to maintain a healthy weight, you'll get discouraged and stop trying. If, instead, you take it to mean that you haven't worked hard enough yet, you should expect the opposite effect. You'll be motivated to keep going and try to lose weight.

According to the psychologist Carol Dweck, people hold one of two theories about their own intelligence. Some people believe their intelligence can develop with practice. They hold a "growth mind-set." Other people believe their intelligence is static and cannot be changed. They hold a "fixed mind-set." These theories in turn guide the lessons they learn from negative feedback. Those who believe that intelligence can be developed through dedication and hard work will learn from negative feedback that falling behind means they should work harder. Those who believe intelligence is innate and fixed and therefore that no amount of practice can change it, learn from negative feedback that they're unintelligent, which discourages further learning.

So who intuitively develops a growth mind-set? Who works harder in the wake of negative feedback? As it turns out, we all have a growth mind-set or, at least, the ability to develop one.

COMMITMENT AND EXPERTISE

Think about a goal that's important to you, something you're absolutely committed to. Maybe it's something mundane, like staying clean; or something that defines you, like being a parent or a teacher. Either way, the more committed you are, the less likely you are to ask yourself

121

"Am I committed?" and the less likely it is that negative feedback will make you doubt your commitment. For example, if you're committed to your personal hygiene and someone points out a stain on your shirt or a funny body odor, you won't reevaluate whether being clean is important to you. You'll run to the shower or change your clothes. And if parenting is central to your identity, when your child is angry with you, you don't reevaluate whether you still want to be their parent. Instead, you focus on the best way to fix things; you take care of your child.

The more committed you are, the less likely you will be undermined by negative feedback. But if you aren't yet committed, you may take negative feedback as a signal that you're not committed. And the less committed you are, the harder it is to stay motivated in the wake of failure. If you've just started working at a car dealership and find yourself on the bottom rung of the salesperson leaderboard (ouch!), you might decide that selling cars isn't for you.

Experience and expertise have a similar effect on our ability to take negative feedback as a sign of lack of progress rather than a sign that we should give up. As people gain expertise and therefore become more secure in their commitment, they're more motivated by negative feedback. They learn from negative feedback that they need to work harder. A car salesperson who's been selling cars for decades wouldn't be discouraged to find herself at the bottom of the leaderboard; rather, she'd be motivated to get back on top. People who've been working on the same goal for years, or maybe decades, don't doubt their commitment, so the only possible inference from negative feedback is that they should work harder. They've developed a kind of growth mind-set.

Stacey Finkelstein and I found this pattern in a study that compared how experts and novices respond to feedback on their recycling habits. Undergraduate students who were either members or nonmembers of an environmental organization received feedback on their recycling habits. Half of them were praised for correct recycling habits, while the other half were informed of the ways they had been recycling incorrectly. Because recycling is complicated, we didn't have to lie to anyone in telling them what they did right or wrong. Almost everyone makes some mistakes while recycling, and almost everyone does it right in some ways, too. Telling the highly committed members of the environmental organization what they were doing incorrectly motivated them to take further action. Everyone in the study entered a lottery to win $25. When the study was over, before the lottery winner was announced, we asked everyone how much of their winnings they'd donate to help the environment. Members of the environmental organization who got negative feedback about their recycling practices were willing to donate more money than those who got positive feedback. Among nonmembers, this negative feedback didn't have the same effect. Instead, nonmembers were more motivated to donate their winnings after being told what they were doing right.

It's easier to tolerate negative feedback when we have experience or expertise. We already know that we can do what we've set our mind to and are eager to get it right. Because of this, negative feedback won't only provide useful information but might even increase the expert's motivation. Further, with expertise, negative feedback becomes rarer, as experts get it right more often than novices. A professional piano player, for example, plays well most of the time. Rare feedback conveys unique and useful information, which is why highlighting a professional pianist's mistakes would be more informative for his practice than highlighting all that he does right.

SEEKING AND GIVING FEEDBACK

Commitment and expertise not only change our response to negative feedback; they also change the feedback we seek. Though people tend not to look for negative feedback when setting out with a goal, commitment somewhat changes this. Committed experts seek more negative feedback than novices. When you're confident in your ability and actions, you're more open to learning how you can improve.

Finkelstein and I first discovered this in a study in which we asked our American college students who were enrolled in beginning- and advanced-level French classes which type of instructor they preferred: one who emphasized what students did well and provided feedback on strengths, or one who provided constructive feedback on students' mistakes. We found that students in advanced classes were more open to having an instructor who provided negative feedback than those in the beginner classes. When you've long been studying a subject, you're less concerned that negative feedback will crush your commitment and anticipate that it might even motivate you to work harder.

Much of these lessons about who can and can't tolerate negative feedback are intuitive. In general, we give more negative feedback to people we perceive as experts or as highly experienced. Most of us don't need to master motivation science to know not to be too harsh with beginners. You would know, for example, not to be too critical of a child who's learning to play basketball and keeps missing the basket, just as my yoga instructor, whom I've only been taking classes with for a few months, knows to go easy on me. We found this in a study that tested how employees give feedback in the workplace. People who watched an employee's presentation gave harsher feedback the longer they assumed the presenter had been working at the company.

STAYING MOTIVATED IN THE WAKE OF NEGATIVE FEEDBACK

Knowing what we now know about how people typically respond to negative feedback, how can we be sure that we learn from and stay motivated by our mistakes?

Ask about progress: To sustain motivation, we want the lesson from negative feedback to be about our lack of progress, not our lack of commitment. Asking ourselves certain questions in response to failure or negative feedback could help. For example, asking, "Do I feel I haven't made progress?" will prompt us to frame the negative experience in a way that might motivate us to make progress. You might feel you're progressing too slowly and be motivated to pick up the pace. Asking instead, "Do I feel uncommitted?" will result in reevaluation of your commitment, and the likely conclusion will be that your commitment is low. You might infer you aren't cut out for the task or that this goal isn't for you, and your motivation will decrease.

Asking about progress is easier if you already feel confident about your commitment. Your confidence in your ability and prospects is often a better predictor of whether you'll master a skill than your actual ability and prospects. When you were learning to walk as a toddler, it was your confidence in your inner power, not your proven ability, that guided you. The same happened when you were learning how to read and write. And it wasn't until you swam your first lap that you knew you could stay afloat. Children commit to mastering these skills without any prior evidence that they can do them. It's self-confidence rather than evidence that gets them to embark on a task in the first place. It also protects you from the adverse effect of negative feedback along the way.

Learning mind-set: Another remedy involves adopting a learning mind-set that emphasizes growth. When you learn, your goal is not to "get it right" but rather to improve your skills. While mistakes and setbacks move you further away from your goal of getting it right, they move you in the right direction in terms of your goal to improve a skill. When you mess up a recipe, you may not have a delicious dinner, but you've learned a valuable cooking lesson. So if you set your goal to learn, rather than do something perfectly, you've still made progress even when you've failed.

Training in growth mind-set is a tested remedy for increasing resilience to the adverse effects of experiencing frustration, difficulty, or failure. To develop a growth mind-set, you'll have to understand that learning requires experiencing and persevering through difficulty. People who undergo this training understand that the brain is not static, but rather that it constantly learns and develops when you confront and overcome challenges. Whether you've failed or succeeded, if you're able to learn from the experience, your brain grows. In one study on growth mind-set, David Yeager discovered that a training of less than an hour helped ninth graders who had low GPAs get better grades in core classes a few months later.

Distancing: A third remedy involves distancing ourselves from the experience of failure. Recall that people learn from others' failures just as much as they learn from others' successes. When your ego isn't getting bruised, you're less likely to tune out. By distancing yourself from your own failure—for example, by imagining it happened to a stranger—you should be able to learn and stay motivated.

Advice giving: Finally, a fourth strategy for sustaining motivation in the wake of failure involves giving advice to someone who is struggling with a similar issue. Consider something you're struggling with. It could be your finances or controlling your temper. Now, think of the advice you could give another person struggling with this problem. Most people hesitate to give advice about something they haven't yet mastered. After all, how can you help others with something you don't do very well yourself? But I encourage you to go ahead. Research suggests that giving advice can help you regain motivation and restore confidence.

To give advice, you have to search your memory to figure out what you've learned about how to (or not to) go about your goal. This memory search reminds advisors just how much they know. Further, in the process of giving advice, you form specific intentions and lay out concrete plans of action, both of which increase motivation. And if that's not enough, giving advice also boosts self-confidence.

Eskreis-Winkler, Angela Duckworth, and I tested the power of giving advice in a study where middle school students either gave motivational advice to younger students or received such advice from teachers. Those who gave advice spent more time on their homework over the following month. This phenomenon was not unique to young students. Other experiments found that adults struggling with saving money, controlling their temper, losing weight, or seeking employment were more motivated to pursue their respective goal if they were asked to give advice compared with if they received expert advice. For example, unemployed people who gave advice to others were more motivated to look for a job than another group of unemployed people who learned from The Muse, a job-searching website, about the critical role of social networking.

HIDDEN FAILURES

In the news, we often hear stories about the struggling chef who took a big financial risk and opened her own restaurant, only to become extremely successful and wealthy. We hear about struggling musicians who eventually make it big and play concerts all around the world. Or we hear about the likes of Bill Gates and Mark Zuckerberg, both of whom dropped out of Harvard to start tech companies (Microsoft and Facebook, respectively) that became two of the most influential businesses of our time. Based on these inspiring success stories, you may conclude that dropping out of college, opening a restaurant, and pursuing a career in music are wise financial decisions. After all, these stories seem to end only in success.

But what if you were making these choices knowing how many people open restaurants that close less than a year later, or spend their whole lives trying to make it in music but never play outside local bars, or drop out of college to start the next big tech company and flounder?

We live in a world of asymmetric information. We hear about when people succeed far more than we hear about when they fail. If you were also to hear stories of failures, you might realize that the decisions above usually aren't financially wise. On average, college dropouts make less money than those who finish college, and most restaurants and musicians never make it big. Because you don't hear these stories of failure, at least not as frequently as you hear the success stories, your learning is biased.

Most people shout out their good news. We use social media to broadcast a promotion or a college acceptance; we post photos that capture the highlights of our life. If you judged me by the photos I share on social media, you'd assume my life is a long, sunny vacation even though I live in Chicago, where it's often very cold. We don't broadcast a job we lost or a school that rejected us, or those long, blustery winters. Bad news tends to be held close to the chest.

In general, we also choose to broadcast our positive news to a bigger audience. We announce our engagement to whoever might be willing to listen; we might even put an ad in the paper. In contrast, we announce a breakup to only a small circle of close friends.

You can easily spot this asymmetry. Try running a Google or YouTube search using the words "success" versus "failure." You'll find that "success" yields more than twice as many results.

This might lead us to believe that successes are simply more common. But this is an unlikely explanation for the world of asymmetric information. We hear more about successes than failures even in environments where failures are more common or as common.

Take admissions decisions as a prime example. Top colleges in the US reject over 90 percent of applicants. Yet you've probably heard more stories about people getting admitted to a college than about people getting rejected. Sports games, too, require both failure and success. By definition, in almost every game played, one team wins and one loses. Success is as frequent as failure. But when we looked at reports of sports games in the *New York Times* since 1851, we found that stories about winners outweighed stories about losers by a large margin (for every use of the word "lost," the newspaper used "won" 1.4 times). We don't hear about failures even when they're frequent.

Possibly, then, failures are hidden because the audience is biased: if people prefer to hear about successes, communicators will tailor success stories to their audience. Indeed, contrary to the common belief that newspapers thrive on bad news, in our analysis of *New York Times* articles, and not only the sports section, we found twice as many articles about successes as about failures. When you check the news, you're much more likely to see a light, fun story about a celebrity than a grave report on the dire state of public education. Even during the COVID-19 pandemic, the *Times* used the words "success" and "happy" more than "failure" and "sad."

Another reason for the asymmetry in available information is our desire to protect our ego while presenting ourselves in a positive light. You'll be more impressed if I tell you about the awards I've won than those I was nominated for but didn't win; therefore, I only mention the wins on my résumé. Similarly, it's an open secret that every scientific discovery was preceded by many failed experiments. Thomas Edison strategically described the reality of failed experiments when he said, "I have not failed. I've just found ten thousand ways that won't work." Scientists' daily job is to sort through failures. Occasionally we discover something of interest. But we don't write about our dead-end ideas; we keep those to ourselves.

Besides the human tendency to keep failure as secret as possible, the success-to-failure asymmetry also stems from the false belief that failures don't contain useful information. If you believe you've learned little to nothing from failure, you keep the experience to yourself. And because figuring out the lesson learned from failure can be tricky, most experiences of failure remain private.

An illustrative experiment had research participants choose which information to share with another person to educate them: either information they knew was wrong or information that had an equal chance of being right or wrong. They could say "I thought the answer was 'A' and I was wrong" or "I thought the answer was 'B' and have no idea if I was right." The majority of the participants preferred to tell someone that they didn't know if they were or weren't right rather than reveal when they were certainly wrong, even though telling someone that something is definitely wrong better helps them figure out the correct answer.

This experiment used a simple task to explore the psychology underlying our hesitation to share what we've learned from failure. The results shed light on our tendency to happily *recommend* a class, a product, or a potential date to a friend and our corresponding hesitation to tell our friend about a class, a product, or a potential date they should *avoid*. This psychology results in a world of asymmetric information, one where failures are hidden and successes are everywhere. What are the implications of this asymmetry for successful goal pursuit?

As it turns out, hidden failures hide superior information. Failures often provide better and richer information on how to succeed than successes do. Negative information on failures has two features that often make it superior: it tends to be unique, and while it is rarer, it is also more elaborated.

Negative information is unique

The first sentence in Tolstoy's *Anna Karenina* reads, "Happy families are all alike; every unhappy family is unhappy in its own way." Motivation researchers agree. Negative information on failure is unique. In contrast, like recipes for chocolate-chip cookies, recipes for success are mostly the same. So two pieces of negative information tend to be different from each other, while two pieces of positive information tend to be similar to each other, which is just what Alex Koch, Hans Alves, Tobias Krüger, and Christian Unkelbach discovered.

According to these researchers, the difference in diversity happens because the spread of successful instances of something—their statistical variance—is smaller than the spread of unsuccessful instances of that same thing. Consider personal traits. For any trait, there's a relatively narrow range of what we would consider desirable or good. Displaying too much or too little of a given trait would be considered undesirable or bad. Take friendliness, for example. All friendly people behave similarly in social interactions—they're polite and kind and genuinely interested in what people have to say. Displaying too much friendliness would be undesirable; a person who is overly bubbly and talkative at a group gathering, being sure to speak to every person, is considered attention-seeking. Displaying too little friendliness is also undesirable; the person who sticks close to the wall at a party is considered shy. Being needy is very different from being shy, yet both labels stem from the amount of friendliness a person shows; people who get friendliness wrong are potentially very different from each other. The same principle applies to a quality like generosity. All generous people are similarly willing to share their resources, but they can miss the mark by either being too stingy or too careless with their money or time. Once again, those who "fail" to be appropriately generous are potentially very different from each other. The difference between the stingy person and the careless person is larger than the difference between the two generous people. In general, if we both get something wrong, your mistake is likely different from my mistake. There will be more information in your failure because your failure is unique—different than mine.

This has implications for the information we collect about pursuing our goals. For many goals, the various means or paths for getting it right are more alike than the various ways by which we can mess things up. One person can exercise so much that she injures herself, while another exercises so little that she's out of shape. These mistakes carry unique information for a health-conscious person. Whenever mistakes, failures, or negative information are more diverse, there's more for us to learn. If, when we fail, we fail in a unique way, each of us will have a unique contribution to make when we exchange information about our failures. If we all succeed in a similar way, there's not much information we can gain from sharing our experiences.

Negative information is elaborate

We move through life expecting things to go well. So when something does go well, we don't feel we need to explain why; it was, after all, exactly as we expected. If something goes wrong, to the extent that we didn't tune out and instead actually noticed the discrepancy, we feel compelled to provide an explanation. If we can't ignore a failure, we might as well make sense of it.

This tendency to explain negative outcomes is apparent in everyday semantics. Good milk is not called "good milk," it's simply "milk." In contrast, milk that has gone bad is referred to as "spoiled milk." Positive states are what people expect, requiring no further explanation; negative states require elaboration. If you show up to our meeting on time, you don't explain why you arrived when you did. If you're late, you feel the need to tell me that the bus was late or that you hit horrendous traffic on your way in.

Because negative experiences call for precise explanation, many languages contain more words to describe negative emotions than positive ones. If you feel bad, you want me to know that you're sad but not angry or frustrated. To get it right, you rely on a rich vocabulary of negative emotions. If you feel happy, you're less concerned about being precise in your description. If I mistake your happiness for joy or amusement, so be it. These emotions overlap anyway.

Take product reviews as an example of our tendency to elaborate on negative experiences. Negative reviews of products are less common than positive reviews. We don't like to share information about a product that failed us. However, when negative reviews are written, they tend to be more precise. If you're happy with your new shoes, there's a good chance you'll post a brief review (e.g., "Great shoes!"), but if you're unhappy and decide not to hide your feelings from yourself or the world, you might write a whole paragraph explaining whether the sole, shoelaces, design, or shipping failed your expectations.

The result is that negative evaluations and analyses of failures, despite being rare, often provide better information than positive evaluations and analyses of success. An interesting illustration of this comes from a study that asked people to guess which of several restaurants was more highly ranked based on reading either only positive or only negative reviews of each restaurant. Positive reviews were awfully similar; all positive reviewers mentioned they loved the food, making it impossible to distinguish between the best restaurant and ones that were less highly ranked. Negative reviews offered a wide range; some mentioned too-high prices while others described the dry food. So those who read negative reviews had an easier time identifying which restaurant was best.

Negative evaluations even predicted future performance. People who read only negative film reviews were able to predict which movie would win the Oscar. People who read only positive reviews could not.

Put these two together—that failures are unique and information on failure, though rare, is elaborated—and you get a recipe for success. Namely, learning from failure.

QUESTIONS TO ASK YOURSELF

This chapter has explored why people often learn too little from failure. Negative feedback can lead you to tune out and stop paying attention, so that you don't learn. In extreme cases, it results in learned helplessness, so that you learn the wrong lesson. Here's the paradox: failures are hidden, but when we're willing to elaborate on and learn from them, we gain valuable information. Realizing that negative outcomes provide unique information that's critical for success, we should learn to both seek out and learn from information about failure. Start by asking these questions:

1. What makes you committed to your goal? What makes you the expert in pursuing your goal? Feeling confident that your

goal is within reach will make it more likely that you'll learn from negative feedback.

2. Can you think about pursuing goals in terms of growing your abilities rather than proving these abilities? Keep in mind that whether you succeed or fail in a goal, you always learn.

3. Can you give others advice based on your personal mishaps? Try articulating the lessons you've learned in the format of advice to another person.

4. What can you learn from observing others' successes and failures? Learning from others' mishaps is often easier.

5. When identifying the best path to a goal, can you pay close attention to information on failures? Don't limit yourself to your own failures. Listen to those who have failed, as well as succeeded, and extract lessons from their experiences.

Part III

COMPETING GOALS

SØREN KIERKEGAARD, A NINETEENTH-CENTURY Danish philosopher considered to be the first existentialist, argued that "purity of heart is to will one thing." Research on motivation deems this admittedly inspiring advice both inaccurate and impractical. You'll always want more than one thing at a time. You might simultaneously want to shop, eat, work, and play. Even as you read these words, you probably can't help wanting to do several other things. According to Gallup surveys, half of Americans don't have enough time in the day to do what they want to do. For those of us who experience this shortage of time, goals pile up faster than we can address them.

Pursuing goals sequentially—that is, finishing one before starting another—is unrealistic. For one, goals take time to accomplish. Some goals can take a lifetime. You can't wait to get your degree before finding a relationship, just as you can't put your health on hold while you work to launch your career. Moreover, we have multiple goals because we're complex organisms with many needs living in an equally complex world. We simply have no other choice than to address several needs (and wants) at once.

Despite how unrealistic Kierkegaard's directive to "will one thing" is, there's a kernel of wisdom in his words. When we try to achieve multiple goals at one time, problems can arise. And if we want to succeed, we need to pay attention to the obstacles we might face along the way. My advice? Replace the nineteenth-century philosophy with this more psychologically sound, albeit less inspiring, adage: pick your battles.

When it comes to goal pursuit, picking your battles means prioritizing some goals and postponing others. You juggle your goals, deciding which one should get your attention at what moment. Along the way, if you're lucky, you may even find ways to achieve multiple goals simultaneously. If you're lucky enough to find love with a personal trainer, you can knock out a relationship goal and a fitness goal in one fell swoop. But that perfect combination might be hard to come by. When we have different goals in different areas of our lives, these goals tend to pull us in their own, independent directions. If going after a promotion is like throwing a dart at a target, then other goals, like adopting a puppy or training for a marathon, are the gravity that pulls the dart away from the bull's-eye.

Motivation science uses the phrase "goal system" to describe how we organize our goals in our minds. Each of our goals is connected to the set of means that help us achieve it. This set of means can be considered our "subgoals." Each goal is further connected to a set of overriding goals, or "big-picture" goals for our lives. If your goal is to run a marathon, one subgoal may be to purchase new sneakers, and one overriding goal may be to be healthy and fit. If your superordinate goal is to achieve success in your career, your goal may be getting a promotion and the connected subgoal might be to be more punctual.

Parallel goals, such as developing a career and supporting your family, are connected in either "inhibitory" or "facilitatory" links. Your career goal will facilitate your family goal if you believe a stable job helps to support your family. These goals can, on the other hand, inhibit each other if you view your career as a distractor from your family or fear that your family distracts you from your career. Our specific goals and the ways we perceive that they interact with each other are as unique to us as individual snowflakes. Still, the principles governing all goal systems are universal, and understanding them allows us to set smarter goals and choose better actions in pursuing them.

Throughout this section, you'll learn how to create an effective goal system (Chapter 9), how to recognize when temptation and lack of self-control will get in your way (Chapter 10), and about the importance of patience in managing multiple goals (Chapter 11). Though you'll never will only one thing, you'll learn how to pick battles so that you can win.

9

GOAL JUGGLING

I WANT TO WRITE a book. I want to get back in shape. I want to get together with a friend. I want to spend time with my spouse. I miss my kids. I want to do something about all of these desires today. This is my internal monologue, and we haven't even made it to lunch.

How does the presence of everything else we want to do influence the likelihood we'll achieve any one of these things? To answer this question, we need to first understand our goal system: the relationships between our focal goal, the other goals we simultaneously hold, each goal's means of attainment, and the overriding goals each goal helps achieve.

Whenever goals are served by the same set of actions, one goal inevitably facilitates the other. A homemade lunch is both cheaper and healthier, so bringing my lunch from home to save money can also support my healthy eating goal. Yet when goals are served by different actions, pursuing one goal can undermine or conflict with another. My homemade lunch may be both cheaper and healthier, but it undermines my goal to get to work on time, as I'm a slow cook and my morning is already busy. When a goal conflicts with other goals, you can expect a rocky path; it's hard to stick with a course of actions that undermines another goal that's important to you.

In a goal system, the motivational principle that governs pursuing multiple goals is that of "maximizing attainment." According to this principle, we choose actions that make as much positive impact on as many goals as possible while minimizing the negative impact on our other goals. You might choose to be honest both because it's ethical and because it helps build strong relationships. But if honesty hurts your relationship—as in telling your boss she's going about a project backward or telling your friend you think her new dress is ugly—you'll think twice. Advancing your ethics might not be worth undermining your chance at a promotion or hurting your friendship.

The principle of maximizing attainment constrains our choice of actions. We either look for a compromise (e.g., between honesty and relationship maintenance) or prioritize our goals. Depending on the configuration of our goal system and how the means to each goal interact, we sometimes balance between goals, doing a little bit of this and a little bit of that, and other times choose to attend to a single goal while trying to put all other goals out of sight and out of mind.

THE PRINCIPLE OF MAXIMIZING ATTAINMENT

When we have multiple goals at once (which all of us do, all the time), we organize them on a hierarchy. Think of the way animals are classified first by kingdom, then phylum, then class, order, family, genus, and finally species. Your goals follow a similar structure (illustrated in Figure 2). At the top of the hierarchy are general and abstract goals, such as desires for social connection, wealth, and health. These are served by subgoals or means. You might set the subgoal of making new friends in order to cultivate social connection. These subgoals or means are in turn served by their own subgoals or means. You may decide to join a gardening group in order to make friends who share your interest in plants. Apart from a few top-of-the-hierarchy goals (for example, leading a meaningful life), each goal we pursue is also a means to other goals.

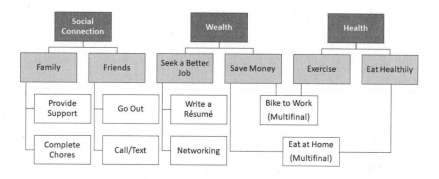

Figure 2. *A simple goal system. At the top are three general goals, each served by subgoals. Each subgoal, in turn, is served by its own means of attainment. The means listed on the right are multifinal; they serve two subgoals simultaneously. Biking to work combines exercising with economical commute. Homemade meals tend to be healthier and cheaper.*

Further, within a goal system, some means are "multifinal": they serve several goals simultaneously. You can think of this goal configuration as "feeding two birds with one scone," the more animal-friendly version of the famous figure of speech. Take biking as a prime example. Biking is a healthy, environmentally friendly, and affordable mode of transportation. Because it has the potential to serve many goals—the aims to exercise more, reduce your carbon footprint, and save money—it's a multifinal activity.

By the principle of maximizing attainment, multifinal means are desirable. You would prefer to do something that helps you achieve more than one goal at a time. But the more goals we hold, the harder these combinations are to come by. Think about a time when you stood in a food court, staring around you, at a complete loss as to what to eat. While there are endless possibilities to satisfy your hunger, the reason you sometimes feel like you can't find anything you want to eat is because you're trying to satisfy a host of other goals while you make your food choice. You may simultaneously want your food to be tasty, healthy, inexpensive, something you haven't had for a while, and something that won't take too long to prepare. After all, you're busy. You don't have all day.

To study the process by which more goals imply fewer lunch options, Catalina Köpetz, Tim Faber, Arie Kruglanski, and I surveyed people entering a food court around lunchtime. We asked some people to write down their goals for the rest of the day as they entered the food court. Next, everyone listed all their acceptable lunch options. Out of a dozen food shops, with many dozens of meal offerings, how many lunch options did people actually list? As it turned out, not that many. And those who listed their goals for the day identified even fewer acceptable lunch options. Thinking about everything you set out to do for the afternoon may remind you that your time is limited, that you need to stay fully alert, and that your lunch had better keep you full until dinnertime. In other words, you're left with a sandwich.

Sadly, the same process happens when searching for a soul mate. While your focal goal might be to find romance, other goals, such as being financially comfortable or dating someone your family approves of, might constrain your options. You might say you're looking for love when you're actually looking for love, financial support, and parental approval. These additional background goals may seriously cut down your set of choices.

When setting up a goal system, you might also run into "equifinal" means—means that all serve the same goal. This goal configuration is best captured by the saying "All roads lead to Rome." For example, biking, golfing, and rock-climbing can all serve your fitness goal. Equifinal means are interchangeable. Any one would work.

Equifinal means often pose a competition. Pursuing each one makes the others redundant. You might bike in order to exercise, but once you sign up for a new gym class, you might quit biking—both activities help you achieve your fitness goal, so you feel compelled to choose. But remember that biking could be serving other goals, too, such as your desire to save money on gas or to be more green. In this case, the gym class undermines only one of the several goals biking serves, so it's likely you'll continue biking once you've joined a gym.

While equifinal means compete with each other, their mere presence increases your commitment to the goal. We discussed in Chapter 5 that an important ingredient in building commitment is knowing that your goal is within reach. With equifinal means, you realize there are multiple paths to where you want to be, which is encouraging. This increase in commitment is most critical for beginners who aren't sure about the feasibility of achieving their goal. When a new gym user learns about the variety of exercising options her gym offers (from dance classes to treadmills, steppers, and a swimming pool), she becomes more motivated. Even though she might never sign up for the boxing or hula-hoop classes, knowing these options exist reassures her that something will fit her style; and this helps motivate her to put on her workout clothes and head to the gym. But while a variety of means gets you more committed to start on a goal, it might not help if it's introduced after you've already committed to a given path. Once you've settled on a Zumba class, you won't be more motivated if you hear about the water aerobics one.

WHAT MAKES MEANS RIGHT

Pandas enjoy eating bamboo more than I'll ever enjoy anything I have ever eaten or will ever eat. I know this despite not having any direct way of assessing panda bears' subjective enjoyment of their food. I know because no single food ever fully and finally satisfies my palate. The panda's diet, in comparison, consists almost entirely of the leaves, stems, and shoots of bamboo. For the panda, satisfying hunger (their goal) is associated with one activity only: eating bamboo. Bamboo is by definition the most delicious food the panda will ever eat. Nothing else comes close.

We humans, in contrast, have many foods that satisfy our hunger. And each of these foods also satisfies a host of other considerations, such as meeting our budget and impacting our health goals; our foods are both equifinal and multifinal. Given the number of associations between the foods we eat and the goals they serve, there's no single food we would happily resign ourselves to eating for the rest of our lives.

This is just one example of how having too many ways to satisfy a goal can result in not having a single way that feels totally right. By the principle of maximizing attainment, we look for activities that serve several goals, such as an exercise that also helps us get around. The problem with having one activity that serves multiple goals is that with each additional goal it serves, our perception that this activity is the "right" means for us decreases.

The mental link between a means (be it an activity, an object, a person, or a bamboo shoot) and a goal weakens the more other mental links exist for that means and for that goal. If a means serves several goals or if a goal has several means, the means-goal link is diluted. When the mental association between the path to the goal and the goal itself is weaker, the goal is less likely to come to mind when pursuing this path, and the path is less likely to come to mind when looking for ways to achieve the goal.

When the mental link is strong, an activity, an object, or a person may seem highly instrumental for achieving the goal. Suppose you can't think of a better way to exercise than biking. So biking is strongly related to exercise in your mind. But if you recognize that there are other ways to exercise that you'd like just as well (biking is equifinal), or that there are other goals you can achieve by biking (biking is multifinal), biking seems less instrumental for exercising. You can think of many other ways to stay in shape and also many other reasons to bike. As a result, your dedication to biking for exercise might dwindle.

Because of this dilution, we often forgo the principle of maximizing attainment in favor of "unifinal" means—actions, objects, or people that help us pursue one goal only and are therefore strongly associated with that single goal.

As you may recall, we had a very similar discussion about dilution in Chapter 3. There, I explained that multifunctional products often fail because they seem less instrumental for each of their functions. A laser pen may seem both like less of a laser pointer and less of a pen, though in reality it's both. Other inventions suffer from a similar fate. An ironing board that folds into a wall mirror or an umbrella that is also a coffee holder are very real and creative inventions that didn't catch on because they seemed less instrumental for either of the functions they were meant to serve.

We reject multifinal means whenever the increase in the number of goals they achieve cannot compensate for how much less useful they seem for the focal goal. This might happen because we care very little for these additional goals. The extra benefits may provide no or little personal utility for us. Take kosher food. If you don't care to eat kosher and your grocery store has a kosher section, I'd bet that you steer clear of it. You assume this food was made to serve both one's palate and a religious lifestyle. That double association makes you doubt that it actually tastes good. Indeed, Itamar Simonson, Stephen Nowlis, and Yael Simonson found that advertising ice cream as kosher reduced nonobservant consumers' interest in it. Instead of ignoring this irrelevant benefit of the advertised ice cream, potential consumers took it as a sign that the ice cream wouldn't taste as good.

Perhaps an even more impressive demonstration of the bias against multifinal means comes from the preference for products or activities that serve one goal while also undermining another goal (the opposite of multifinal). People falsely infer an increase in gain from the presence of pain—as the (often misleading) saying goes, "No pain, no gain." Jane Fonda originally popularized this (ancient) phrase as a motto for exercise in her 1980s aerobics videos, but it has taken on greater meaning since. For example, one study found that many people believe a mouthwash that causes an unpleasant burning sensation is better at eliminating germs than a pleasant mouthwash. Learning that an activity or a product undermines one goal (to not experience pain) might make it seem even more useful for another (killing germs).

The same psychology can explain the rash, self-destructive decisions teenagers are prone to making. Teenagers often knowingly choose to become addicted to cigarettes and to try potentially addicting, and illegal, substances like alcohol and other drugs. They don't do this for the initial enjoyment—your first cigarette or beer is hardly enjoyable. Instead, they make these choices because they want to fit in. But why would self-harm be the ticket to a desirable social group? One reason is that self-harming behaviors undermine other basic goals, like being healthy and safe. Smoking sends a clear signal that you want to belong to a group of smokers, as it offers no other immediate benefits upon initiation and comes with a large cost. Starting to smoke is a sacrifice that teens are willing to make because they have a strong need to belong.

A similar analysis applies to behaviors that are harmful to society at large, such as joining extremist groups. People often turn to extremism as a means to achieving significance and respect. And for them, joining extremist groups seems to satisfy the goal of achieving respect exactly because it undermines other goals such as creating a comfortable life or treating others with kindness.

Altogether, while we seek multifinal means to maximize attainment across multiple goals and seek equifinal means to increase goal commitment, these paths to a goal come with a cost. Some activities or objects would feel less instrumental for achieving our focal goal exactly because they serve more than one goal, or because they are substitutable. When we prioritize a focal goal much more than the others, we often prefer activities or products that are unifinal, serving only this one goal. And because unifinal means feel good— pursuing them is like achieving the goal itself—they're even more desirable. When you engage in a highly instrumental, unifinal means, you're intrinsically motivated. It feels right and you just can't think of a better way of doing it. It's why avid runners often can't picture life without running. It's also the reason pandas must love eating bamboo.

GOAL TRADE-OFFS

If you value eating organic food but also want to save money, you'll be pulled in two different directions. Eating organic tends to be expensive. So how do you resolve the conflict between these two goals: buying organic food and staying on budget? How do you make trade-offs between them? Do you compromise by seeking middle ground or by alternating between organic and nonorganic, or do you prioritize one of these goals while giving up on the other?

There are two opposite approaches for resolving goal conflicts. When you compromise, you strike the balance between two or more opposing goals so that you partially satisfy them all. No single goal will be fully achieved, but no goal is completely left behind. You choose to make progress on all fronts. Alternatively, when you prioritize, you devote yourself to one goal at the cost of the others. We compromise when we balance career and family. We prioritize when we postpone starting a family in order to advance our career, as well as when we give up a career to be there for our family. We compromise when we balance healthy and indulgent foods. We prioritize when we strictly adhere to eating healthily, but also when we give up on healthy eating altogether.

When we sense we've made sufficient progress on a goal, we tend to compromise. Considering the progress we've made, we feel we can relax our efforts and attend to other, conflicting goals (as we saw in Chapter 6). This type of compromise can sometimes become more of an excuse to let go of an important goal. If you behave inappropriately—being rude to a family member or not tipping a service provider—because you perceive yourself to be good, you engage in what motivation research refers to as "licensing behavior." You act as if pursuing a goal allows you to take actions you wouldn't otherwise be able to justify to yourself. Pursuing the goal is a "hall pass" that excuses inconsistent future behavior.

For example, people may seek a compromise between doing

what's right and doing what's easy. In this case, being right makes them feel licensed to take the easy route. Benoît Monin and Dale Miller documented this licensing behavior when they invited male Princeton students to evaluate some blatantly sexist comments. The students rejected these statements, as we would hope. And yet they subsequently allowed sexism to cloud their judgment when evaluating job candidates. After patently disagreeing with statements like "Most women are better off at home taking care of the children" and "Most women are not really smart," these men rated a job in the construction industry as being better suited for men than women. In this case, men felt more empowered to express sexist views when they had just declared their supposedly feminist views. Other studies found that white Americans who voiced support for Barack Obama just before the 2008 election felt licensed to make ambiguously racist statements afterward (again stating that certain jobs are better for white people than Black people). Although voting for Obama really didn't imply that voters were civil rights advocates, it did make some people feel they could be excused for expressing racial discrimination. An egalitarian action, such as supporting a Black candidate, felt as if it excused bad behavior.

But we don't always compromise when we see progress made on a goal. We prioritize when we feel our actions express our commitment to our goal. Rather than feeling satisfied with our progress, these actions renew our commitment and make us want to do more. Increasing our commitment to one goal decreases the appeal of conflicting ones. So in the examples above, if the first action increases our commitment to racial and gender equality, it would decrease the likelihood of subsequent discriminatory behavior.

We also compromise when we seek variety. We want to have an assortment of products or experiences instead of sticking with a single favorite. For example, if you pack your snacks for the week every Monday morning, you most likely select an assortment to increase the variety of your meals that week. Given the time to think ahead, most people predict they'll enjoy a variety of snacks. On the other hand, if you grab a snack every morning before work, you're more likely to choose the same favorite snack each time—you prioritize that snack choice. With only a few seconds to make your choice, you choose the same thing over and over because most people actually enjoy less variety in their food than they'd predict.

The "diversification effect" is another example of compromise—this compromise is between means to a goal, instead of between conflicting goals. You diversify whenever you divide your resources across several investments. You could invest your money in a variety of assets, since you don't know which one will be profitable (therefore compromising on several paths to successful investment). You could also invest your energy in a variety of first dates, recognizing that you don't know who might become your significant other. Either way, you're investing in multiple means to a goal. Prioritizing, in contrast, leads to seeking consistency, repeating a set of behaviors. When you prioritize, you focus on your relationship with a single partner.

Unsurprisingly, the ultimate compromise is the "compromise effect": a preference for moderate choices and a distaste for extremes. Moderate or "middle" options satisfy several goals partially and no goal fully. When you order the medium coffee, buy an average-priced phone, or go on a medium-length hike, you compromise between saving money and getting a better product or between sightseeing and relaxing. Given how common the compromise effect is, sellers rely on your preference for middle grounds to increase the appeal of their products. All they need to do is add an extreme option to a choice set, thus making the item you may have previously considered extreme the "new middle" or the "compromise." A restaurant, for example, might add an expensive bottle of wine to its menu to boost sales of what used to be the expensive option and would now be a moderately priced option, encouraging patrons to perceive this option as their middle ground.

Despite the frequent appeal of moderation, we often resist

compromises, choosing instead to prioritize. We might not think, for example, that a combination of cheap and expensive bottles of wine will work well at a dinner party, and we would hesitate to serve wine to just half of our guests to balance between generous hosting and financial constraints. In these cases, we prioritize either the financial goal or being considered a generous host.

CHOOSING TO COMPROMISE VERSUS PRIORITIZE

Several factors determine whether you seek to compromise or prioritize when pursuing multiple goals, the first of which is whether you see your actions as reflecting who you are as a person. Do your actions tell you or the world something about your identity or morals?

If you'd answer yes to that question, then you'd tend to prioritize. In such cases, compromising is like sending mixed signals about who you are, so you avoid it. Buying an electric car but leaving all the lights on in your home might send mixed messages to your neighbors about your environmental concerns. After you purchase the car, you'll be more likely to turn off the lights.

Take a study in which Franklin Shaddy, Itamar Simonson, and I tested for compromising versus prioritizing in snack selections. An experimenter offered passersby two free snacks from a display containing bags of relatively healthy veggie crisps and more indulgent potato chips. In this baseline condition, about half the people chose one of each snack; these people sought variety. They were compromising. But when the display included a sign asking people whether they were a "health-conscious snacker" or an "indulgent, fun-loving snacker," only a few chose one of each. The sign hinted that this choice would reflect on the snacker's identity. Under these conditions, most people chose the same snack twice so that they could convey that they were pursuing a single goal. They prioritized. This experiment demonstrates how cues in our environment that make an action seem like a reflection of identity influence our approach to making goal trade-offs.

To illustrate another reason people tend to prioritize, I ask that you give your honest response to the following two questions: 1. Would you sell one of your organs for $500,000? 2. Would you accept payment for sex?

If these questions made you cringe, you're not alone. Many find them uncomfortable, even inappropriate. They're what Philip Tetlock refers to as "taboo trade-offs": trade-offs that appear morally wrong because they trade a sacred value (the human body) for a secular one (money). When it comes to moral dilemmas, people prefer solutions that fully satisfy the sacred consideration and neglect the secular ones. They endorse prioritizing, and in this case, health comes before wealth.

This is not to say that taboo trade-offs are objectively wrong, only that many people see them as such. Whether these types of trade-offs are objectively wrong is a philosophical debate, and philosophers prefer their debates to remain unresolved. So if you evaluate actions by their consequences, in which case you're a "consequentialist" philosopher, you should embrace compromises even if they feel uncomfortable. But if you evaluate actions by the ethical principles that guide them, in which case you're a "deontologist" philosopher, you believe taboo trade-offs are morally wrong. As a deontologist, you endorse prioritizing goals.

Take buying a car. When choosing a car, you most certainly will need to trade off safety with financial goals, as more expensive cars tend to carry higher safety ratings. A person who sees this purchase as a moral dilemma and thinks like a deontologist would choose the car with the highest safety rating they can afford. A consequentialist, or a person who thinks about this purchase with few to no moral implications, would search for the compromise—a car that has a sufficiently high safety rating and isn't too expensive. This person is compromising between safety and price.

Whether you compromise or prioritize further depends on the relationships among the actions that achieve the goals. So, for example, if reading this book substitutes for watching a TV series, you'll switch to watching TV once you've finished reading just to mix things up. If you think this book complements others, you'll be more likely to read a complementary book soon after you finish this one. The general point is that if one action substitutes for another, people seek compromise, as pursuing the goal via one route frees resources to attend to something else. When substituting reading for TV, finishing a book frees up time for your show. On the other hand, if actions complement each other, people seek to prioritize goals, as pursuing one route makes similar routes more attractive. When reading to gain knowledge about a specific topic (say, behavioral science), finishing one book makes you want to grab another.

One factor that pushes you toward making compromises is the presence of numerical information. Consider people's choices between options that come with a number, such as horsepower for engines or square feet for apartments. Whether it's the number of calories, a price tag, or a subjective rating of quality, when we see numbers, we tend to seek compromise. For example, if you were given the choice between a broccoli-cheddar soup and a Greek salad, you might not order half of each. But if the soup and salad come with nutrition labels that advertise them as having 800 and 200 calories respectively, the half-soup, half-salad special starts to seem like the right choice.

Another factor that makes compromise more attractive is the nature of the goals under consideration. Recall (from Chapter 5) that for accumulative goals such as working out several times in a week, the "marginal value"—the added value from each extra action—declines. On my vacations, I like short hikes because after a few miles I know I'll no longer get the same benefits in the next few miles. The added value of continuing to hike is diminishing, which calls for switching to something else, such as time at a hotel spa.

When it comes to goals with decreasing marginal value, like hiking, we seek compromises. As another example, many parents believe spending time with their children is critical for good parenting. But spending all their time with their children seems excessive as the added value declines. These parents seek to strike a balance, or a compromise, between parenting and other areas of their lives, like career and leisure.

In contrast, prioritizing goals is more attractive when we pursue goals with increasing marginal utility (i.e., all-or-nothing goals). When the reward for pursuing a goal comes only once you've achieved it, you're likely to prioritize that goal until it's complete. For example, when we learn to drive, the more progress we make, the less likely we are to stop training and switch to something else. Consistency is valuable because learning to drive only halfway is no better than not learning at all. You'll get a driver's license only if and when you finish the training.

Finally, the order of attending to our goals also impacts the trade-offs we'll make. Compromises that move us from less important to more important goals are more desirable than compromises that seem to move us in the opposite direction. As the joke goes, while your priest won't allow you to smoke while praying, he might let you pray while smoking. If you don't smoke or pray, think of this example: adding fruit to ice cream is considered a sensible dessert, one that balances health with taste. Yet adding ice cream to fruit seems too decadent. When presented in this order, most people would prioritize health over indulgence.

QUESTIONS TO ASK YOURSELF

This chapter is about juggling multiple goals. At this point, you should be able to understand the relationships between your main goals and the means by which you pursue them. These means include activities, objects, and even the people who help you. You should also be able to identify the trade-offs you're making or need to make to ensure that the highest-priority goals are addressed. Here are a few questions to ask yourself as you consider your multiple goals:

1. Can you draw your goal system? Start by listing your broadest goals. For example, you could list "career, relationships, health, and leisure." You probably have more goals that are unique to you, like volunteering or helping the environment. Below each goal, list the main subgoals or means that serve it. For example, under "health," you could write "exercise, walking, sufficient sleep, and balanced diet." Worry less about completeness and more about not leaving out a central piece. Make sure to draw the connections between the subgoals or means. Draw a solid line for facilitating links and dotted lines for inhibitory links. So if exercising helps you sleep better, draw a solid line between these means. If exercising requires that you get up super early and lose sleep, draw a dotted line instead. You have now drawn your goal system.

2. Can you identify your multifinal means? These are ways of pursuing a goal that also help you achieve other goals or subgoals. By the principle of maximizing attainment, you want to pursue them. For example, buying a new computer helps with both your freelance career and your wish to watch more Netflix.

3. Can you identify your equifinal means? You should choose among these means, as they are substitutable.

4. Can you identify goals that have only one means? You should make sure to allocate resources to this means, as you have no other way to achieve the goal.

5. What trade-offs should you be making, for example, between career and family, academic and social activities, or staying healthy while having fun? For which conflicting goals should you seek a compromise? For which goal conflict should you

seek to prioritize one goal over the other? When choosing the appropriate solution, consider whether a goal is central to your identity, or whether you see pursuing it as a moral or ethical issue, in which case you should seek to prioritize it. If, alternatively, the added value for continuing to pursue a goal diminishes with each additional action, you should seek a compromise instead of prioritizing.

10

SELF-CONTROL

THE BOOK OF GENESIS in the Bible tells the story of Lot's family, who lived in the land of Sodom. As the story goes, two angels came to Lot one night as he sat at the city's gate. "The outcry to the Lord against its people is so great that he has sent us to destroy it," they told him. As dawn approached, the angels pleaded with Lot and his family to flee to the mountains and not to look back at the destruction of the city. Lot, his wife (who's never given a name), and his two daughters ran, but as fire and brimstone rained upon the land, Lot's wife gave in to temptation and looked back. The instant she turned her head to look, she was transformed into a pillar of salt.

Lot's poor wife is often used as an example of the importance of self-control. Self-control, as is implied by its name, is what it takes to overcome the self. It's your ability to stick with an important goal (like the angels' directive not to look back) when you're tempted to do something that goes against it. A self-control dilemma is the ultimate goal conflict. It involves choosing between what you believe you ought to do and what you want to do instead. You may need to go to work but feel tempted to stay in bed for another hour. Exercising self-control is hard because momentary desires (like wanting to get more sleep) can be at least as powerful as overarching goals, and they can pull you in the opposite direction. You may desire to eat, drink, sleep, smoke, use social media, spend money, or have sex, to name just a few. According to Wilhelm Hoffmann and his colleagues, you feel some desire about half the time you're awake. And about half of those desires are in conflict with your other goals (not to eat or drink, to stay awake, and so on).

Not all difficult goal conflicts require self-control. Choosing among several career paths or deciding whether to marry your partner can be excruciating decisions, but they don't require self-control. A decision involves self-control if you can clearly see one option as the right choice and another as the temptation. This might not happen right away, as we're good at tricking ourselves, but when it's brought to your attention that self-control might be a factor, you should be able to clearly distinguish between what you *should* do and what you're tempted to do. A problem isn't about self-control if it isn't clear that one choice is a temptation. When both choices have potential, it's simply a difficult decision. Choosing a career is rarely a matter of self-control, as any job has its merits.

When self-control is involved in your goal conflicts, it matters what type of goal you're pursuing. When you're pursuing an approach goal that involves taking an action, self-control helps you to persevere, to push forward when you're being pushed back. You may keep working when you're tempted to quit. In the case of avoidance goals, exercising self-control helps you forgo temptation. You may skip a glass of wine, sex, or raising your voice at someone because in your particular situation, these tempting possibilities don't align with your more important goals.

As a society, we've thought about self-control nearly as long as we've been able to think. These dilemmas make a regular appearance in ancient mythologies. Though the biblical couple Adam and Eve had an abundance of food in paradise, they were tempted to eat the one piece of forbidden fruit (likely because it was forbidden—recall ironic mental control from Chapter 1). Adam and Eve failed to exercise self-control. The Greek myth of Odysseus and the sirens similarly tells a story of self-control. Resourceful Odysseus wanted to hear the sirens' beautiful song without following them to his death, so he plugged his sailors' ears with beeswax and tied himself tightly to the mast. Once tightly secured, Odysseus no longer had the option to follow the sirens. With a little bit of self-control at the outset, he eliminated the need to use self-control later on. We call this self-control strategy "pre-commitment."

In modern times, self-control has been associated with academic achievement, employment, financial savings, and being able to stay in a relationship. When Denise de Ridder and her colleagues analyzed the results of more than 100 studies, they found that people who report having strong self-control also report that they're happier and have more love in their lives. In contrast, lack of self-control was associated with low relationship commitment, binge eating, alcohol use, occasional speeding, and crime.

These studies may make it seem that some people were born with ironclad self-control. But the truth is that we were all born with very little ability to control ourselves. We develop self-control as we grow up, and some develop self-control more quickly.

The rate of growing self-control matters. In one longitudinal study, Mathias Allemand, Veronika Job, and Daniel Mroczek examined the relationship between the development of self-control between ages twelve and sixteen and various life outcomes at age thirty-five. As part of the study, German adolescents reported their ability to exercise self-control once a year. They rated their agreement with statements such as "I often start new things and don't manage to finish them," "I feel that I have a quite weak will," and "I often give up at the first sign of difficulty." If you reject these statements, it's a sign that you have high self-control. Some twenty-three years later, those who were growing their self-control ability at a higher rate—they had much better control at age sixteen compared with age twelve—reported that they were happier with their intimate relationships and more engaged at work.

While the rate of growing self-control varies, developmental studies find that for most of us, self-control improves from childhood through adolescence to adulthood. Self-control gets easier as we grow older. The Go/No-Go task nicely illustrates this fact. To study impulsiveness, a team of cognitive psychologists created what's likely the most boring computer game ever invented. They constructed a game in which people were supposed to press a key on their keyboard whenever they saw a GO sign. They were not supposed to press the key if they saw a NO GO sign. But as remarkably simple as these instructions sound, it turns out that this game was easier said than done. Because the GO sign appeared frequently and the NO GO sign was relatively rare, people got into the habit of pressing the key every time a sign popped up and therefore found it difficult to stop pressing on NO GO. Inhibiting an action requires self-control. Interestingly, Go/No-Go research shows us that people become better at this task as they grow older. The brain regions that are responsible for self-control, and the connections between them, take many years to fully mature. This may explain why teens tend to be more impulsive.

Even for adults, it's often quite difficult to exercise self-control. To overcome yourself, generally speaking, you have to manage both steps in a two-step process: detecting and then battling temptations. You detect a temptation when you realize that you shouldn't do something even though you want to do it, or that you should do something even though you don't want to. Detecting a temptation isn't trivial because most temptations aren't explicitly announced (as in the Go/No-Go task) and have a negligible impact if indulged in moderation. One beer won't make you an alcoholic, taking office supplies for personal use just once won't make you a thief, and the one time you left your wet towel on the floor of the bathroom didn't destroy your relationship. In moderation, each of these is a totally acceptable, harmless behavior.

The problem is in accumulation. Given that grabbing a beer with friends will make a lovely night while bingeing on a lot of beer might ruin a lovely night, at what point do you identify "having another glass of beer" as a temptation?

The second challenge is to battle temptation. Knowing that temptation is a huge barrier to most people's goals, behavioral science has discovered many strategies people use to bolster their self-control. These self-control strategies operate by increasing your motivation to adhere to the goal and decreasing your motivation to give in to temptation. For example, you might choose to keep your liquor in a locked cabinet and leave the key on a different floor while keeping your water bottle within reach as you move around the house. Luckily, there are even more strategies you can employ to battle temptation, and they don't involve locked cabinets.

DETECTING TEMPTATION

In 2013, the cyclist Lance Armstrong, who won the Tour de France seven times, admitted to using performance-enhancing drugs. As part of his confession, he argued that he didn't think his behavior was wrong because he assumed all the top riders were using steroids. He said, "I went in and just looked up the definition of cheat and the definition of cheat is to gain an advantage on a rival or foe that they don't have. I didn't view it that way. I viewed it as a level playing field." For Armstrong, it seems, doping didn't pose a self-control conflict. And assuming he indeed didn't detect a problem, he had no reason to try to resist.

Some self-control conflicts are immediately apparent. If you're allergic to peanuts, you know that the tray of delicious warm peanut butter cookies your colleague brought to work will make you sick. You have no problem detecting that you ought to stay away from these cookies. But if you've recently decided to eat fewer sweets, a tray of cookies delivered to your office might not raise a red flag. Rather than thinking about it as a temptation to be avoided, you might view these cookies as a one-time indulgence.

A single cookie will have a negligible effect on your sugar intake, and if everyone else is enjoying them, you might as well join the party.

Most everyday temptations resemble the dieter's situation more than that of the person suffering from a peanut allergy. For these temptations, a single indulgence will not risk missing the overriding goal. Be it dessert, a cigarette, overspending, or speeding, a single instance will probably have no consequences for your long-term prosperity, which makes it hard to see it as a temptation to be avoided.

Ethical violations, like Armstrong's choice to use steroids, can also be tricky to detect. Many of our everyday ethical violations can only be identified as temptations when we view them through the lens of ethical dilemmas. If you've ever omitted critical details about your résumé in a job interview (like avoiding precise dates so you don't have to explain unemployment), pirated software, or bluffed in negotiations, you likely weren't seeing these as temptations. Instead, you may have thought these were normative behaviors—that "everyone does that." When I ask my students whether they would engage in each of these behaviors, I typically find that around half say they would. More interestingly, the vast majority of the students who say they would do these things also believe everyone else in the class would do just the same. These people don't detect an ethical problem in the questions I pose because believing that everyone else would do it too poses no threat to their ethical reputation, and so there's no self-control conflict between their ethical reputation and the immediate benefits of getting the job, getting free software, or getting a better deal.

To identify a self-control conflict, at least one of two conditions must be met: the behavior under consideration must seriously undermine a more important goal, or it must undermine the way you see yourself.

Condition 1: Undermining the goal

The supply room in the business school at the University of Chicago, where I work, has boxes and boxes of pens. While I'd never imagine taking a whole box home, I have no problem with grabbing a single pen from time to time. I start off using them in my office, but those pens have a tendency to sneak into my bag, attached to a paper I'm working on, and end up at home. Over my eighteen years of teaching, I've probably brought a boxful of pens home.

Pilfering pens every now and then doesn't make me an office supply thief, but if I recalled how many pens I'd already taken home every time I'm tempted to grab another one, I might be more careful about keeping that pen in my office and out of my bag. Detecting a temptation is easier if you think about it in bulk. Most of us can recognize that buying a three-gallon bucket of ice cream will clearly ruin our diet, but it's harder to see a pint of ice cream having the same impact, even though a pint of ice cream quickly adds up to a gallon if you buy one every week. The ability of single-instance decisions to cloud the impact on our goals is the reason many smokers choose to buy their cigarettes by the pack rather than a ten-pack carton. This way they can trick themselves into guilt-free smoking. Because the cost of a single temptation is negligible, it's too easy to round it down to zero and discard the harm. To identify temptation, you may want to mentally multiply your actions before taking one. Before filling your wineglass, consider the health impact of every night you'll drink too much this year. Or, before yelling at your partner for leaving dishes in the sink, consider the impact on your relationship of all the times you'll lose your temper.

In a study that explored this point, Oliver Sheldon and I asked employees how likely they'd be to engage in various questionable work-related behaviors like calling in sick to take the day off or taking office supplies for personal use. For instance, we had them imagine they woke up one morning and just couldn't bear the thought of going into work. Some considered only that day—one day in which they wanted to fake sick so they could take a break. Others were told that this would be a particularly hectic year at work and they'd face this choice seven times. As we expected, people who thought about taking an unnecessary sick day in isolation reported greater intention to actually fake sick. The same pattern was true for other behaviors, like taking office supplies and intentionally working slowly to avoid additional work. Deciding to go against your moral compass is easier when you consider just a single instance.

You're also more likely to detect a self-control dilemma when you make a decision that affects multiple occasions; we call this using a "broad decision frame." If you decide in advance what to eat for lunch every day this month, you'll probably choose healthier foods than if you decide on lunch just before noon each day. Thirty lunch decisions are more consequential than one, as healthy choices add up. You may even set a rule: no more than one glass of wine per dinner. Rules, by definition, refer to a broad set of decisions, which means they take into account the accumulating impact of giving in to temptation across many opportunities to indulge.

But as positive as this way of thinking can be, you'll need to be wary of falling into certain traps. Broad decision frames are only useful if you don't use tomorrow's virtues to justify today's vice. You fall into this trap each time you promise yourself to start saving next month, start studying on Monday, or start your diet tomorrow. In these cases, a broad frame allows you to give in to, rather than resist, temptation. The risk here is in trying to balance goals with temptations in the form of "temptation today and goals tomorrow." Tomorrow is always in the future; it never becomes today. Recall our discussion from Chapter 9 of prioritizing a single goal versus seeking a compromise. When you're concerned about giving in to temptation, it's better to prioritize the goal than to seek a compromise between a goal and a temptation.

Take a study in which Ying Zhang and I left free snacks outside a lecture hall for our hardworking University of Chicago students. There were two choices: a bag of carrots or a chocolate bar. During some hours, these snacks were presented in two separate bowls, while during others, they were mixed together in the same bowl. After setting out the bowls, we simply watched. What we saw was interesting. When two snacks were served in separate bowls, two-thirds of the students chose carrots. When the two snacks were in the same bowl, only half of the students chose carrots. Our hypothesis was that separate bowls indicated separate purposes, while mixing snacks in the same bowl implied that they go together. Even though most of our students only made one choice (thanks to social norms that implied they should take only one snack), the impression that carrots and chocolate balance each other out, which we gave by mixing them, was enough to obscure the idea that chocolate is a temptation and persuade students to make the less healthy choice. You may have fallen into the same logical trap when choosing carrot cake or yogurt-covered pretzels over other sweets. These foods seem to suggest that a balanced diet has a mix of sugar, fat, and a little bit of something healthier like fruit, veggies, or probiotic-rich yogurt, making it harder to detect a self-control conflict.

It's therefore easier to detect a self-control conflict when temptations aren't mixed with a goal. When we separated the carrots from the chocolate bars, we implied that one is better than the other and more people chose the carrots. We also found that more health-conscious people made healthier choices. This makes sense, as you would expect more health-conscious people to eat healthier food. Interestingly, however, being health-conscious doesn't translate into healthier food choices when healthy and unhealthy foods are mixed together. When fruit and candy are served next to each other on a snack tray or when fried chicken, croutons, and cheese are served on top of a pile of lettuce, many health-conscious people fail to detect a self-control conflict and eat these less healthy foods. Something as simple as separating healthier and unhealthy foods on a menu—for example, using a "healthy corner"—can help people detect a self-control conflict.

Another way to help you spot moments when self-control could be a downfall is to think ahead. Who will you be in ten or twenty years? And how will that future you feel about what you're doing now? Envision your future lifestyle and dreams. What will your profession or hobbies be? Will you marry or remarry? Will you have children or grandchildren? And no less critically: Will you care to be mentally and physically healthy? Will you wish you had done something differently?

Being reminded of your future self puts you in a very broad decision frame. Whatever decision you make today, you should be able to envision making it again and again over many years. So instead of asking yourself whether it's okay to procrastinate, cheat, smoke, or drink today, you should ask yourself whether it's okay to do so for the rest of your life. Multiplying a small temptation by the number of times you would succumb to it in the course of your life will surely make it too large to ignore. And if you think a decision you make today is diagnostic of all future choices, you'd better make the right decision today.

Thinking ahead also makes you more psychologically connected to your future self so that you care more for the person you'll become. People vary by how psychologically connected they are to their future self. If you're highly connected, you expect to share memories, intentions, beliefs, and desires with the person you'll be in the future. You feel intimately familiar with them. If you're lowly connected, you think of your future self as almost a stranger.

The philosopher Derek Parfit argued that if you feel connected to your future self, you should care about her welfare. You'll take actions today that will benefit her in the future. But why would you sacrifice your present welfare to benefit a stranger? If you feel distant from your future self, you'll make choices that benefit you in the present. Why, for example, should you save for retirement if you don't feel close to the person you'll be when you retire? For the lowly connected person, sacrificing the present to benefit the future seems very unwise. Imagine, for example, putting $100 in a savings account, expecting to get $150 in five years. If you feel connected to the person you'll be in five years, this could be a good deal. You should go ahead and invest in that person's financial resources. However, if that person is a stranger to you, why would you give away good money to benefit them? Why should you care about their ability to afford a vacation or pay their mortgage?

While philosophers are concerned with the "normative answer," that is, what we should or shouldn't do, psychologists are concerned with the "descriptive answer": in this case, how feeling connected can help you detect temptations in your environment. Feeling a greater connection to our future self helps us detect a self-control problem by making us care more about the long-term implications of our actions.

College students are a good example of this. Many students draw a line between the present, which is being in college, and the future, which is the rest of their lives. They further recognize that graduation is an important milestone. It's the point when the present ends and the future begins. But college students vary in how much they think graduation will change them as a person. In one study, Daniel Bartels and Oleg Urminsky had college seniors read passages that described their imminent graduation either as an event that would change their identity or as a relatively minor event with little personal impact. Some read that "the characteristics that make you the person you are will likely change radically around the time of graduation." Others read that these characteristics "are established early in life and fixed by the end of adolescence." Then the researchers told their participants that they'd be holding lotteries to win a gift card for either Target or Expedia—and that they could choose to get a $120 gift card immediately or to get more money on a gift card (up to $240) after one year. Given that an event that will change your identity makes you less connected to your future self, the scientists expected students who thought graduation would change who they were to want immediate, smaller gift cards. And indeed, that's what they found. Seniors who read that graduation would change them felt less connected to the person they'd be in one year and therefore prioritized their present self.

Marriage is another good example of this psychological phenomenon. People who believe marriage will forever change them might be more likely to give in to temptation, such as cheating on their fiancé before their wedding day. Expecting that whoever you are as a single person will have little to do with the person you'll be when you're married might serve as an excuse to let go while you're still single. To detect temptation, it's best to remind yourself that who you are today and who you'll be after marriage, after graduation, and in ten years or twenty, are remarkably similar.

Condition 2: Undermining the self

As we've heard time and again, "breakfast is the most important meal of the day." I agree, but not necessarily for the reasons we've been taught. Sure, what you eat (or don't) for breakfast can impact your energy for the rest of the day. But more important, what you do first thing in the morning has a big pull on your identity. Indulging at breakfast will send a stronger—albeit wrong—signal about your identity as a health-conscious person than indulging in a late-night snack.

Actions that make your identity are important to you. These are the actions you'd say describe who you are, and they influence how you and others see you. These actions might be public or otherwise grab your and others' attention. Attending a book club every month (a frequent and public choice) better describes your identity as a reader than telling a neighbor about a book you read. And eating a healthy breakfast (which you do first thing in the morning) grabs your attention and therefore has a stronger hold on your identity as a "healthy person" than midday snacking. For identity-defining actions, it's relatively easy to detect a self-control conflict. When a particular choice will impact how you define yourself, you pay close attention to steering away from temptations. In contrast, actions that don't define your identity seem unnoticeable and temporary, which makes it harder to harness self-control.

So, for example, when you sign a document, you attach your identity (you've literally attached your name) to your action. Given that your true self isn't a reckless cheater, having to sign a document encourages you to be accurate and honest. That's the reason forms ask for a signature in the first place; it's not just proof of accuracy and honesty but also *motivates* accuracy and honesty.

You can also use identities you *don't* hold to encourage the behavior you want. Jonah Berger and Lindsay Rand discovered this in a study in which they gave Stanford University freshmen flyers that said, "Lots of graduate students at Stanford drink." Freshmen said they wanted to avoid looking like graduate students, so those who read that flyer reported drinking less alcohol than those who read a more typical flyer saying, "Think when you drink. Your health is important." Once binge-drinking is associated with an identity you don't hold, even if it's a positive identity, you'll think twice about drinking. Such a simple strategy is often all it takes to detect a self-control problem.

Another simple strategy stems from the "middle problem" we talked about in Chapter 7—we relax our effort in the middle of pursuing a goal. This motivational decline results from the tendency to see beginning and end actions as stronger signals of your identity than middle actions. And because beginning and end actions impact how we see ourselves, it's easier to detect a self-control conflict at those moments. So, for example, Maferima Touré-Tillery and I found that college students who were trying to save money were more likely to relax their financial goal in the middle of the year. They were more likely to plan all sorts of unnecessary purchases, ranging from new wallets to designer jeans, if they thought about springtime as the "middle" of their academic year than as the beginning of spring term or end of winter term.

But what if pursuing the goal, rather than giving in to temptation, is inconsistent with your identity? Take the overriding goal to lead a healthy lifestyle. While people in America generally see a healthy lifestyle as part of their group identity, this isn't the case for all social groups and all health behaviors. As a Jewish person, I don't associate my ethnicity with athleticism. So, while I personally care to be athletic, reminding me of my Jewish heritage will not make me care to exercise more. Similarly, the backlash against Michelle Obama's 2010 Healthy, Hunger-Free Kids Act, which required healthier school lunches in American schools, was fueled by people's feeling that nachos and pizza represent who they are—their true identity—more than yogurt and greens. Indeed, many people don't subscribe to the belief that restrained eating, exercising, or refraining from smoking are behaviors that characterize their social group. They might not associate their race, ethnicity, or social class with eating foods Americans typically deem healthy. In general, when temptations are identity-inconsistent, they make it easier to see a problem. But when it's the goal that appears inconsistent, it's especially hard to detect a self-control conflict. After all, our identity fuels our motivation.

BATTLING TEMPTATION

Identifying a self-control problem is only step one. Now you need to *exercise* self-control. Self-control strategies counteract temptation, canceling out the influence of temptations on your goal. This works either by increasing your motivation to adhere to the goal or decreasing your motivation to give in to temptation. Some self-control strategies can also do both. The result of exercising self-control is that two opposing forces with similar motivational pull—a goal and a temptation—get further apart, with the motivation to adhere to the goal getting significantly stronger than the motivation to give in to temptation. For example, instead of losing your temper while simultaneously wanting to stay calm, you'd want to stay calm more than you'd be willing to lose your temper, so you don't blow up.

Stronger temptations, unsurprisingly, elicit more forceful self-control. Imagine getting ready to lift your desk. If you expect the desk to weigh very little, you'll approach it with relatively less force than if you expect it to be heavy. Similarly, if you expect only a minor temptation, you'll exercise less self-control than if you expect it to be extremely hard to resist. You might not be too worried about a temptation to drink too many mimosas at brunch, but the worry that you'll be tempted to drink too much at a dinner party is stronger. Accordingly, you're likely to exercise more self-control at the party than at brunch.

It's important, then, that you correctly judge the strength of the temptations you'll face. As long as your expectations are well calibrated, you'll be prepared to fight temptation off. But if you don't correctly estimate the strength of a temptation, you'll fumble. When you underestimate it, you'll be underprepared and exercise too little self-control. You might underestimate how tempted you'll be to lie in bed, so you turn off your alarm clock and end up oversleeping. When you overestimate temptation, you might exercise too much self-control (which isn't always a good thing). If you overestimate how tempted you'd be to sleep in, you might wake up several times to make sure you haven't missed the alarm and end up ruining a good night's sleep.

Not only do we sometimes fail to estimate the strength of temptation, we often also encounter unexpected temptations for which we're, by definition, unprepared. Having no advance warning makes it harder to exercise self-control. Take my weakness for cookies. As a professor, I attend a lot of faculty meetings. When I first started going to these meetings, I was caught off guard by the freshly baked cookie that always sat at the bottom of our lunch boxes. Unprepared to face my temptation, I always gobbled it up. Now that I've learned from years of experience (and regret), I can easily avoid the cookies. I set a rule to never eat cookies in faculty meetings, relying on a broad decision frame to remember that these cookies are not a one-time indulgence. But even now, if you offered me cookies when I wasn't expecting them, I would happily eat them. Unless I'm prepared to exercise self-control, I usually say yes to cookies.

To explore the effect of expectations, Ying Zhang and I invited people to complete an anagram, which is a puzzle that scrambles the letters of several words into new words. For example, the word "times" makes "items," "mites" makes "emits," "seat" makes "east," and "teas" makes "eats." Our research participants faced the temptation to give up as soon as the task got difficult. Knowing that, we told some people that the puzzle would be difficult. Those who expected to have a hard time planned to work harder and did indeed stick to the puzzle longer than those who were told the task would be easy. In telling people they'd have a hard time, we were setting up their expectation to face a temptation to quit, which in turn made them ready to persist.

In this study, the participants' telling themselves and the experimenter that they'd work harder served as a self-control strategy (a kind of pledge or a self-imposed deadline, as we discussed in Chapter 2). But there are plenty of other self-control strategies people use. Most strategies fall under two basic categories: those that change the situation itself and those that change how we think about the situation.

Self-control modifies the situation

At some point in your life you may have had a friend who ended a bad relationship and then (maybe after a few drinks) was tempted to call her ex. Anticipating that she'd probably want to make that call when she felt lonely, in a moment of clarity before the drinks started flowing, your friend deleted his phone number. In theory, she had three options: (a) she could call her ex; (b) she could delete his contact information and not call him; or (c) she could keep his contact information and not call him. The reason she deleted her ex's number is that she didn't trust option (c) to truly exist. If she had her ex at the tip of her fingers, she knew she wouldn't be able to resist the temptation to call him when she felt lonely. Deleting his number smartly saved her from herself.

In behavioral science, we call what your friend did "pre-commitment." A pre-commitment strategy involves eliminating temptation before you're tempted; you eliminate certain foods from your house or contacts from your phone because you know both that you like them too much and that they're unhealthy. A gambler might pre-commit to leaving his wallet in the hotel room, taking only a set amount of cash into the casino with him. When the money is gone, the temptation to continue gambling has been eliminated. By similar logic, you could put your money in a retirement savings account to prevent yourself from spending it. Alternatively, you may commit to an earlier-than-necessary deadline at work to encourage yourself to get going on an annoying project you were assigned (recall our discussion of challenging targets in Chapter 2). Either way, your pre-commitment makes it possible to stick to an important goal.

A pre-commitment strategy can also involve tying yourself to a certain position, not literally as Odysseus did in tying himself to the mast, but figuratively. Think of publicly announcing your engagement or, alternatively, your breakup. Either way, publicly announcing the status of your relationship makes it harder to reverse course. Consider a study in which Yaacov Trope and I offered to pay people for getting a physical exam. When we told some people that the exam would be uncomfortable, they were more likely to postpone getting paid until after they'd completed it. By making compensation contingent on completing the exam, these participants risked that they might not get paid at all. But this also made it more likely that they would follow through with the exam. When you insist on getting paid only after you complete the work, you increase the likelihood that the work will get done.

A pre-commitment strategy works on either eliminating temptation (as your friend did when she deleted her ex's number) or securing the goal (as our study participants did when they accepted payment only after finishing their physical). Either way, this strategy defies a basic principle in economics: you can't have too many options. By economic analysis, adding options to your choice set might not improve your situation, but it can't hurt. You can always forgo the options you don't like, as in deciding not to call that ex despite having his contact information. But by a self-control analysis, pre-commitment makes a lot of sense. Temptations are easier to forgo when they're unavailable.

Another effective strategy doesn't eliminate temptation but makes it difficult to swallow. This is the strategy of imposing penalties on yourself for giving in to temptation and rewards for sticking with your goals. A study by Xavier Giné, Dean Karlan, and Jonathan Zinman illustrates this nicely. These researchers offered smokers who wanted to quit a savings account in which they deposited funds for six months. If they quit smoking within that time period (tested with a clean nicotine urine test), their money was returned; otherwise, their money was forfeited to charity. Following the success of this program, Karlan joined up with two other economists to found stickK, an online commitment platform. The platform invites you to make a "commitment contract"—a binding agreement to pay a certain amount of money to an "anti-charity"—an organization that you don't support—in case you fail to follow through. For example, a left-leaning user recently created a contract requiring him to wake up on time for sixteen weeks. The user committed to donating $80 to the National Rifle Association if he ever hit Snooze and slept for another hour after the alarm went off. Not wanting to support the dissemination of guns in America gave the user incentive to get up on time.

People also reward themselves for adhering to a goal. Celebrating milestones, such as meeting your monthly savings goal or finishing one year of college, is a way to increase the appeal of your goal and therefore increase the likelihood you'll stick to it.

People might even literally move closer to their goals while keeping their distance from temptations. When you want to limit alcohol consumption, you might pull your glass of water toward you and push away your half-empty glass of wine. Motivated students may deliberately select dorm rooms that are closer to the library and farther from Frat Row. And on an interpersonal level, people keep their distance from those who exert a bad influence while staying close to those who are helpful in pursuing long-term interests.

Self-control modifies how you mentally approach temptation

Let's go back to the story about your friend and her ex. There's a situation in which your friend doesn't delete her ex's number, but instead spends the entire night complaining to you about how horribly he treated her. Over drink after drink she tells you how he'd pick fights over the tiniest things, how he'd lie about what he was doing or where he was going, and how he'd lose his temper and call her horrible names. While a night of drinking and complaining might seem like a typical breakup ritual, it actually serves to bolster her self-control. Reminding herself of what a horrible person he is keeps her from calling him, because who wants to date a horrible person?

What your friend has done here is modify how she mentally approaches the situation. Although complaining about her ex poses very little risk to her, modifying the situation can be a costly approach to battling temptation, as it reduces your flexibility in responding to it. For example, you may have felt uncomfortable when I described anti-charities. If the sleepy liberal overslept once, he'd have to make a donation to the NRA, and he'd severely regret his choice. While oversleeping was within his control, external circumstances some-times prevent us from following through on our goals, in which case imposing penalties on ourselves will only result in having to pay the penalty on top of missing the goal. The saver who lost her job might regret putting her money in a savings account now that she needs to pay high withdrawal fees to pay her rent. Once the pre-commitment has failed to motivate action, you'll wish you'd never made it in the first place. Other times, our priorities truly do change. Marriage is a commitment to stay loyal to someone for as long as we both shall live. But many people hesitate to make that pre-commitment, anticipating that they might someday fall for someone else. If you anticipate a change in your circumstances or your taste, you should rightly hesitate to pre-commit.

This is where "softer" self-control strategies, like the one I described above, come in. These strategies change how people mentally ap-proach the situation, rather than changing the situation itself. If you anticipate a self-control conflict, one way to stack the deck against temptation is to remind yourself what makes the goal attractive and what makes temptations less so. Mentally, you bolster the goal and devalue the temptation. You could, for example, remind yourself that a workout at the gym will make you feel great, or that the cupcakes your colleague brought to work are too colorful to taste good.

Interestingly, because people engage in this strategy as they prepare themselves to resist temptation, they tend to devalue available temptations more than unavailable ones. For example, we might tell ourselves that our single neighbor isn't our type because we want to protect our relationship with our partner. But if that neighbor enters into a committed relationship, we'll feel safe to admit that she really is attractive. As a result of exercising self-control, available temptations appear less tempting.

Take a study conducted in a campus gym by Kristian Myrseth, Yaacov Trope, and me. As gymgoers were on their way out, we offered them a choice between a health bar and a chocolate bar. Almost everybody chose the health bar, as these were all health-conscious people who didn't want to send the wrong signal. But how much more appealing was the health bar compared to the chocolate bar? The answer, it seems, depends on when you ask. We asked some gymgoers which bar they thought would taste better before they made their choice. These people rated the health bar as much better than the chocolate bar. Those who we asked after they'd chosen, however, thought that the health bar and chocolate bar were equally appealing. Before choosing, these gymgoers actively inhibited the appeal of the temptation, telling themselves (and the experimenter) that a chocolate bar is not very good. But once a choice had been made and the chocolate bar was no longer available, gymgoers could admit it looked delicious. While we often devalue unchosen options to justify our choice after we've made it—call it the "sour-grapes effect" or cognitive dissonance—when it comes to self-control evaluations, forgone temptations become more appealing because we no longer need to protect ourselves from pursuing them.

Another self-control strategy involves mentally distancing yourself from the self-control dilemma. If you were tempted to pick a heavy pasta dish while out with friends, you could ask yourself what a health-conscious person would choose to eat. If you were tempted to buy an expensive pair of headphones, you could ask if you'd still want to buy them next week. You can distance yourself by imagining the dilemma occurring to a different person, in the far future, or in a faraway place. Thinking about what your advice would be to someone who faced a similar dilemma or what you would do if you had to make the decision next year helps you choose the goal over the temptation.

Embedded deep in this strategy is self-talk. We regularly talk to ourselves; after all, we can always trust ourselves to listen. But people vary in how they self-talk. You can use "immersed self-talk," which takes the I/me, first-person perspective. You could be asking, for example, "What do I want?" Or you can use "distanced self-talk," which takes a third-person perspective. You would be asking, for example, "What does [Your Name] want?" As Ethan Kross has documented, distanced self-talk gives us better control over emotions than immersed self-talk. One study involved college students who, like all students, were nervous about their job prospects. These students were asked to explain why they were qualified for their dream job to a panel of expert interviewers, an anxiety-provoking task for anyone. Those who were guided to use distanced self-talk were better able to control their anxiety. These students asked themselves "How does [My Name] feel about preparing for their presentation?" which helped them better control their emotions than those who asked themselves "How do I feel about preparing for this presentation?" Asking yourself in the third person why you feel something and how you plan to deal with it helps suppress negative emotions because it feels somehow as if it's happening to someone else.

Another method of distancing yourself involves thinking of temptations in "cool" terms, that is, cognitive and emotionally neutral terms. In one of the first self-control studies, the psychologist Walter Mischel explored how three-to-five-year-old children resist eating marshmallows in a famous study that became known as the marshmallow test (more on this in Chapter 11). Children who were encouraged to mentally distance themselves by imagining the marshmallows as cool, nonappetitive objects—for example, "white, puffy clouds" or "round, white moons"—were better able to resist eating them than those who imagined them as the appetizing objects they are, thinking of them, for example, as "sweet and chewy and soft."

Changing how we think of the situation may further involve setting the intention to adhere to a goal and forgo temptation. College students who were asked to list the number of hours they would spend on their course work on a given day listed more hours if they were first asked to list the number of hours they planned to spend on leisure. On the other hand, college students who were asked to list the number of hours they would spend on leisure listed fewer hours if they were first asked to list the number of hours they would need to spend on their academic work. In both cases, we asked students to think about both temptations and goals. Thinking about temptation first led them to plan to spend time on their goals, and thinking about goals first led them to plan to avoid temptation. This study illustrates the process of counteracting temptations: you motivate yourself to pursue a goal when you encounter temptation and motivate yourself to avoid a temptation when important goals are at stake.

THE EXPERIENCE OF EXERCISING SELF-CONTROL: DEPLETING YET UNCONSCIOUS

Battling temptation is tiring and even harder to do when you're exhausted to begin with. Roy Baumeister and Kathleen Vohs call this "ego depletion." Health workers, for example, skip mandatory hand-washing more often later in their workday. And doctors are more likely to prescribe unnecessary antibiotics the longer they've worked a shift. For tired physicians, prescribing antibiotics is tempting because patients often demand them, and physicians want to do something more concrete than telling you to wait for test results or until your symptoms go away.

The lesson we can learn from tired health workers is that because exercising self-control is effortful, you may want to make decisions that involve self-control early in the day. Whether you're deciding on your diet or considering an impulsive purchase, it's best to wait until you're alert enough to make the right choice.

Popular magazines (and some scientific research) may correctly portray self-control as effortful but mistakenly portray it solely as a conscious process. You might imagine yourself feeling torn between the devil and the angel, sitting on opposite shoulders and whispering conflicting advice into your ears. But the reality is that your self-control is much more efficient than that. When you skip an unhealthy dessert or an advertisement for a gadget you shouldn't buy, or when you calm yourself during a heated debate, you're often controlling yourself unconsciously.

Most of the time and under most circumstances, we control ourselves without paying attention to what we're doing. This subconscious fight to resist temptation is immensely helpful—if you consciously weighed the pros and cons of nearly every decision you made, you wouldn't have time for much else.

Unconscious strategies are very similar to the self-control strategies we've already talked about, with the upside that they don't require attention and don't wear out our energy as much. You don't need to be aware that you're exercising self-control to glorify your goal or downplay your temptation. When you want your relationship to succeed, you exaggerate the positive qualities of your partner and downplay the attractiveness of other potential partners (as you might have done with that attractive single neighbor). You make the goal more attractive than the temptation without realizing that you're thinking this way to protect your relationship. When people exercise self-control, they automatically evaluate their goals more positively and evaluate their temptations more negatively. You might associate eating healthy food with feeling proud and successful and associate eating unhealthy food with feeling shameful.

Similar low-level self-control processes also help you keep your goal in mind when you encounter temptation. When a health-conscious person is confronted with a burger, they immediately think of their health and are more likely to eat something else instead. Similarly, people who are trying to save money might bring their bank account to mind when faced with the temptation to buy something just because it's on sale. To illustrate this process, one study had research participants first list their goal-temptation conflicts; for example, one person wrote "study-basketball," so we can assume they needed to study but were tempted to play basketball. Another person wrote "faithful-sex," so you can imagine their dilemma. Using a computerized task, it was then found that people were faster to read their goal words after the tempta-tion words were briefly flashed in the same location on the computer screen. Temptations bring to mind the goals that override them in such a way that people are mentally prepared to perceive these goals.

Unconscious self-control also helps steer you toward your goal and away from temptation, as Paul Stillman, Danila Medvedev, and Melissa Ferguson discovered. Their study used another computerized task. In this task research participants saw two images of foods, like an apple and an ice cream bar, on opposite sides of the monitor. Their task was to draw a line from the bottom center of the screen toward the food that would help them meet their health and fitness goals. The question of interest in this paradigm is how straight the line is — do you go directly to the food that's healthy, or is your line tilted a bit in the direction of the food that isn't healthy? As it turned out, those with better self-control were able to draw straighter lines; they were implicitly resisting the temptations on the other side of the screen and going directly to the healthy food.

People's ability to exhibit these low-level responses sheds light on what's going on under the conscious surface. They explain, for exam-ple, why some people automatically push their wineglass away when they want to be sure not to overdrink, or why you can automatically move your gaze away from an advertisement for a new laptop you'd like to buy before you get your next paycheck.

These low-level responses are frequent, and with practice they become a habit. You probably don't need to motivate yourself to brush your teeth. You've learned to associate "getting up in the morning" with "brushing my teeth." Maybe you've similarly learned to associate certain foods (for me, that would be doughnuts) with an "I'll skip that" response. As Wendy Wood discovered, once you've formed a habit, the context triggers your behavior directly, regardless of whether you've set an explicit goal or exercised self-control. With practice, resolving self-control conflicts becomes easier. You might not even need to remind yourself of the goal or even involve your self-control at all.

When you haven't yet established a habit, you can try setting implementation intentions and start practicing. According to Peter Gollwitzer, a simple implementation plan can go a long way. Once you've set a goal, add a plan in the format of "I will do [goal-directed actions] when [situation X] arises." You may say, for example, "I'll do yoga once I wake up" or "I'll put my glass in the sink as soon as I finish my first glass of wine." An implementation intention, once set, reminds you to do what you've said you'll do once you encounter the cue you set (waking up, or taking your last sip of wine). Usually, we're able to enact set plans almost automatically, again relying on our subconscious to do it for us.

Overall, while recognizing that self-control can be hard and will often leave you tired, we can remind ourselves that with practice and set intentions self-control can become automatic. Eventually, you might form a habit, which bypasses self-control. You won't need to think about what you should do (and what you shouldn't) at all. You simply act in a way that's beneficial for you.

QUESTIONS TO ASK YOURSELF

By now you should be able to distinguish between the challenge of detecting a self-control problem and that of battling temptation. And you should be able to recognize which self-control strategies fit each of these challenges. Getting familiar with your self-control arsenal should increase your confidence that you can resist temptations, as well as help you develop some strategies to increase your chance of success. Here are the main questions you could ask yourself to improve your self-control:

1. Know your enemy: What are your main temptations? What are some situations under which you're most likely to succumb to temptation?

2. How can you make it more likely that you'll detect self-control dilemmas? Possibly think about decisions in bulk, assuming that whatever you decide to do today, you'll do each time you face a similar situation. Think of yourself in the future. You are your future self's best friend; what can you do for that person today? Evaluate how your decisions reflect on your identity. Is there an identity that stands in the way of pursuing your goals?

3. How do you battle temptation? Consider making a pre-commitment to help you achieve your goal and rewarding yourself for progress made. Think about how you would mentally approach temptation. What makes pursuing your goals so much better than giving in to temptation? Can you distance yourself from the situation, use self-talk by asking what [Your Name] should do, and challenge yourself with high expectations?

4. When planning to resist temptation, how do you protect yourself from challenges like limited resources and feeling depleted? Plan for extra goal protection when you're tired toward the end of the day. Or form a habit.

11

PATIENCE

AS THE SAYING GOES, good things come to those who wait. But waiting is no fun. Whether you're waiting for your grilled-cheese sandwich to reach the perfect temperature or for your investment to mature, waiting is hard. The English word "patient" refers to both a person who's able to wait and a person who's in need of medical treatment. The double meaning isn't accidental. Both words have the same origin as "the one who suffers." Waiting is painful.

One reason waiting can be so difficult is that waiting often requires you to forgo something smaller, sooner, in favor of something larger, later. It also requires that you keep your cool, staying calm when you can't get what you want in the moment. These requirements may remind you of our talk about self-control in the last chapter. That's because being patient often relies on self-control, so much so that motivation scientists sometimes equate being patient with exercising self-control. Indeed, one of the classic paradigms for studying self-control, colloquially known as the "marshmallow test," which I mentioned in Chapter 10, actually assesses patience.

The famous marshmallow test dates back to the 1960s, when psychologist Walter Mischel set out to study how young children delay gratification. The test typically offers kids a choice between two food rewards. In the original study, children were brought to a room and sat at a table that held a single marshmallow. Researchers told the kids that if they could wait before eating the marshmallow (usually, the waiting would last ten to twenty minutes, though the kids wouldn't know that), they could have two marshmallows. Then the researchers left the room and watched what happened when the kids were left alone with their sweet treat. At any point during the wait, the children could've changed their minds and eaten their one marshmallow immediately. The number of minutes they waited before deciding that enough was enough defined their "patience score."

Think of something that's very tempting to you, like a glass of wine, a slice of freshly baked chocolate cake, or your Twitter feed. Imagine sitting in front of the temptation with nothing to do but wait. The wait time is unknown to you, but you believe that once it elapses, you'll get something better: a more expensive glass of wine or more time to spend on Twitter.

Using the marshmallow test, researchers initially identified the strategies children used to help themselves wait. Kids who were able to distract themselves (some sang songs or came up with games to play with their hands and feet; some even tried to fall asleep) and kids who thought about the food reward in nonappetitive terms (a marshmallow could be a white cloud, as we discussed in Chapter 10) were able to wait longer. Things got significantly more interesting when, around a decade later, Mischel and his colleagues went back to these children—by then adolescents—to see how they were doing. They found that preschoolers who had been able to be patient in the face of a tempting marshmallow were doing better cognitively and socially as adolescents. They got better grades and had more friends.

These marshmallow test data have been analyzed several times since then, and although by no means will the ability to exercise patience in one instance determine a child's future, delaying gratification at a young age tends to partially predict important life outcomes.

Research like the marshmallow test tells us that patience at an early age predicts positive outcomes later in life. But it doesn't tell us why. What is it about patience that enables success? Is it that patient people have stronger willpower? Are they smarter? Do patient children trust that good things really do come to those who wait so they're more likely to finish their homework before going to play outside? Motivation science suggests it's a combination of these factors plus more. But to address these factors, I need to start with why waiting is so hard in the first place.

WHY WAITING IS HARD

Waiting is a necessary evil. Most of the larger rewards we aspire to in life can take years of waiting. You save for retirement for decades before reaping the rewards of your effort. And if you want to move up at work, you might need to spend several years earning an online degree or going through a training program. Waiting is even a recipe for better health. The patient who's patient is the one who's willing to wait before asking for potentially unnecessary antibiotics or surgery. Yet waiting patiently isn't easy.

Waiting is hard because we're wired to discount our futures. In our mind, what happens to us in the future is worth less simply because it won't happen right now. A promise for $100 in a year, for example, will make you less happy than getting $100 now. You'll similarly be less excited about the opportunity to see your girlfriend next month than about being able to see her today.

Situations that require you to wait go against your human nature. They require forgoing an immediate option with higher appeal in favor of a delayed option with low appeal. For example, saving requires turning present income, which you highly value, into future income, which you value less. So when my eight-year-old son gets his allowance, he can either spend it or save it. Given that he values the money more if he can use it right now, it's no wonder he doesn't save.

To describe the speed at which future outcomes lose their appeal, we can refer to "discount rate." If you're patient, you have a low discount rate: you value future outcomes almost the same as present ones. You'll be okay having to postpone seeing your girlfriend because you value future love similarly to present love. If you're impatient, you have a high discount rate: you value future outcomes much less than present ones. You won't wait for love because you care about having it now much more than you appreciate having it later.

Regardless of how low your discount rate is, we all typically have a high-enough rate that we prefer immediate rewards. We're willing to accept less and pay more if we can get the thing we're waiting for right now. This is one reason airlines increase the price of flights the closer you get to departure. You're willing to pay more for a flight that's scheduled for tomorrow as opposed to one that is scheduled in a couple of months. Broadway shows also cost more if you buy tickets for a show that's happening tonight versus in a few weeks. And when shopping online, you're not just willing to pay more for one-day delivery, you expect to.

Realizing that we're impatient creatures is half the battle, as it prepares us to fight against impatience. But we also have to know the specific factors that determine just how impatient we are.

WHAT CAUSES IMPATIENCE

A keen observer will have noticed that successful tech companies like Apple have become masters at exploiting impatience. Whenever Apple comes out with a new, updated version of the iPhone, the company announces the new phone long before they're ready to release it. Besides the announcement that it's in development, you don't hear much more about the phone—what it'll look like or what it'll be able to do. In 2000, Dr. Arnold Kim capitalized on the impatience this strategy creates by founding a website called MacRumors. The website publishes unofficial information about Apple's new products. Each post about the rumored features of the newest iPhone or iPad satisfies the impatient tech lover as they wait. Eventually, Dr. Kim's blog became so successful that he decided to quit medicine and dedicate himself to the lucrative work of spilling Apple's secrets.

Apple's and MacRumor's success tell us that the longer someone stands to wait, the more value they assign to a product. But also that people have a hard time waiting. Generally speaking, if you're willing to wait, you both stand to get more and feel that what you get is more special. After all, your new phone will feel more precious if you've waited several months to buy it. Given that waiting is hard but will make you value what you've been waiting for, what specific factors make people impatient?

Lack of willpower. When we give in to temptation, we often chide ourselves for having very little willpower, so it likely comes as no surprise that a lack of willpower, which is your ability to exercise self-control, increases impatience. When Angela Duckworth, Eli Tsukayama, and Teri Kirby analyzed the marshmallow test data, they found a correlation between how much willpower parents and teachers said children had and how long these children waited for their reward. Kids who seemed to have more willpower were also more patient. But these studies also found that children's cognitive ability predicted the amount of time they could wait. So willpower cannot be the entire story. Having a strong mind, on top of a strong will, predicts the decision to wait. Smarts matter because a child who's able to fully reason through the benefits of waiting will be more patient. And being smart in pursuing delayed benefits is useful for adults, too.

Similarly, in a recent reanalysis Walter Mischel and his colleagues published after he passed, willpower at ages seventeen to thirty-seven predicted how much money a person had made by age forty-six. While in this analysis the single preschool marshmallow test score didn't predict midlife financial performance, parents' ratings of their children's willpower and, later, participants' ratings of their own willpower, did.

Lack of trust. How long should you wait before you give up? When waiting, this is a question you implicitly ask yourself. Put yourself in the shoes of a kid sitting in front of a marshmallow waiting for some grown-up to come back and say you can eat it. How long should you wait before concluding that the experimenter is never coming back? Or consider waiting for the bus at midnight. How long should you wait before you conclude that the bus isn't running anymore and start walking home? Note that I'm asking how long you *should* wait, not how long you *would*.

You surely would not wait forever. At a certain point, you should no longer trust the experimenter or the bus to come. You should conclude that the larger-later option is not really an option and decide to go for the immediate alternative, whether it's less candy or the walk home. You lose patience because you don't see the point in continuing to wait.

A main reason people are impatient is because they don't trust that waiting will pay off. They might not trust others to deliver on their promises, or they estimate the remaining wait time as simply too long. Often, the longer you've waited, the less trusting you become. If the bus hasn't arrived after thirty minutes (when you expected it to be just five minutes), it's more likely that it won't arrive tonight. And so patience declines over time.

Some evidence for the effect of trust comes from the marshmallow test. It was found that children from stable home environments tended to wait longer. If you grow up in a predictable environment, you trust adults to deliver on their promises. You might even decide to go to graduate school, delaying a steady paycheck by a few years, because you trust it'll pay off. In contrast, children from less stable environments are more suspicious of the adults in their lives. Sometimes, adults deliver on their promises; other times, they fail to do so. When children from lower socioeconomic backgrounds grow to be more impatient adults, it's often because they learned that the world is untrustworthy. If you learned to be suspicious of adults as a child, you might skip graduate school or undersave because the notion that good things come to those who wait doesn't quite resonate with your personal life experience.

Lack of care. How does the love of marshmallows influence a child's willingness to wait for two marshmallows later instead of receiving just one marshmallow right now? How does the love of coffee influence a coffee fanatic's willingness to wait until he makes it to his boutique coffee shop instead of buying coffee at the first coffee shop he sees? As you may have guessed, the more you care for something, the longer you're willing to wait for more of it or a better version of it. Love is patient, after all.

When you love something, whether it's marshmallows, coffee, or seeing a big number in your savings account, there's a big difference between the inferior and the superior versions of it. Tech enthusiasts believe there's a big difference between the currently available phone and the one that will be released next fall. Expecting a large difference, you're willing to wait. On the other hand, if you're like me, a phone is a phone, just like coffee is coffee. Why wait for a new model that's only slightly better than the one I could buy now? Given that I don't fall in love with machines, I'm an impatient consumer of technology.

In a study that documented just how patient love (or even just liking something) can be, Annabelle Roberts, Franklin Shaddy, and I asked research participants to choose between getting a T-shirt that would fit them perfectly in ten weeks or getting a T-shirt one size too large this week. Presumably, a T-shirt that's slightly too big can still be worn at home and will make for cozy pajamas, but you probably won't wear it when you want to look your best. Either way, waiting on the mail can be hard. The catch was that some people made this trade-off for a T-shirt design they really liked while others made it for a design they thought was just okay (based on how they rated twelve designs we showed them). We found that people were willing to wait the extra nine weeks for a T-shirt that fit, but only if they loved the design. When making the decision for a design they liked less, they were less patient. Other studies found that, for products ranging from coffee, beer, and chocolate to cheese and breakfast cereal, the more people liked the product, the more patient they were in waiting for a larger portion to be delivered next month over a smaller portion right now.

Note that while love increases your willingness to wait—you'd choose the larger-later over the smaller-sooner option—your experience while waiting will be more difficult. When you love something, you find it harder to keep your calm while you're waiting. The longer you wait, the more agitated you become. Indeed, in a study that investigated how desire for a consumer product changes over time, Xianchi Dai and I found that the longer people waited, the more they desired the product, but only if they liked it a lot. If they had good substitutes, they actually desired it less the longer they had waited.

You may have experienced this if you've ever traveled abroad. Many students who study abroad and spend several months in another country eventually find that they miss the food from their home country. In our study, the longer students traveling to Hong Kong had to wait to eat a homey dish, the more they looked forward to it.

While growing up in Israel, I felt similarly during the Passover holiday, when religious tradition prohibited the sales of foods that contain flour. I started to really miss bread. Inspired by my own experience, in another study, Dai and I surveyed people who abstain from chametz foods during Passover, and, indeed, they desired these foods more the longer they went without them. But the growing discomfort happened only if people hadn't identified satisfying substitutes for the desired foods. When observant participants considered having matzah (which substitutes for bread), flourless cake (which substitutes for cake made with flour), or potato dishes (which substitute for pasta dishes), the amount they missed flour-based foods didn't grow much over time. A similar phenomenon was observed when people were instructed to abstain from social media. One study asked Facebook users to stop using

Facebook for three days. People who didn't have good substitutes, like Twitter or Instagram, desired to use Facebook more and became more impatient over the course of the three days.

Having substitutes means that you like something, or someone, less. On the one hand, you find it easier to wait. On the other hand, you might not bother to wait.

A *desire to get this off your mind.* Recently, I paid $20 to a colleague I owed $15. When she reminded me that I owed her, I grabbed my wallet and found only $20 bills. I pulled out a bill to hand to her, but she shook her head, insisting that she didn't want to take more than I owed. I insisted right back. I'd rather pay $20 now than $15 at a later point. Why was I impatient to pay my debt, even though it cost me $5?

We often associate impatience with wanting to get money or other goods as soon as possible. Yet people are also impatient to close debts, in which case they can't wait to give their money away. When we asked people, the majority said they'd do what I did because it's better to overpay now to close small debts instead of leaving the debt open until they have the exact amount. Moreover, the majority of people also preferred to be underpaid now over leaving a debt open. So, for example, most people prefer to pay $20 now than wait until they can pay $18, and most people prefer to receive $18 now than wait until the person who owes them can pay $20.

These decisions reveal that people are impatient. They're willing to lose money to close debt sooner. The reason people prefer to close a debt sooner regardless of whether they owe or are owed is that they dislike open goals. People want to achieve goal closure.

Take the choice between doing more work now versus less work later. One study found that people prefer to transcribe more alphanumeric passwords (e.g., 3atAmynZ5P) today than fewer passwords in one week's time. Why? Doing the work now allowed them to cross it off their list. For a similar reason, some people choose to pay their credit card bill once it's posted and before it's due, and in another study, the majority of surveyed people said that if they needed to get vaccinated, they'd rather get a painful shot today than wait to take a painless pill in one week.

We become more eager to complete the goal, and therefore more impatient, the closer we get to its end state—recall the goal gradient effect in Chapter 5. Think of a time when you were getting ready to go on vacation. How difficult was it to focus on work, housework, or anything other than getting on the plane, train, or automobile that would get you to your vacation? We also become more agitated as we get closer to the end of the line in the DMV, regardless of how long we've already waited. Feeling closer to the end of a waiting period makes people restless. You find it harder to continue waiting and can't wait for the waiting to end.

Altogether, there are several reasons people are impatient. You might have weak willpower or low trust. You might not care enough or be too eager to finish. Before I explain how to fix these problems, keep in mind that at times, impatience isn't a problem. Instead, it can be an adaptive response to your environment. It's not the case that people should always wait. If you're hungry or tired, for example, a small immediate gratification could keep you going. Whether it's an afternoon snack or a short nap, a small gratification allows you to optimize your mental and physical functioning. You might correctly prioritize immediacy over quantity. And if you always wait for something better later, you might never get to enjoy the moment. That's not the way to live a happy life.

REMEDIES: HOW TO INCREASE PATIENCE

Patience is incredibly important in life. Patient people are more likely to graduate from college, as it requires forgoing an immediate but potentially less interesting job in favor of a later but potentially more satisfying career. Patient people also tend to save more money, as they're willing to put funds away for the future rather than spend them now. They're better at keeping their cool while stuck in traffic or standing in line at the coffee shop. And they're less likely to ruin their appetite by snacking too much before dinner. But patience, as I said before, is fickle. We all have some patience and we're all sometimes impatient. So how do you build patience when you need it to work in your favor?

Distraction. In his most famous experiment, the mathematician John Edmund Kerrich flipped a coin 10,000 times. The total percentage of heads and tails varied wildly at first but gradually converged around 50/50, providing a demonstration of the Law of Large Numbers. Though it proved to be an important discovery, Kerrich ran this experiment to distract himself. In the 1940s, he was held in Nazi captivity and passed his time waiting for the end of World War II by flipping a coin. Not knowing how long it would take to be freed, he remained patient by passing the time doing something, even though it was a rather mundane task. Children in the original marshmallow studies also used this strategy. When they kept themselves busy making up songs or stories, they were distracting themselves so they wouldn't have to think about the marshmallow in front of them.

What Kerrich and the marshmallow testers demonstrate is that pushing the wait out of mind is an effective way to increase patience. Find something else to do and try to forget you're waiting. It's easy to wait if you're not aware you're waiting in the first place.

Make your decision in advance. If I offered to give you $120 in six months or $100 now, which would you choose? What if I offered $120 in a year and a half or $100 in a year? Many people would choose $100 in the first scenario but $120 in the second. Either way, I'm asking you to wait six months for an extra $20. So why are people willing to wait when they'd already have to wait at least a year for their money? The answer is that distance increases patience. When the options are close, we tend to choose a smaller-sooner reward, but when there's distance to either option, we choose the larger-later reward.

This example demonstrates one strategy to increase patience: make the decision to wait in advance. According to the "advanced decision" technique, you'll be more patient if you decide between the smaller-sooner and the larger-later options ahead of time, when they're both scheduled in the far future. It's easier to wait an extra month for a better product or a better price when the waiting takes place next year rather than now. Our perception of time is nonlinear—the difference between now and next month seems larger in our mind than the difference between one year from now and one year plus one month.

Another reason people switch their answer is because of what motivation researchers call "hyperbolic discounting." People are initially quick to discount future outcomes but discount these future outcomes more slowly later on. So in your mind, a sum of money is worth much less if you're to get it in six months, but it isn't worth much less if you get it in a year and a half rather than a year from now.

Pigeons benefit from having to make advanced decisions, too. If they choose in advance, pigeons opt for the larger-later reward. In one study, Howard Rachlin and Leonard Green had pigeons choose between a small, immediate reward (a peck on a key that produced two seconds of access to grain immediately) and a large, delayed reward (a peck on a key that produced four seconds of access to grain, delayed by four seconds). The pigeons were impatient; they preferred the small, immediate reward. However, when the researchers introduced a constant time delay of ten seconds, making the immediate reward appear in ten seconds and the delayed (larger) reward appear in fourteen seconds, the pigeons started switching to pecking on the key that offered the delayed reward. They therefore switched their answer to the question "Are you willing to wait an additional four seconds for more grains?" depending on whether their decision was made way in advance, in which case they were patient, or just before the immediate reward became available, in which case they were impatient.

We can use this principle to increase patience. All we need to do is introduce more time before the smaller-sooner option becomes available. If, for example, you knew you could only afford to take one trip over the summer, you'd be better off planning your trip in advance. If you were forced to make a choice right now about whether you'd take a weekend trip this weekend or a weeklong trip next month, it'd likely be hard to resist booking a weekend escape. But what if your choice was between a weekend vacation in three months or a week-long vacation in four months? No matter how much you're aching for a vacation, you'd likely be able to wait an extra month for the longer trip. After all, you already have to wait. It's also easier to skip paying expedited delivery fees if paying shortens the delivery from ten to five days than if it would shorten it from five days to next day.

Wait to choose. Thomas Jefferson once said, "When angry, count to ten before you speak. If very angry, a hundred." In saying this, he endorsed another strategy to increase patience, the "wait-to-choose" technique. This technique involves postponing the decision on how to respond (choose the option that benefits you now versus later) until after you hear about the options and think about your decision for a while.

The wait-to-choose technique introduces a deliberation time in which you get to assess the options and appreciate the advantage of getting something better if you wait a bit longer. As a result, you become more patient. For example, in one study, Dai and I asked people to choose between entering a lottery for a merely okay digital audio player that was available in fifteen days or for a better player that was available in forty days. Some people waited to make the lottery choice, while others chose immediately. Those who waited thirteen days before choosing were more likely to wait for the better model than those who had made their choice immediately. Waiting to choose made people appreciate getting a better model of the audio player more, and therefore made them more willing to wait for it.

Address the cause of impatience. Other techniques to increase patience directly address the causes of impatience we discussed earlier. If the cause of impatience is a lack of willpower, we can improve self-control, for example, by reminding ourselves that the future will one day be our present. Alternatively, we can increase the degree to which we feel connected to our future self. Psychological connectedness is a tested technique for increasing patience. For college students, using virtual reality to generate an image of themselves at age seventy increased their intentions to save for retirement, just as writing a letter to their future self increased their propensity to exercise.

If you're impatient because the future is uncertain, increasing your confidence in future outcomes will make them worth the wait. For example, you can set an automatic payment of credit card debt in the present, making it less likely that you'll forget to pay your bill on time. Or you can demand that a payment stay in escrow until you're eligible for it. This is a common practice in real estate, where sellers are more comfortable waiting for money when buyers submit their payment to a third party, such as the title company. And if the cause of impatience is lack of love for the larger-later reward, you can remind yourself what's special about the reward and why you care about it in the first place. It might even happen spontaneously as you employ the waiting-to-choose technique; as you wait, you may value the waited-for options more. This psychology is at play when you grow fonder of products as you wait in line. When you invest in something, you learn to appreciate it.

But when the stakes are small, you may want to quickly close the goal in order to take it off your mind. In this case, there are technological solutions to help you. You could put a reminder on your calendar to follow up later or schedule your emails to be delivered at a future time, for example. And if you're concerned that you'll forget to use a coupon, you're probably not alone. A large proportion of coupons and gift cards are never redeemed. But if you're worried that your impatience to use a gift card or coupon will lead you to buy something you don't really need, a calendar reminder to use your discount at a later date might be handy.

Be patient for the sake of others. Finally, you might be more patient if you enlist others to join you in the wait. If we both decide to wait, the waiting will be easier. And if your benefits depend on my ability to wait, that might be even more effective at increasing my patience. A couple that sets a joint savings goal may be better able to achieve it than individuals with no joint goal or social support. Take a study that used a modified version of the marshmallow test, but this time handed out cookies. In this study, Rebecca Koomen, Sebastian Grueneisen, and Esther Herrmann assigned some children to pairs. Within each pair, the children got the larger-later reward only if both independently decided to wait. Children were more patient when they realized that eating their cookie too early would not only cost them but would cost their partner a second cookie, too.

Next time you find yourself waiting for a sandwich, an investment, or anything in between, try some of these strategies. You'll be more patient in the end.

QUESTIONS TO ASK YOURSELF

Few people describe themselves as patient. Most of us, myself included, feel we could benefit from being willing to wait a bit longer. Below are some questions you can ask yourself as you work to become more patient and therefore strive to get the larger-later rewards in life.

1. Are you more patient in some contexts than others? Are you making shortsighted financial, medical, academic, or other decisions?

2. When you're impatient, are you mainly concerned about making shortsighted decisions or feeling agitated, even angry, about having to wait? Is it both the decision and the experience that are difficult for you?

3. Why are you impatient? There are several possible reasons: lack of willpower, lack of trust that good things will happen if you wait, not caring enough for the delayed rewards, or maybe there's already too much on your mind.

4. How can you become more patient? Consider distracting yourself, and the advanced-decision and wait-to-choose techniques. You may also increase your sense of connection to your future self or your trust that future outcomes will materialize. Alternatively, remind yourself what you like about the waited-for items. Or use technology to get things off your mind and ease the experience of waiting. Finally, you could make the decision to be patient with others and for the sake of others. Indeed, working with others is the final ingredient in motivating yourself (see Part IV).

Part IV

SOCIAL SUPPORT

HERE I AM, WRITING about social support in the midst of the COVID-19 pandemic. I'm at home, where I've been isolating from the world with my family for many months. Social distancing is the name of the game. I haven't seen my colleagues or friends in months, and I don't know when I'll see my parents next. The week before my university closed, a colleague reached out his hand to me before immediately pulling back. We stopped shaking hands a few months ago. My three-year-old neighbor waved at me this morning, and I waved from a distance before her mother pulled her away. We no longer hug our adorable little neighbors.

For many, this era of reduced social contact has provided a daily reminder of just how critical others are in helping us stay motivated. Having colleagues, friends, and family by your side makes it easier to push forward. So, while we've all been advised to use our time in quarantine to exercise, read, learn a new skill, eat more healthily, and learn to work from home, it's harder to attend to these goals without your people around you. There has been no time quite like this year to evaluate the importance of social support in motivating us to achieve our goals.

It's also a perfect time to write about how we, as humans, are programmed to join forces with other humans in working together toward goals that we share as a group. While people are physically isolated, a new sense of community is emerging. We join a single purpose as we fight a common enemy, and our success depends on each person doing their part. Our ability to coordinate with others in pursuing a shared goal is being tested across the globe. If we can succeed at this challenge, there's a chance we can tackle other globally shared goals as well. There's hope that the skills we develop during this crisis could be used to reduce pollution or fight climate change.

In this section, we'll talk about how others help us achieve our goals. Motivation science explores several possibilities. Some involve the mere presence of others in our lives. Especially if we consider people to be role models, their expectations and actions motivate us to achieve our goals. They may also lend a helping hand to encourage our progress or to help us stick with something important. As humans, we have evolved to help each other. We feel distressed when a baby cries because we hear their call for help, and we feel an urge to do something about it even if they aren't our baby. We're ready to provide help to others as well as receive it.

Further, others work with us to accomplish shared goals. We've all heard the saying "teamwork makes the dream work." We know we should never be tempted to credit a single individual with a company's success or a scientific discovery. Neil Armstrong didn't land on the moon by himself; countless others helped. Indeed, the bigger the achievement, the likelier it is that others were involved. A lesson I'm reminded of during quarantine: you may only need two people to make a baby, but it really does take a village to raise that child.

Several features of our motivational system allow us to efficiently support each other's goals and pursue shared goals. First, we pay a lot of attention to the people around us. We dedicate most of our thinking to other people. Unless your mind is completely occupied—and how often is that?—it tends to wander. And when it wanders, it tends to wander toward other people. Maybe you're imagining what someone else is doing or what they think of you.

To get a sense of how much attention we pay to other people, consider the ease with which sports fans perform "the wave." Fans accomplish this complicated coordination effort all the time in stadiums of thousands. Even young children can clap their hands together in perfect unison, an ability that only improves with age as they become more attentive to others.

We also seek others' company. As humans, we're social animals; we thrive in groups and fall ill when alone. No matter whether you identify as an introvert or an extrovert, to some extent you need to be with other people. Social isolation is so unnatural to humans that it's considered a harsh and often cruel and unethical punishment. Solitary confinement has been identified as a major cause of mental illness, one that can lead to death.

Moreover, we're usually ready to work with others, whether as a team or as partners. When we meet someone new, we evaluate how we can work with them. We typically start by noting other people's social status; that is, their position in the social hierarchy. When we know if someone has more or less power than us, whether they're superordinate, subordinate, or equal to us, we know how to work with them. We seek out information on others' power because it tells us how we ought to relate to them in pursuing shared goals.

So we know people pay close attention to others, seek others' company, and are ready to cooperate with others. Combine these features with the understanding that important goals require the support of others, and you should start to get a sense of why social support is critical for successful goal pursuit. Whether you wish to get in shape or overcome a pandemic, you'd better join forces. But the question remains: How do we work with others in a way that's optimal for success?

Part IV seeks to answer this question by addressing the various aspects of social support and how to create a social network that helps your goals. Chapter 12 is about pursuing your own goals in the presence of others. You might look up to your role model or join a Zumba class to achieve your health goals. Chapter 13 is about pursuing goals with others. These are goals that require joint effort, like winning a soccer game or making a scientific discovery. Chapter 14 explores implications of social support for successful relationships. It explains why you're drawn toward those who support your goals and away from those who stand in the way.

12

PURSUING GOALS IN THE PRESENCE OF OTHERS

MANY OF US, MYSELF included, are quick to use "we" to describe others' actions and achievements. Think how many times you've heard someone say "we won the game" or "we landed on the moon." Though most of us are neither professional athletes nor astronauts, it feels natural to use "we" to describe these achievements. By virtue of the pronoun "we," it's difficult to distinguish between something you and I did last weekend versus something Neil Armstrong did in 1969. The ambiguity in our language is in large part because there's no psychological need to make such a distinction. The boundaries between others and ourselves are far from clear-cut.

Psychologists use the concept of "self-other overlap" or "psychological overlap" to account for the perception of overlapping identities between ourselves and others. Imagine a Venn diagram where one circle represents your identity and the other circle represents the identity of someone close to you. There's likely a lot of overlap between the two. This diagram captures the psychology of how we think of others who are close to us: they're separate from us, but not entirely so. The closer you are to someone or to a group of people, the greater the overlap you perceive between your identity and theirs. The two of you are intertwined; you're separate parts of a combined whole.

This perception of ourselves intertwined with others produces a number of interesting phenomena. For example, you may take time to recognize a trait that's unique to you and be much quicker to identify the traits you share with a close other or your group. If you and your partner both like classical music, you'll immediately report that you're a fan of Mozart. If you like classical music while your partner prefers jazz, you'll take a little longer to recall your personal preference because you don't share this musical love as a couple. It's easier to remember aspects of your personality that you share with your partner and that are therefore characteristic of you together.

This psychological overlap with others, especially with those who are close to us, is key to understanding the various and often surprising ways by which the mere presence of people influences our motivational system. When others pursue their goals in parallel to you—for instance, when you exercise, shop, work, or carry out your daily activities in the presence of a friend, partner, sister, or coworker—you might conform by working harder. Others increase your motivation. They might even serve as role models. Alternatively, you may also relax your efforts in response to others' actions. If you don't sufficiently separate others' actions from what you did or didn't do, it can be too easy to feel satisfied with the progress you've noticed—even if someone else did the work.

CONFORMITY

As a young girl, I used to do macrame. For those fortunate enough to be unfamiliar, it is, in essence, a craft that involves tying a (traditionally white) cotton string into a series of knots that can be used as wall décor. It didn't require a lot of creativity, as I was meticulously following precise directions, and I never thought the outcome was especially pretty. I never wanted to hang it on my own wall. But all the other girls my age were into it, so I assumed macrame must be cool.

In choosing our hobbies and our professions, in deciding what to buy and what to eat, and, more broadly, in setting our goals, we tend to conform to other people. We would like to have or say what they have had or said.

In what's now considered a classic experiment in social psychology, the psychologist Solomon Asch sought to bring conformity to the lab. He invited students to participate in what they thought was a test of their vision. Each student sat in a room with several other students. The group saw a series of boards, each showing a comparison line and three lines next to it. Their job was to identify which line was the same length as the comparison line. Unbeknownst to the participants, the experiment was about conformity, and the other people in the room only pretended to be naïve participants; they were "research confederates," that is, they were actually part of the research team. The vision test was rigged against the one actually naïve participant in each room. When the boards were presented, the confederates all pointed at the same wrong line, one that was either too long or too short (sometimes quite obviously so). The real participants, who were always the last ones to give their answer, often agreed with the false statement, pointing at the wrong line as well. Expressing dissent when everyone has reached a consensus can be unpleasant, even if it's only about the length of a line. Rather than openly dissent, participants went along with the wrong answer.

When another group of participants was invited to privately write their answers on a piece of paper (supposedly because they were late to the experiment), few conformed. Asch's experiment demonstrates conformity that's based on compliance. The participants conformed in public to an answer many of them rejected in private (unless they were truly concerned about the quality of their vision). We conform all the time in public, even if we privately don't agree. If everyone around the dinner table praises the wine, you might speak in favor of its aroma and body even if you're really unimpressed by it.

Under extreme pressure, compliance can turn into obedience. You might wear heels to work even though you believe they're designed to torture women because all the other women in your office wear heels. You feel that to be taken seriously you need to dress like them and you don't wish to lose your chance at a promotion over shoes. The same social pressure is on display in Stanley Milgram's famous experiment testing whether people would inflict pain on others in order to conform. Research participants were told to deliver what they believed to be strong electric shocks to research confederates who failed to answer a question correctly. Though these people personally rejected the idea of inflicting pain on someone for being a slow learner, they did as they were told. Fortunately, the "shocks" weren't real and the participants caused no harm.

In contrast with conformity that's based on compliance and obedience, most everyday conformity involves at least some degree of genuine acceptance of the judgments or ideas expressed by other people. When we conform, we usually internalize others' preferences and behaviors. We believe that other people are onto something.

The different types of conformity tell us something about the different reasons people choose to follow others in the first place. One is that there are certain social benefits to being an agreeable person — for one, people tend to like you better. Often, people strategically agree with others in order to keep being liked and accepted. If you're a rebel, you're probably missing out on these benefits. This is "normative conformity." You may agree outwardly with what someone else did or said but might not agree inwardly. Just like the participants in Asch's lines experiment, a person showing normative conformity runs the calculation and determines that it pays off to say you agree even if you don't. In your heart, you may reject the idea that listening to classical music is diagnostic of superior musical taste, but you'll play along and rave about a classical concert you attended because you believe it will connect you to the right crowd.

Another reason people conform is that they suspect others have figured out what's best to do or say. This type of "informational conformity" results from the information others' actions convey about best practices, correct answers, and, more generally, which goals are worth pursuing. If you see a long line in front of a coffee shop, you'll assume that shop has incredible coffee. Other coffee drinkers' choices give you a kind of proof that this cup of espresso shouldn't be missed. This is why I used to do macrame; I trusted that my friends knew what was fun. When your friends or online community recommend a recipe or hairstyle, you assume they know what's best.

Often, others *do* have useful information to share with you. And the more people you ask, the more likely you are to get it right. The wisdom of the crowd often suppresses the wisdom of a single person within the crowd. This is why you may choose to consult the combined ratings of thousands of moviegoers rather than blindly follow your coworker's movie recommendation. This is also why we let the market, basically a crowd of people, decide the value of stocks through trading rather than relying on the evaluation of a limited number of expert economists.

Of course, even large crowds are not always wise. How else could you explain that the US has not yet elected a single woman president? But even if you don't think the people around you are especially bright, there's yet another reason to conform to them: you conform because you're part of the crowd. The crowd is made up of "your people."

Indeed, a main reason people conform is that they don't hold clear-cut boundaries between themselves and the person or people to whom they conform. Instead of "they," we say and therefore think "we." This is the difference between saying, "My parents want me to be a doctor" and "My family wants me to be a doctor"; in the latter statement, you're included in the group of people who want you to pursue medicine. You've internalized other people's views and goals because they're part of you.

To demonstrate this lack of boundaries, think of the ease with which you adopt another person's experiences in a movie or a book. If you watch a movie scene in which a tarantula crawls on someone's neck, it'll likely make you shiver as if it were happening to you. You adopt the unpleasant sensation as well as the immediate goal of getting this bug off your neck. You have formed a psychological unit with that fictional person, adopting their experiences and goals. You conform.

Naturally, we overlap more with close friends and family than with strangers or fictional characters, and so we conform more to our close circle. We form a "shared reality"; we experience the world in a similar way and adopt similar viewpoints to theirs. We care about the social issues they care about and we follow their fashions and fads. If friends have a goal, we share that goal with them. After all, we're parts of a single whole.

WHEN CONFORMITY TURNS INTO COMPLEMENTARITY

Those we're closest to exert the greatest influence on us—but this doesn't mean that we always mimic their actions and thoughts. At times, conforming by following others' steps might be undesirable. We teach young children to share their toys, for example, because it's not a good idea for everyone to reach for the same toy at the same time. They should take turns and diverge their interests rather than mimic each other and fight for that toy. Later in life, we learn that we should never show up at a party wearing the same clothes as our friend, no matter how much we love her dress, and that a polite conversation requires switching between speaking and listening rather than speaking at the same time. The general rule across these examples is that we learn to seek actions that complement rather than overlap with or repeat what others do.

What determines whether people seek to conform (repeat) versus complement each other's actions? Why do you sometimes jump onto a goal your friend started and other times skip it because they're doing it?

The experience of psychological overlap accounts for both patterns of coordination. You respond to others' actions, preferences, and goals similarly to how you would respond to your own. You ask yourself: Given what "we" just said or did, is it best if I repeat this statement or action, or should I go for something else?

People tend to conform to what others say. As we discussed in Chapter 5, once you say something, you boost your commitment. So if I express that something is important to me, I would be more likely to express this view again and follow through with action. By the principle of psychological overlap, if my partner says that something is important to him, I infer it's important to us as a couple. My commitment increases, so I'm also more likely to express this view and follow through with action. For example, if my partner decided he'd like to reduce his energy consumption, I'd be more likely to buy energy-saving lightbulbs the next time I was at the store.

But people are less likely to conform to what people close to them do, especially when these actions signal that enough has been done. For example, if my partner brags about all the energy he's been saving riding his bike to work, I might feel that we, as a couple, are already doing enough to cut down on our consumption and that I don't need to act.

The same principle—conforming to ideas and complementing actions—also applies to groups. If I think the people in my group are already behaving ethically, I might be less concerned with doing what's right as an individual, as "we" have already proven we're ethical people. So, in one study, Maryam Kouchaki found that college students who read that students on their campus are more moral than students on other campuses, according to a survey, were later more discriminatory in their hiring practices: they were willing to hire a less-qualified white person over a more-qualified Black person for a police job when the working environment was said to be hostile to Black people. Of course, they thought they were avoiding trouble by not introducing a Black officer into a hostile work environment. But this discriminatory decision won't change the culture. They made the easy but biased choice that someone might make if they felt reassured about their moral standing.

Similarly, perceiving yourself as part of a victimized group can result in lower concern for other potential victims. If I learn that the people in my social group are subject to discrimination, I might worry less about not discriminating against others, as I see "us" as the victim rather than the potential perpetrator. So for me, as a Jewish person, reminders of anti-Semitism across the globe may put me at risk of being less careful about discriminating against a minority job candidate.

In other research, Yanping Tu and I directly compared conformity to others' stated goals to conformity to their actions. We found that because people perceive a psychological overlap with others, they move away from actions others take but conform to goals others say are important. In one study, an experimenter approached pairs of friends sitting around campus, offering them a choice between two flavors of gum: wintermint and sweetmint. If the first person in the pair selected wintermint but was asked to chew it later, the second person in the pair tended to conform. A bit more than half chose the same flavor. But if the first person in the pair started chewing their gum, the second person tended to choose sweetmint instead. Almost everyone chose a different flavor, thereby complementing rather than mimicking the first person's choice.

This research also found that online shoppers conform more to information given through ratings, cues that tell them how much other people like something, than to information on sales, which tells them what other people have purchased. You want the products everyone raves about but not the ones everyone already has, even though these two categories largely overlap. Similarly, online viewers choose video clips based on the number of likes rather than the number of views. You won't necessarily want to watch what everyone has already watched as much as you'd like to watch what others have recommended watching. If everyone else is doing something, you feel, in a way, like you've done it, too. That's why even people who've never read Harry Potter feel as if they have.

ROLE MODELS AND ANTI–ROLE MODELS

Today, my eldest daughter is a successful and confident astrophysicist. But years ago, when she was just starting college, her confidence was low. Almost all of her physics teachers and classmates were men. She didn't feel like she belonged. Luckily for her, one of the few female physics teachers at the school was assigned to be her freshman advisor. This advisor took her job to help budding physicists seriously, especially to help young women move forward in STEM careers. As the first woman hired by the physics department at Yale, my daughter's advisor openly discussed sexism in the field in meetings and at dinners she held for all her mentees. Having her as a role model at eighteen helped my daughter build confidence that she, too, could have a career in the male-dominated field of physics.

Role models are important figures in your life. Your role model is someone to whom you feel close and who displays the qualities you'd like to see in yourself. Even though this person might not know you personally, as when you take a celebrity or a public figure as your role model, you feel you have somewhat overlapping identities. You could potentially be like them, so they inspire you.

As with all others in your life, your role model's stated goals for themselves and others are going to motivate you even more than their actions. So you'll want to choose a role model who doesn't only do well, but also expects themselves and others to do well. The best role model does more than set an example; they set expectations they want you to live up to. An athlete who wants you to be in great shape is a better role model for your own fitness than an athlete who only cares that their fans watch them on TV. And a manager who expects you to succeed is a better role model than someone who's extremely successful at work but who doesn't bother to mentor others.

You should also consider using an "anti–role model." This is a person you want to distinguish yourself from. You'll choose to do something because it's different from what your anti–role model does.

For example, trying to distinguish yourself from a careless manager or a corrupt politician might motivate you to further your education and be a caring and ethical leader.

Anti–role models remind us that there are two very different reasons people choose to diverge from others' actions. At times, you choose complementary actions because you want to get along with others. Coordinating your actions with theirs helps you accomplish that. Other times, you want to "go it alone" and be different from others perhaps because you dislike them or because you want to express your unique personality. Teenagers are a good example of the latter. Teenagers don't necessarily hate adults (or so we think). They mainly reject adults' values because they want to be independent. Even as adults, a group of friends at a restaurant will often order different dishes and drinks because ordering the same thing wouldn't set them apart enough, as Dan Ariely and Jonathan Levav documented. Maintaining a reputation as unique may be a good enough reason to diverge from others.

When it comes to expressing dissenting views and actions, the underlying reason for the dissent will influence what you say or do. If you're motivated by a desire to appear unique, you'll jump on the opportunity to do something that doesn't fit with what everyone else is doing. In contrast, if your motivation is to complement what others are doing, you'll be more likely to do or say something that's both different from and fitting with others' actions. You might choose to be the devil's advocate, for example. While a true nonconformist will express a dissenting view for the sake of argument, someone who aspires to complement others will choose to express a different view that adds a new perspective and potentially suggests a new solution to a problem.

Whether you choose a role model whose goals you adopt or an anti–role model whose goals you oppose, and whether your actions complete or undo the role model's actions, these people influence your actions and therefore play a powerful part in your life.

SOCIAL FACILITATION

At the beginning of this chapter I said that pursuing goals in the presence of others can increase our motivation, but so far I've only covered situations in which others influence us by expressing certain views or through their actions. For the types of influence I've described, physical presence isn't even required. So how does the physical presence of others—who might perform no action and express no goal—influence motivation?

Interestingly, one of the first experiments in the history of social psychology set out to explore this exact question in 1898. It was conducted by Norman Triplett, an American psychologist and an avid cyclist. Triplett noticed that cyclists racing against each other are faster than those racing against the clock alone. Puzzled by his observation, he decided to test whether everyone is more motivated with other people around. He set up an experiment asking kids to turn a fishing reel as fast as possible. Some children wound in the fishing line when standing alone and others wound in the line with another child watching, waiting for their turn. As with the cyclists, most children worked faster in the presence of another person.

Years later, this phenomenon was named "social facilitation." It refers to our tendency to work harder when others are watching. Athletes, for example, perform better in front of an audience. Mental performance also improves when others are watching. You'll be faster to learn as well as generate more arguments in favor of your position when you're in front of an audience. And if that doesn't feel like a basic psychological principle, keep in mind that animals, too, respond favorably to the presence of an audience of the same species. Rats, for example, run a maze faster when another rat is watching behind the window.

The presence of observers increases the performer's psychological and physiological arousal. You assume the audience is evaluating or competing with you, which makes you apprehensive and excited. This arousal, in turn, enhances performance on easy or highly practiced tasks. You'll do more and do it better.

But keep in mind that arousal also hinders performance on more complex and unpracticed tasks, and too much arousal undermines performance altogether. So, for example, if you've just learned to shoot balls into the basket, attempting to play basketball in front of an audience might destroy your ability to do it right. And if you're preparing an important presentation at work, you may want to practice until it feels natural to you. This way, it'll become a well-rehearsed task you can easily do in the face of the anxiety and excitement of other people watching.

Interestingly, having stand-ins for the presence of others, such as a photo of a loved one on your desk or even a photograph of staring eyes, can trigger the social facilitation effect. These cues make you feel like you're being watched, even when you aren't. Such an experience, in turn, motivates you to do well, and to do more, and further increases your cooperation, honesty, and generosity.

Not only will you work harder when you're being watched, you'll also feel like your actions leave a greater mark. When another pair of eyes is watching, we feel as if the magnitude of whatever we're doing has multiplied because two pairs of eyes saw it. This increases our motivation to do the right thing. In a study led by Janina Steinmetz, we found that people believed that the amount of food they ate in public was larger than how much they ate alone, though the portions were the same. These perceptions motivate eating smaller portions in public than in private. In yet another demonstration, individual badminton players believed they had a bigger impact on their team's success and failure the more people were in the audience. This effect motivates players to try harder when more people are watching. When someone is watching, you're encouraged to be your best self.

QUESTIONS TO ASK YOURSELF

The presence of others influences our motivation, even when they're not physically with us. When you're in love, you behave as if your loved one watches and listens to everything you do, say, or think, even when they aren't around. Your loved one motivates you to be your best self. You also rely on your friends and family, among others, to keep you moving forward because they're watching you, even if only in your head.

Here are some questions that will help you design a social environment that motivates you to stick with your goals:

1. Think about the people in your life. Should you conform to their values, including stated goals and actions? Should you instead complement what they say and do? You should probably do both, and it's useful to identify how your goals and actions fit within others' goals and actions.

2. Who should be your role models? Recall that effective role models don't just demonstrate success. Watching sports on TV, for example, doesn't get you in shape. Your role models are the people who expect you to do well.

3. How can you use the power of being watched to facilitate your performance? Whether by performing in front of an audience or working in a public place, when executing highly practiced goal tasks, you can use social facilitation to your advantage. But when learning a new task, try practicing alone.

13

PURSUING GOALS WITH OTHERS

IN 1913, AROUND THE time Triplett noticed cyclists racing faster in the presence of others, in another part of the world, a French agricultural engineer named Maximilien Ringelmann wondered how hard people worked when others were helping rather than merely watching them. To test his inklings, he gathered groups of men and gave them a rope. The rope was attached to a dynamometer, which recorded the force with which the men pulled. Ringelmann found that by themselves, each man pulled hard. But when teams tugging on the rope consisted of several men, each man began putting less strength into his efforts.

We call this motivational deficit "social loafing," and it's something we all regularly experience. Just imagine you're on a lake in a two-person kayak. It's unlikely that you'd put all of your strength into paddling the boat. When you know someone else is there to pick up the slack, you relax. This also happens when splitting the check at a restaurant. If you were eating alone, you'd likely be careful of how much you ordered, not just because you wouldn't want to overstuff yourself but also because you'd be mindful of how much you were spending. But as the number of people at your table grows, so does the amount you'll end up paying. The more people there are to split the check, the more individual diners relax their spending limits. Group projects at school and group meetings at work similarly make us relax our efforts—we don't think as hard as if we were trying to solve a problem by ourselves. Having others participate in the meeting makes it more tempting to zone out. In fact, work meetings only utilize a small proportion of the brainpower in the room.

Social loafing takes place in all groups, from sports teams to organizational committees to symphony orchestras and juries. Whenever we're concerned mainly with how the group performs rather than with who did what, group members are less likely to work hard. This phenomenon is so robust that it's sometimes referred to as the "social disease."

"Free riding" is a similar phenomenon to social loafing, except a free rider doesn't just work less hard in a group; they also strategically make sure to enjoy the fruits of the labor to which they didn't contribute. Someone who avoids paying taxes but enjoys public goods such as highways or public parks is a free rider. At the office, free riders never raise their hand when volunteers are needed, yet they claim their paycheck and the perks that come with the job. At home, free riders never do the dishes or take out the trash.

The reason people loaf or free-ride in groups takes us back to a concept we discussed with the middle problem (Chapter 7): when our actions will go unnoticed, we care less about doing well. In groups, it's often impossible to evaluate the impact of individual contributions. So if the reason we loaf is that no one, not even us, can see the impact of our actions, the solution may be to make individual contributions more visible.

COMBATING SOCIAL LOAFING AND FREE RIDING

In 2010, two viral-marketing specialists, Brad Damphousse and Andy Ballester, started a crowdsourcing website for the everyman. Jumping on the popularity of sites like Indiegogo and Kickstarter, which crowd-source funds for artists and entrepreneurs, they wanted a place for people to fundraise "for life's important moments." They envisioned people using their site to raise money for personal passions like honeymoon trips and graduation gifts. They called it GoFundMe.

Now GoFundMe is a wildly popular fundraising platform. One couple raised nearly $15,000 for chemo treatments for their golden retriever. A seven-year-old girl in California raised more than $50,000 to buy and donate books featuring diverse characters and boxes of crayons with a range of skin tone colors to schools in her community. And a teacher in Colorado raised more than $92,000 to help a student of his—a young boy in foster care—get a lifesaving kidney transplant.

These are huge goals. And while there are many reasons any one GoFundMe becomes successful, Damphousse and Ballester set up their crowdfunding website with two very helpful features: everyone can choose to attach their name to their donation and every donation (big or small) is listed on a separate line.

When giving money anonymously, people tend to give less, as they feel less accountable for their actions. Moreover, when givers can only compare their individual contribution to the total amount that's been raised, their contribution feels like a drop in the bucket. But when names are attached to single donations, people feel accountable and they care both about how much the group raises and about how their own contribution compares with others', so they give more. This effect doesn't stop at donations. When it's clear who did what in a group project at work, people feel more accountable and that their contribution meaningfully influences the success of the project, so they work harder.

What if, though, your contribution wouldn't only be identifiable, but you would also get to contribute first? Inspiring others through your individual contribution is another effective solution in the battle against social loafing. In this situation, the more you do, the more others are inspired to contribute. Other people in your group would work harder because of the example you set. When people see themselves as role models, they're motivated to do more to take full advantage of their influence. An environmental or political activist who posts on social media about preserving biodiversity or signing up to work the polls is probably driven by a desire to inspire others to join these causes. Even the *potential* to influence others can work. When you think about going public with your contribution—be it a monetary donation, a donation of your time, or a stronger effort at work—you remind yourself of the impact of your public actions and motivate yourself to invest.

Another remedy for social loafing involves breaking a large group into smaller ones. In a study that put this idea into action, Bibb Latané and his colleagues asked research participants to clap their hands and shout out loud in a group. The presumed objective of the task was to test how much noise a cheering audience could make. In reality, the goal was to test how the size of the group influences social loafing. The researchers compared the amount of noise participants made when they were in a small group versus a large one and saw that as the number of people in a group increased from one to six, each person started making less noise. When it comes to clapping and shouting, as in kayaking, more helpers means less individual effort. It's no wonder social loafing is a bigger problem for large companies than small start-ups. If you work in a large team, one solution is to break the team into small subteams, with just a handful of people in each.

Lastly, making contributions feel personal can fight social loafing. Some types of giving carry the essence of the person who contributed. Extreme examples involve donating blood or even an organ, in which case you're giving part of your body to assist another person. When people agree to donate blood, they feel a more personal connection to the cause than if they donate the amount of money that would hurt their pocket as much as donating blood would hurt their body. Other types of contributions carry the essence of the helper more symboli-cally. You may give your name, for example, by signing a petition or a document you prepared at work. Your name carries your cultural and familial identity along with your unique identity as an individual within these social groups. And when people give their names by means of a signature, they tend to be more generous and better apply themselves to the job.

Taking all these factors into account, in one study, Minjung Koo and I gave students a ballpoint pen as a gift and then invited them to donate their new pen to children who were short on school supplies. Some students received the pen a moment before we suggested they donate it. Others got to own it for a little bit. They got their gift when they arrived at the lab and were invited to donate it by the end of the experimental session. Because these students had time to develop ownership of the pen, it felt like theirs. We found that owning the pen made pen donation feel more meaningful. Those who got to hang on to the pen for a longer time told us they were more personally committed to the cause of helping children with school supplies.

People are more committed to a cause if they have a chance to make it personal—when the cause communicates something about their identity. For a similar reason, having an opportunity to make a unique contribution, one that only you could make and that relies on your unique expertise and skills, will encourage you to contribute resources to a shared goal. This is one reason bake sales are such a popular fundraiser—only you know your family recipe for the fudgiest brownies. It's also a reason, on the other hand, why it's tempting to relax your effort in a two-person kayak. When kayaking, your contribution is hardly unique.

COORDINATION IN GROUPS

While I've so far described social loafing as a social disease, relaxing efforts while working with others isn't always a bad thing. The underlying assumption in the interventions that combat social loafing and free riding is that people tend to procrastinate when they believe others are working toward a shared goal, thereby causing the group to do worse than it would otherwise. Yet, while selfish motives are partially responsible for the reduction in efforts, they don't account for the whole picture. At times, people relax their efforts in order to coordinate with others.

When working in groups, people can coordinate their efforts by taking turns. As the saying goes, too many cooks spoil the broth. Indeed, when we evaluate what's best for the group, it's unclear that having everyone working together on the same task is ever ideal. If others are working, it can be best for the rest to wait until their groupmates get tired, at which point they can step up and the others can relax.

Beyond turn-taking, there are several other good reasons group members choose to relax when others are working. These group members aren't being selfish; they're coordinating.

It's not selfishness; it's division of labor

In my household, I don't call the repair service when the washing machine needs to be fixed. I don't vacuum the floors, I don't take the dog to the vet, and I don't pick up my child from school. My spouse does all that. Am I a natural procrastinator? Probably (almost everyone is). But my arrangement isn't uncommon. Couples tend to divide household tasks so that each person is almost fully in charge of certain jobs. While I don't do any of the above chores, I'm the one in charge of buying clothes and doing the laundry. I'd like to believe that if it weren't for me, my husband and my son would be walking around naked—or at least, in dirty clothes. I'm also in charge of school drop-offs and answering the phone when the school nurse calls.

Close relationships involve a certain degree of complementarity between two people. Couples complement each other's responsibilities. In one study, Daniel Wegner and his colleagues compared how real couples and pairs of strangers worked together on a memory challenge. The challenge involved learning all sorts of trivia about television shows, science, and other categories. After the teams were given the answers to several trivia questions, they were tested on how well they remembered the facts. Teams made of true couples outperformed strangers.

Their secret was an efficient division of labor. When couples were learning new information, each person focused on mastering the answers in categories they were personally interested in while paying little attention to the other half of the categories, which they assumed their partner would master. If I were the science nerd in our family and my spouse loved to watch TV, we would spontaneously divide the work so that I'd memorize the science trivia while he would pay close attention to the TV trivia. In contrast, teams made of strangers didn't have a natural way of dividing the work. They both tried very hard to remember as much as possible. So, while strangers had a lot of overlapping knowledge, they knew much less as a team.

Of course, this division of labor can come with some downsides. In my household, I have relatively few financial responsibilities. While I hear a lot about research in economics and finance as part of my job, at home, I leave managing our family finances to my spouse. And while I participate in big decisions like buying a new car, I don't do our taxes or manage our bank accounts and mortgage on a regular basis. My spouse does all of that.

While neglecting to handle my household finances allows me to attend to other areas of our lives (like writing this book), it does come with a price. Over time, my lack of engagement will translate into lack of financial knowledge, or what researchers call poor "financial literacy." Financially literate individuals have the basic knowledge to navigate the complex financial decisions that modern life presents to us. They can make wise decisions about how to handle their money. People gain financial knowledge throughout their adult lives, but only as long as they're required to make financial decisions. As Adrian Ward and John Lynch found, if people are part of a household, they gain financial knowledge only if they're the ones in charge of making these decisions for the couple. The person who isn't in charge of the finances remains illiterate.

Off-loading responsibilities to a partner—whether financial or other—may eliminate the need to know in the present but will simultaneously create barriers to making wise decisions in the future. If you off-load knowledge to your spouse, you might not know how to cook, where to shop, or even something as simple as the vet's phone number.

Successful relationships, then, involve some degree of division of labor, where each partner complements the work the other person does, in order to efficiently address all aspects of their relationship and household responsibilities. If your partner is doing the cooking, it would be better if you do the dishes rather than introducing another cook into the kitchen. But beware that this form of otherwise adaptive coordination will backfire if the couple splits up or if one person out-lives the other. While division of knowledge characterizes successful relationships, you shouldn't off-load all knowledge in any specific area of life. In other words, you should never diminish your financial knowledge to a Post-it Note with your bank account number.

It's not selfishness; it's maximizing the benefits for the team

When you're hungry, would you grab a snack from your coworker's snack drawer without asking for her permission? What if she also hap-pened to be your closest friend; how would that change your decision? Or would you consider asking someone to accept a pay cut so that you could get a promotion and a nice raise? What if that person were your partner, who would need to move to a new city with you to make this career change?

Most of us would hesitate to take someone's property without permission, unless that person is a close friend. And we'd never expect someone to compromise their career to allow our career to flourish, unless that person is in a committed relationship with us. But while our behavior in close relationships may appear selfish, our motives usually aren't. The reason we behave as if we're willing to take advantage of our close friends and partners is that, when it comes to close relationships, we consider how our actions will influence the team as a whole. We think it's okay if one person loses less than the other gains because the team as a whole is better off.

The motivational principle that underlies this seemingly selfish behavior is what we call "friendly taking": people are more willing to deny resources to a close friend than a distant one whenever doing so will maximize the total benefits for the collective. We refer to this type of taking as "friendly" rather than as free riding because it's driven by good intentions. As we talked about in Chapter 12, people feel as if their identities overlap with those of close friends, so they pay attention to the total benefits for the group when allocating resources. The result is that they're willing to sacrifice their friend's benefits when it helps them more than it hurts their friend. In the scenarios above, when someone takes their friend's snack or asks their partner to compromise their career, it's because they believe they would benefit more than their loved ones would lose, in which case, the team as a whole has gained.

This doesn't imply that all taking is friendly. When people exploit strangers but treat their friends and neighbors with respect, it's simply because they care more about those who are close to them. People might also exploit their friends for purely selfish reasons. Taking is only friendly when people are more willing to take from someone close to them because they run the mental calculation that, by taking, they make the group better off. So, when walking in the rain, I might accept my spouse's rain jacket because I believe I care about keeping dry more than he cares about getting wet. By giving his jacket to me, he loses some while I gain a lot. And given that I gain more than he loses, as a couple, we're better off.

To explore this effect in a controlled experiment, Yanping Tu, Alex Shaw, and I invited people to come to the lab with a friend to try some chocolate truffles. In the process of signing up for this highly lucrative study, the research participants were invited to choose between two tasting packages. Package A offered "seven truffles for yourself and three truffles for your friend (ten truffles in total)," while Package B offered "two truffles for yourself and four truffles for your friend (six truffles in total)." The participants knew they couldn't redistribute the truffles. They had to choose between the option that benefited them a lot and the option that benefited their friend a little. As we expected, the closer people were to their friend, the more likely they were to opt for the self-benefiting Package A, which also maximized the total for the team. While this choice seems quite selfish, it was driven by friendly intentions rather than the desire to take advantage of a friend. In close relationships, people focus on how much "we" (i.e., their team) get in total, rather than who gets more. They'll choose to get more (but also less), as long as the bottom line is more for the group.

Other studies found that when choosing rewards for themselves and a close friend, people pay attention mainly to the total benefits for them both. Often, they don't even care to find out who gets what. This tendency may explain why committed couples often care to maximize their combined income, even if it means one person is making much more money than the other. This is what happens in our scenario of someone who gives up their job to move to a city where their partner got a promotion. But keep in mind the downside. If no one completely sacrificed their earning potential, the relationship would be more equal, which might be helpful in the long run.

Taking a global perspective, the tendency to focus on maximizing total benefits can also explain why policy makers often worry about the economic growth in their country in total more than the fair allocation of wealth within their country. And again, the downside is that what's better for the country as a whole might be worse for many individual residents.

This tendency to worry less about who gets what further explains why we sometimes take credit for others' ideas. When I talk about motivation research, I sometimes neglect to give well-deserved credit to another researcher. I say "we found," but it was actually another person's finding, which I only read about after it was published. Embarrassing as it is, I'm more likely to neglect to give credit to a close colleague than to someone I don't personally know. A close colleague's ideas blend in my mind with my own; these are "our" ideas, even if not technically mine.

Attention to the total benefits for the group can even be used to rationalize copyright infringement. If you believe taking advantage of someone's work (e.g., using software without paying) helps you more than it hurts them, in your mind the group (this time the "group" being you and them, or the people who have the same interests) benefits as a whole—even though in actuality, it makes you much better off and makes the owner of the copyrights slightly worse off. This friendly-taking phenomenon explains why we often behave as if we free-ride others' effort. It's because we deem it an efficient solution.

It's not selfishness; it's the desire to work when others don't

What would increase your motivation more: remembering that other people have already contributed to a shared goal or remembering that they haven't? Are you more likely to contribute to a group project, for example, if you hear that your team members are hard at work on it or if you hear that they're slacking?

This question may remind you of the discussion in Chapter 6 about what increases motivation: the glass half empty or the glass half full. In the context of pursuing personal goals, I asked whether you'd be more motivated by your own completed actions or your own missing actions. This question becomes relevant again when we evaluate what motivates people to help their group pursue shared goals. Are team members more likely to help when they consider missing actions or completed actions by other people on the team? And when they're less likely to help, are they driven by selfish motives or by wanting to complement others' actions with their own?

As before, the answer to whether completed or missing actions increase motivation depends on the person's level of commitment. This time, it's the commitment to the collective goal as well as to the group. You're more committed to goals that are important for you—they could impact how you describe yourself to another person (e.g., "I work in the hospital"), have long-term consequences (e.g., a multiyear house renovation project), or have a lot at stake (e.g., a product that will determine the fate of your company). You're also more committed to some groups than others. You'll be less committed to a group that you've recently joined, like a new team at work. And if you're newly married, you're probably relatively less committed to your spouse's extended family and their shared goals than to your own extended family because your family has been part of who you are for your entire life.

When you're less committed to a goal or a group, you'll often evaluate whether pursuing this group's shared goal is worthwhile. Should you invest your time, money, and effort in what they've set out to achieve? In this case, others' contributions signal that the goal is both important and within reach. You contribute because others have, and you contribute less if others haven't. Their completed actions therefore increase your willingness to join in. If the kitchen in your new office is clean and organized, for example, you'll make sure to wash your coffee mug. You don't want to stray from the local social norms. If the kitchen is already a mess, you'll feel comfortable leaving the dirty mug in the sink.

In contrast, when you're committed to a group or a goal, you'll often evaluate the pace of progress on that goal. Committed team members choose to invest more time, money, and effort when they feel they should compensate for others' lack of action. In this case, missing actions increase commitment. If your family left a mess in the kitchen, for example, you'd be more likely to clean it up than if the kitchen were in relatively good shape. You don't simply mimic your family members; you compensate for their lack of action.

Koo and I observed these opposite reasons to contribute to a shared goal—either because others are giving or not giving—in a study that assessed donations to a charity designed to help orphans of the HIV epidemic in Uganda in 2007. The organization running the campaign solicited donations across two populations: new and there-fore uncommitted donors and committed donors who had made many contributions to the organization before. We found that new donors were more likely to give when the message emphasized existing con-tributions ("to this point, we have successfully raised $4,920 through various channels"). When they learned how much others were giving, they wanted to give as well. In contrast, regular donors were more likely to give when the emphasis was on missing contributions ("We have successfully raised money through various channels and need another $5,080"). When they learned how much money was still missing, they decided to give. They were helping because others weren't.

Committed people are less likely to free-ride on the work of others and instead are more likely to complement what others are doing. They believe it's more important to pick up the slack by stepping in when others don't rather than following the group. While their actions may look like free riding, they're driven by a rather different motive: they conserve their efforts for when the group falls behind.

Beyond commitment to the cause, our commitment to the group similarly determines whether we would follow versus complement oth-ers' actions. College students, for example, feel committed to helping their fellow students on campus more than young people elsewhere. In one study, student groups generated marketing ideas for products like cell phones and protein bars. Some students were assigned to work in a group with other students from the same university, while others were assigned to work with students from other universities. When working with people from their own school, students compensated for others' lack of action. So, when we emphasized that the group needed more ideas to meet the goal, they were more likely to put their thinking caps on. When working with people from other universities, students followed others. So, when we emphasized that the group already had several ideas, they were more likely to give their own thoughts. Your creativity is often a function of how much you're willing to apply yourself to the creative task. And the more committed you are to helping the group, the more likely you are to be creative when others are struggling.

When we feel close to the people who benefit from our help and suspect that others aren't helping, we help more. This pattern reverses when we don't feel close to the beneficiaries of our help, in which case we help more if others are already helping. These patterns were observed in studies that assessed willingness to help victims of California wildfires in the US as well as victims of political riots in Kenya. Those who felt close to the victims in each of these countries, either because we reminded them that the victims were fellow citizens (in the case of wildfires), or because we described the victims as socially close (e.g., as "our children and families" in Kenya), helped more if they suspected others weren't helping enough. Those who felt less close helped more if they suspected many people were already helping. And, as before, when those who felt close to the victims withheld help, it was more likely because they wanted to complement others' efforts—and therefore help when they were needed most—not because they were selfish.

When you're highly committed and relax your efforts—for instance, when you don't help your child with his homework—it's often because others (most likely your spouse, in this case) are already doing the work. Committed people are looking to address neglected aspects of the shared goal and preserve their resources for when they're most needed. When highly committed, you're not working on a problem just because everyone does it or just when it's trendy. Instead, you're working when others are not.

Notably, committed people are also less interested in symbolic giving. The grocery store register asking for a $1 donation at checkout is mostly symbolic—one dollar won't help very much—and so people committed to the cause won't bother with that small, one-time donation. When you're committed, you want your help to make a difference. You'll be more motivated by an invitation to make an impact—to move things forward—than an invitation to give a small donation to show that you care.

Should we therefore conclude that people are rarely selfish or seeking to take advantage of their group efforts? I would advise against this thought process. Of course, we're often selfish. We also like to conserve our resources. To deny the existence of selfishness or resource conservation would come close to denying our nature as human beings. But while we're often driven by self-interest, our ability to work with others is also inherent to who we are as humans. It's the foundation of any great achievement. Therefore, we should ask when and why rather than whether people seek to work less when others are helping. And when we conclude that people, including ourselves, help too little, we should use the interventions motivation science has given us to combat truly selfish social loafing.

QUESTIONS TO ASK YOURSELF

Realizing that teamwork is necessary for achieving many of our most important goals, we want to distinguish between helpful and unhelpful patterns of coordination between team members. How do you minimize social loafing and free riding? When should team members alternate efforts versus having everyone working simultaneously? How do you motivate yourself to contribute resources to a shared goal? The answers seem to depend on the goal as well as the team.

Here are some questions you could ask yourself to minimize selfishness and maximize healthy coordination between team members, while staying personally motivated to do so yourself:

1. What are the main goals you're pursuing with others? Consider revising your goal system to make sure you include shared goals that require team effort.

2. How do you minimize social loafing and free riding in pursuing shared goals? Consider making contributions identifiable, allowing team members to inspire each other, moving to smaller groups or individual tasks, and allowing team members to contribute in ways that feel personal.

3. When working with others, coordination is key to success. How well does your team coordinate? Specifically:

   - Is your division of labor optimal? Do you minimize overlapping tasks and knowledge while not undermining your independence in case the group makeup changes?

   - Does feeling close to someone sometimes lead you to act selfishly despite having good intentions? Would you ask your partner, for example, to make compromises you would never ask anyone else to make?

   - Can you motivate yourself by focusing on the work others didn't do (the glass they left half empty) for when you're highly committed and focusing on the work others did do (the glass they left half full) when your commitment is lower?

14

GOALS MAKE A HAPPY RELATIONSHIP

SOON AFTER I HAD my first child, I started drifting away from my childless friends. When they asked me to go to the movies, meet up for dinner, or get a drink at a new coffee shop, I almost always said no. When they told me tales of first dates both good and bad, I couldn't relate. And when I told them that we finally got my baby to sleep for four hours straight or how worried I was about whether she was eating enough, they had nothing to say in return. When I tried to laugh about silly commercials that claimed I needed both a cradle and a crib—which are essentially the same thing—they didn't see the humor. Eventually, they stopped asking me to go out and I stopped telling them about what was happening in my life, which mostly revolved around my daughter.

The issue between my friends and me was deeper than a simple lack of interest in conversation topics. Our life goals had diverged. We often drift away from friends after something so major happens that it shifts the makeup of our lives. And because my friends and I were pursuing different goals, we had a hard time supporting each other.

Supporting each other's goals is important in any successful relationship. Yet, in most relationships—be they friendships, family, or romantic relationships—each person is more concerned with feeling helped than providing help. The infamous breakup line "It's not you, it's me" is always true, for every relationship. According to motivation science, your relationships are generally about you. Specifically, they're about connecting with people who facilitate your goals.

The people in your life not only help you meet your *relationship* goals—a spouse makes you a husband and a child makes you a father, for example—they also facilitate everything else you've set out to achieve. You pull closer to those who both support and ease the path to your ambitions and push away from those who hinder them. And because both people in a relationship want to feel supported, a relationship is only successful when both feel they're getting something and giving something.

Often, it's easier to provide support if you're sharing similar goals. I say "often," because technically, you can help facilitate goals you don't hold for yourself. It just might be harder. Goal alignment helps to make happy relationships. We form friendships with people who hold similar goals and therefore encourage us to stick to what we want. In elementary school, you might have made friends with kids who liked to play on the monkey bars as much as you did. In high school, your friends may have been into the latest fashion and supported your goal to look good and be cool. At work, you've probably formed friendships with people who uphold your values of hard work and honesty (and who watch the same TV shows or read the same books). Over time, as we grow and our interests change, friendships cool down and friends drift apart. It's natural for high school friendships to dissipate, for example, when you go off to college and form friendships with people who share similar academic and life goals. These new friends are more useful for you, and you're useful for them.

Of course, sharing the same goals doesn't guarantee a supportive relationship; it only increases the odds. Your colleague who competes with you for a promotion shares a similar goal but might try to sabotage your professional success. In this case, the person who shares your goal is the last person you'd consider a friend. On the other hand, your parents might support your academic and professional goals even if their own paths in life were vastly different. One doesn't need to have earned a college degree to support one's child doing so. Ultimately, what matters is that a relationship helps rather than hurts your goals. If a parent doesn't support their child's wish to become a writer, an artist, or a chef, their relationship is likely to cool down.

Marriages will also fall apart when partners don't support each other's goals. And while it helps to have similar goals, it's not necessary. Your partner might be an aspiring artist while you can barely doodle a flower, an avid cook while your signature dish is fried eggs, or a health care provider while you faint at the sight of blood. Setting aside these differences, you can still help each other succeed.

The supportive people in your life encourage you to stick with your goals and push you when you're falling behind. They expect you to be successful but are still impressed by your successes. They might also provide resources—like the partner who can only fry eggs but who buys you a nice pie plate or makes sure you always have a clean pot when you need one. They might take on greater responsibility in other areas of your shared life to empower you to pursue your goal—like my husband, who took on extra child care when I wanted to write this book. They may even help you pay the bills when pursuing your goals requires money.

CHANGING GOALS, TRANSITIONING RELATIONSHIPS

Just as when I had kids, when our goals change, so do our relationships. Beyond the macro changes—big life stages we go through, like becoming a parent or starting a new job—there are micro changes to your goals. Goals fluctuate daily. This morning, I was homeschooling my son, who's stuck at home due to the pandemic and largely dependent on his parents' limited ability to teach a second-grade curriculum. His newly virtual homeroom teacher was instrumental in helping me. In the afternoon, I was back to my university job. Schoolwork was completed and my son's teacher was no longer the person I could rely on. My goal had shifted and so had the people who were helping me.

These fluctuations matter. We move toward and away from people as we prioritize or deprioritize the goals they can help us achieve. When it's the right time to attend to a goal or when we feel we're falling behind, a goal gets high motivational priority. As a result, we draw closer to those who are instrumental to achieving it. Once the goal has sufficiently progressed and its motivational priority reduces, we feel less close to those people.

In a study that examined how goal progress influences relationship strength, Gráinne Fitzsimons and I asked college students to list a person whose existence in their lives made it easier to do well in school and another close person who had nothing to do with their academic success. Some were then asked to focus on what they had already achieved in school, while the rest focused on what they needed to do to achieve their academic goals. We wondered how recalling prior academic progress versus the work they had yet to do would influence how close people felt to the people they listed. As you might expect, those who thought about the academic progress they needed to make said they felt closer to the friend who would help them get there. However, when students thought about the progress they'd already made, they felt equally close to both friends. Making progress temporarily lowered the motivational priority of academic success, which cooled down feelings of closeness to helpful others.

The tendency to pull closer to those who support our goals can have surprising consequences. For one, we're more grateful to people before they help us than after. Of course, you'll feel appreciative once the help was provided and the task is completed, but not as appreciative as just before the help is given. This is because appreciation of a helper depends on how much you still need them. When you're motivated to work on your goal and think someone will be helpful, you feel grateful. Once you're done, you switch your attention to a new goal and feel less gratitude to the person who has just helped your previous goal.

To illustrate how appreciation peaks before help is provided, Benjamin Converse and I conducted a study that staged a trivia game styled after *Who Wants to Be a Millionaire*. As in the game show, "contestants" needed to answer trivia questions to win a prize and were able to use a "lifeline" to get help on one of their questions. We found that contestants were more appreciative of the helper after they asked for an answer and before they got one than after they won the round with the information the helper provided.

This pattern isn't intuitive. If you're helping someone move into a new apartment, you usually expect they'll be more grateful after you've set down the last box than while you're still packing up. Similarly, most health care providers would expect patients to be more appreciative after treatment is done than while it's still ongoing. And while restaurant patrons might be more thankful for service— and be willing to give higher tips—while they are still being served, restaurants generally ask for tips after the service is completed. Knowing when appreciation peaks will keep you from feeling disappointed by the amount of gratitude you receive.

CONNECTING THROUGH GOALS

In 1894, a young woman from Poland met a man in France. She had just finished degrees in physics and mathematics at the Sorbonne in Paris. He was a professor of physics at the School of Industrial Physics and Chemistry. Together, they'd revolutionize chemistry, physics, and medicine, but at the time they were simply two intelligent, passionate people falling in love. Marie and Pierre Curie quickly bonded over their shared intellectual passion and were married a year after they met at the town hall in Sceaux, where Pierre's parents lived. They used the money they received at their wedding to buy bicycles, as cycling was another shared interest. To break up the monotony of studying day after day in the run-down shed that the principal of Pierre's school allowed them to use for their experiments, Marie and Pierre would go on long, adventurous cycle rides.

Now we know their names as the scientists who discovered two of the elements on our periodic table: polonium and radium. And particularly, we know Marie Curie as one of the first women to achieve such amazing scientific success. In 1903, Marie and Pierre jointly won the Nobel Prize in Physics with Henri Becquerel for their study of spontaneous radiation. It was Pierre who insisted that Marie also be named. Marie won a second Nobel Prize, this time in chemistry, on her own eight years later.

Marie and Pierre Curie were able to make such incredible discoveries in part because they connected over the shared goal of finding a new element (Pierre actually gave up his research on crystals to pursue it). But their strength as a couple came from connecting over many goals: their scientific goals, their bicycling goals, the goal of raising their daughters, Irène and Ève, and I'm sure other goals that the history books don't tell us.

Throughout their lives, this famous couple utilized several of the mechanisms by which our goals connect us. First, as discussed above, we connect to those who hold similar goals. It's easier to get along with someone who wants the same things you do. When Marie and Pierre first met, they immediately bonded over their scientific interests. And when you first met your partner, you may have discovered that you both like hiking and cooking. It was your commonalities that first sparked an emotional connection.

Second, we connect by supporting others' goals and feeling that our goals are supported by them (as Pierre supported Marie in insisting she be named on their Nobel Prize). In this way, helping each other pursue our goals is fundamental to social connection. When you sit at the table each night and ask your partner about their day, brainstorming a polite way for them to talk to their coworker about picking up the slack, you're instrumental to their career goals. When your partner notices how agitated you've been each night when you come home and eases you into talking through the stress of a looming deadline, they're supporting your career goals. Support is a two-way street, and if one person in the couple is supported without being supportive, it's likely that person is more satisfied in the relationship than their partner.

Beyond these two mechanisms of connection, we also connect through shared goals. When you pursue a goal alongside friends, colleagues, family members, or a partner, you experience a deep sense of connection with that person or people. Goals that require joint effort glue the group that pursues them together. Marie and Pierre Curie worked tirelessly together, day in and day out, in that run-down shed as they attempted to isolate polonium and radium. You and your partner may be saving for a house, taking care of a pet, or planning a trip to New Zealand. No matter the goal, the fact that you need each other to succeed brings you closer together. In fact, if you find you're drifting away from a partner or a friend and want to hold on to your relationship, finding a new goal you can strive toward together could help deepen your bond. You could sign up for a painting class with your partner or join a spin class with your friend.

As a fourth mechanism, we also connect by holding goals for other people and having them hold goals for us. Marie and Pierre Curie, like most parents, wanted their daughters to do well in school. We assume they cared mostly about science, which could've prepared their oldest, Irène Joliot-Curie, to win her own Nobel Prize in chemistry in 1935 (following in her parents' footsteps, she won with her husband, with whom she was working).

When we set a goal for a family member or a friend, like wanting your sister to succeed in her new job or wanting your friend to complete her marathon, we feel more connected to that person. In turn, we feel closer to the people who set goals for us. But when you hold a goal for someone, that person will only feel more connected to you if they also hold the goal for themselves. Asking your brother or sister to read more books or exercise regularly might evoke feelings of annoyance or even resentment if they don't already want to read or exercise. They might feel that you're trying to control them. Keep in mind that you should only hold a goal for someone if that person also holds that goal for themselves. If you want something for me that I don't already want for myself, I won't feel closer to you.

The result of these various mechanisms of goal connection is that our individual goals influence the goals of our friends, family, and partners. I want my goals to be similar to my partner's goals and I want them to be goals that he would support. I both share goals with him and set goals for him. I can therefore expect our relationship to shape our goals. Some motivation researchers go as far as to suggest that people in a romantic relationship have a joint goal system. These researchers analyze the goal system of the couple: what these two people want together and for each other. Similarly, large teams, such as an extended family or an organization, can be seen as having a joint goal system, where the team has identified a set of goals and the means of attainment and has decided on the connections between these goals as either competing with or facilitating each other.

But while two or more people often have a joint goal system, this system doesn't replace their individual goal systems. Not everything we want is part of a relationship with one other person. Some of our goals are truly personal, and others involve an entirely different social group. Moreover, a shared goal doesn't necessarily serve everyone who shares it equally. It could be central in one person's goal system and peripheral for another. Let's go back to our couple who decides to move to a new town because one partner was promoted. The partner who had to give up a career for the move now has to take on a larger share of household and child care responsibilities and is expected to support their partner emotionally during the career transition. So that career goal benefits one partner much more than the other. Although we've made great strides in women's equality over the last several decades, this scenario still comes up for many women, who feel they're expected to forgo personal goals to support the couple's goals.

These women's personal goal systems are then compromised by their commitment to the joint goal system they pursue as a family. Regardless of the overlap between their own goals and their goals as a couple, family, or friends, people usually don't share their entire goal system with any individual person.

This interdependence between people's goal systems has some intriguing implications, such as outsourcing goal pursuit to someone else. In close relationships, when we consider how others help us achieve our goals, in particular the goals that they, too, have for us, we feel less motivated to help ourselves, trusting others to keep us on track. Many children outsource the pursuit of personal hygiene to their parents. From the child's perspective, if their parent reminds them to shower, there's less need for them to remind themselves to do so. And in one study, college students who were reminded of their parents' support (or pressure) to achieve academic excellence exercised less self-control in motivating themselves to study. Knowing that someone else will make you stick to certain goals makes you feel less personally responsible for them.

Connecting through mundane goals. When you think about connecting with people over goals, you probably picture only big goals like raising a family or moving up in your career. These are mostly the goals I've described so far. But we make connections over small goals all the time. When you start walking your dog with a neighbor, that's a connection you've made over the small goal of getting your dog some exercise. We also make social connections over exchanging books or recommending music. I, for example, often connect with my colleagues over a cup of tea and with fellow Israelis over hummus and tahini, two favorite Middle Eastern foods. While getting food into our bodies is a mundane and basic goal, those who feed us or those we eat with are often considered friends. It's no wonder the English word "companion" comes from the French *compagnon*, which is literally "one who breaks bread with another." And the word *huoban*, which means "friend" in Chinese, is constructed from the character *huo* for cooking and *ban* for companion. Feeding someone, or even just eating with them, connects you to them.

Even young children rely on basic goals to create a social bond. Christine Fawcett and Lori Markson found that three-year-old kids prefer to play with a puppet that, in a pretend game, "chooses" to eat the food they like. This trend continues through adulthood. In one study, strangers who ate similar foods trusted each other more and were better able to cooperate with each other. On the other hand, people who cannot share a meal due to food allergies or culturally imposed restrictions often feel lonelier during a meal. Not being able to pursue basic goals with others undermines social connection. If your child is sensitive to gluten, you should probably worry less about him missing out on eating a delicious slice of cake or pizza at birthday parties and more about the lack of social connection that not being able to eat the same foods as his peers engenders. And if your teenager is eager to start drinking, they might not be going after the taste or feeling tipsy. Their true reason may be to connect with friends who are already drinking. If you wish to steer them away from alcohol, start by encouraging them to connect with friends over other goals.

Often it's intuitive to use these insights to ensure that we connect with others. Parents connect to their newborn through fulfilling this little person's basic needs, such as feeding and washing. The rest of us can serve a meal, take care of neighbors' plants while they're on vacation, and offer friends sunscreen (on a sunny day) or a scarf (when it's cold) to create a social bond. While we've not developed a love potion (at least, not yet), we have discovered scientific methods of bringing people closer together using their goals.

FEELING KNOWN

As I write this, we're in the era of social distancing and self-isolating, which are scientifically proven ways to slow the spread of COVID-19. But as people all over the world distance themselves from friends and family, health professionals as well as social scientists are reminded of the negative effects of social isolation. Being alone is its own health risk, one that we're acutely aware of these days.

To estimate the health risks of lacking social connection, Julianne Holt-Lunstad, Timothy Smith, and Bradley Layton analyzed data from approximately 150 previously published studies. They found that social isolation is comparable with smoking, alcohol consumption, and lack of physical activity in reducing life expectancy. And even though causality is hard to determine in these correlative studies—as you know, umbrellas don't cause rain, but they tend to appear when it's raining—existing data suggest that social connectedness might be more important to your health than losing that extra little bit of weight.

But not all social connections are worthwhile. To get the amazing health benefits, your social connections have to be meaningful. What makes a social connection meaningful, a connection that's actually good for your mental and physical health? Be it with your neighbor, colleague, teacher, family member, or partner, a true connection is with someone who can support your goals. To be able to do that, at the most basic level, this person must know you and make you feel known.

When you feel known, you sense that the person with whom you interact "gets" you. They understand why you do what you do—even when you did something others may find peculiar or foolish—and why you think the way you do. They grasp your needs and wishes. The person who knows you is therefore the person you'd want on your team and the one whose advice you'd accept. Feeling that another person knows you is not only the basis for a stable romantic relationship, it's also the foundation for professional relationships and for your relationships with your doctors and your teachers, to name a few. It even determines which political candidates will win your vote—it'll likely be the ones who seem to understand your needs. When it comes to intimacy and romantic relationships, feeling known is even more critical. Many breakups happen because one partner feels that the other doesn't "get" them.

Of course, feeling known is not the same as being known. If you've never tested their knowledge, you might be giving too much credit to someone you assume knows you well. At times, we might even feel known by people who don't actually know we exist. For example, when we experience a psychological connection to artists, athletes, or celebrities, we feel as if these people know us, though realistically, we know they can't. Also, those who actually do know us might know less than we think they do. And we usually know the people in our lives less than we assume.

Take a study that compared how much people thought they knew their partner to how much they actually knew about them. The study worked somewhat like *The Newlywed Game*. In one version, William Swann and Michael Gill first asked couples to guess how their partner would answer a series of questions about their sexual history and then rate how confident they were in their guess. Participants predicted their partner's answers to questions about how many past sexual partners they'd had, how often they'd used condoms, and how many dates they'd usually go on before having sex. People could easily make a guess on these questions. They were confident that they knew their partner well. But they were often wrong. You think you know your partner better than you do. Moreover, the longer you've been in a relationship with someone, the more confident you are that you know your partner well. But you would still get many answers wrong.

Don't beat yourself up too much, though. Remember that this truth also applies to your partner. You think you know your love better than you do, and they think they know you better than in reality, too. What's more, each of you probably thinks the other knows you better than they actually do. In general, people overestimate how well others know them.

Accepting that how much people actually know you often falls short of your expectations, you should realize that, regardless of how much someone truly knows you, *feeling* that you're known is the foundation of a satisfying relationship. Furthermore, feeling that you know someone matters less for your own satisfaction with the relationship.

To demonstrate this point, consider the all-too-familiar experience of forgetting someone's name. If you get the impression that I've forgotten your name, you might feel our relationship isn't as close as you'd initially thought. Now, what if you were the one who forgot my name? From your perspective, forgetting my name doesn't tank our relationship as much as the reverse.

Or you may run the following thought experiment. Choose a friend, a sibling, or a romantic partner, and think how you'd answer these three questions:

1. How well do you know this person's goals and aspirations?
2. How well does this person know your goals and aspirations?
3. How satisfied are you with your relationship with this person?

My experiments with Juliana Schroeder revealed that the answers to questions 1 and 2 separately predict the answers to question 3. But when we compared two forms of relationship knowledge—feeling known and knowing someone—feeling known (question 2) was often more critical to experiencing closeness in a relationship.

For most of us, there's only one unique relationship in which supporting the other person takes precedence over supporting the self: a parent's relationship with their child. When parents answered the above three questions with regard to their grown children—how well do you know your child, how well does your child know you, and how satisfying is the relationship—the extent to which they knew their child predicted their relationship satisfaction more than the degree to which their child knew them. When it comes to my own adult daughters, I'm happier and more satisfied that our relationship is doing well when they share with me rather than when I share with them and feel they're listening.

So you're less known than you think, and you know less than you assume. You care more about feeling known than about knowing. And you didn't know this about yourself until now. The implications are that we should all be more modest in how much knowledge we assume exists in any relationship and pay special attention to knowing the people in our lives to be able to support their goals and maintain close relationships.

EMPTY VESSEL

Some relationships are highly instrumental. Your real estate agent, the person who cleans your office or home, and your hairdresser are people you invite into your life to help you meet specific goals. While you hope they know you well and can attend to your needs, you may have less interest in knowing them and understanding their needs. These instrumental people are often seen as "empty vessels": you see only the characteristics that make them a good real estate agent, cleaning person, or hairdresser, rather than their whole personality.

Health care providers, for example, often seem more than human to us. When we're sick and need care, they're there to help and we forget that they're whole people who might get frustrated or tired. In a study that explored these empty-vessel perceptions, people who needed to see their primary care physician rated their doctors as less able to feel both negative feelings such as pain, hunger, and tiredness, and positive feelings such as happiness, relief, and hope. Yet they also rated their physician as better able to perceive emotions in their patients. You assume your physician, your teacher, and the person who cleans your home are all there for you and are therefore able to grasp your feelings without having feelings of their own.

The extreme version of seeing someone as an empty vessel is objectifying that person, seeing them only as a tool to fulfill your goals rather than as an individual on their own. Some men, for example, objectify women by equating a woman's worth with how sexy they think she is. For these men, a woman is a tool for satisfying sexual desire; she's not considered to have human thoughts and feelings of her own. Interestingly, people who are objectified come to perceive themselves through the gaze of others, engaging in what is considered "self-objectification." According to the psychologist Barbara Fredrickson, many women internalize the perspective of those who objectify them in such a way that they see themselves as primarily physical objects. While perceiving others who are instrumental as empty vessels is far from full-blown objectification, these two phenomena share the tendency to see someone as little more than a necessary instrument for achieving one's goals.

When interacting with a service provider, it's tempting to ignore their human experience. But empty-vessel perceptions don't end there. If you're in a management position, it's unfortunately tempting to treat your employees as if they're merely workers. Or if you've read enough dating profiles, you may have noticed that more people want someone to take care of them than want to take care of someone. People say they're looking for someone who will make them laugh, rather than looking to make someone laugh. Most dating profiles are self-focused; they present the person seeking love as someone looking to be supported. When you want to adopt a puppy, you say you have love to give. When you're looking for a romantic relationship, you say you want to feel loved.

What's surprising is that dating profiles are meant to serve as a personal advertisement. People are marketing themselves, hoping their profile will attract the attention of the right person. They should be written so that the reader will find them attractive, which we've learned is driven by how the author will support the reader, not the other way around.

Indeed, when people are asked to create a profile explaining why they would be the ideal partner, they write more attractive profiles than when left to their own devices. And this doesn't end with dating profiles. Whether you're looking to hire someone or to reconnect with a friend, it's best to get into the mind-set of supporting their goals.

To keep ourselves from seeing people as empty vessels, we can be more other-oriented in our interactions with the people around us. When we're attuned to supporting others, we're more attractive to them. This way, we stand a better chance of having people in our lives who are attractive to us.

To get support, you need to be supportive. There are two possible mistakes you could make. First, you might offer a new friend, romantic partner, or coworker too little help. The relationship may work for you. You're feeling known and your goals are being fulfilled. But it might not last long. If you aren't facilitating someone's goals, they're likely getting very little from connecting with you. Second, you might be facilitating someone's goals but not getting help in return. In this kind of relationship, you give without getting back. You might have a relationship like this with a family member, a partner, or a colleague at work. These relationships are asymmetric and therefore hard to sustain over time. You might want to ask for more—or walk away.

QUESTIONS TO ASK YOURSELF

People connect through their goals. We want our friends, family, and partners to know us so that they can help us achieve whatever we set out to do. The extent to which another person supports your motivation predicts how satisfied you are in your relationship.

You should accordingly develop insights into the roles of those around you in your goal system. They're not only instrumental to meeting your relationship goals; they facilitate all other goals. Your personal trainer facilitates your goal of "keeping in shape" just as your partner might facilitate your goal of "getting a promotion," for example. You should also consider how you, in turn, play a role in their goal system. Would they say you facilitate their emotional and intellectual growth? Would they say you help them stay healthy? Finally, keep in mind that while our relationships support our goals, it's also possible to develop goals with the sole purpose of deepening a relationship. These are goals that will be facilitated by the relationship and may involve anything from developing a new skill (rock-climbing or baking, for example) to acquiring a new purpose in life (promoting social justice, for example). To do all of this, you can start by asking:

1. How well do you know the people in your life? Do you know their goals, needs, and aspirations? How well can you draw their goal system? If you're struggling, start asking questions, making observations, and taking mental notes.
2. Do the people in your life know your goal system? Is it possible you've been too quiet or ambiguous about what you want?
3. What do you do to facilitate your partner's goals? What do they do that helps you achieve your goals? What needs to be changed?
4. Can you develop goals, like a new hobby, that will serve as glue for a relationship? This can be a goal that allows you to be supported and support someone in turn.

ACKNOWLEDGMENTS

This book was, for a while, a mother-daughter project. I wrote the first version with the help of my daughter Shira, who provided valuable feedback and edits as well as endless inspiration as she stayed motivated through difficult medical school classes and exams. My other daughter, Maya, and my son, Tomer, also inspired me as I wrote, with self-driven Maya finishing her PhD in astrophysics and Tomer teaching me countless lessons about the development of motivation as he finished first and then second grade. By my side was my best friend and husband, Alon, who keeps us all together. His love and support energized me. Without my family, I don't know that this book would be filled with such heart and soul. I'm grateful to them.

I'm grateful also to my scientific collaborators. Much of the research I describe in this book was conducted with dozens of brilliant scientists I'm glad to call lifelong friends. I'm grateful to Yaacov Trope and Arie Kruglanski, my two mentors who opened the door for me to study motivation. I'm further grateful to my mentees: Ying Zhang, Minjung Koo, Jinhee Choi, Kristian Myrseth, Benjamin Converse, Xianchi Dai, Stacey Finkelstein, Rima Touré-Tillery, Luxi Shen, Yanping Tu, Juliana Schroeder, Kaitlin Woolley, Janina Steinmetz, Franklin Shaddy, Lauren Eskreis-Winkler, and Annabelle Roberts, among others. I owe my most important discoveries to our partnerships.

I'm grateful to my colleagues at the University of Chicago and at

Yale. I spent hours discussing the ideas in this book with them. They helped me polish my arguments, often without even knowing.

Finally, I'm in debt to Max Brockman, my literary agent, who encouraged me to write this book; Kasandra Brabaw, who helped me add color to my black-and-white stories; and to my editor, Tracy Behar, who kept me focused on the message my stories tell.

NOTES

PART I

CHAPTER 1

5 **Exercise in my management class:** Subarctic survival exercise, by: Human Synergistics, Inc.

7 **An autographed book:** Thaler, R. H. (2015). *Misbehaving: The Making of Behavioral Economics.* New York: W. W. Norton.

8 **People don't want to invest in means:** Shaddy, F., and Fishbach, A. (2018). Eyes on the prize: The preference to invest resources in goals over means. *Journal of Personality and Social Psychology,* 115(4), 624–637.

8 **Cultivating an abstract mind-set:** Fujita, K., Trope, Y., Liberman, N., and Levin-Sagi, M. (2006). Construal levels and self-control. *Journal of Personality and Social Psychology,* 90(3), 351–367.

9 **Those who had high expectations lost more weight:** Oettingen, G., and Wadden, T. A. (1991). Expectation, fantasy, and weight loss: Is the impact of positive thinking always positive? *Cognitive Therapy and Research,* 15(2), 167–175.

11 **"White bears":** Wegner, D. M. (1994). Ironic processes of mental control. *Psychological Review*, 101(1), 34–52.

12 **An approacher or an avoider:** Carver, C. S., and White, T. L. (1994). Behavioral inhibition, behavioral activation, and affective responses to impending reward and punishment: The BIS/BAS scales. *Journal of Personality and Social Psychology*, 67(2), 319–333.

12 **When people feel they're in power:** Keltner, D., Gruenfeld, D. H., and Anderson, C. (2003). Power, approach, and inhibition. *Psychological Review*, 110(2), 265–284.

13 **When avoidance versus approach framing provides a better fit:** Higgins, E. T. (2000). Making a good decision: Value from fit. *American Psychologist*, 55(11), 1217–1230.

14 **Pursuing approach and avoidance goals feels different:** Higgins, E. T. (1997). Beyond pleasure and pain. *American Psychologist*, 52(12), 1280–1300.

CHAPTER 2

17 **Once a target has been set, you see anything below it as a loss:** Heath, C., Larrick, R. P., and Wu, G. (1999). Goals as reference points. *Cognitive Psychology*, 38(1), 79–109.

18 **"Loss-aversion":** Kahneman, D., and Tversky, A. (1979). Prospect theory: An analysis of decision under risk. *Econometrica*, 47(2), 263–291.

18 **People finish the race just under their set target time:** Allen, E. J., Dechow, P. M., Pope, D. G., and Wu, G. (2017). Reference-dependent preferences: Evidence from marathon runners. *Management Science*, 63(6), 1657–1672.

18 **Closer to gaining the airline's top status:** Drèze, X., and Nunes, J. C. (2011). Recurring goals and learning: The impact of successful reward attainment on purchase behavior. *Journal of Marketing Research*, 48(2), 268–281.

19 "TOTE": Miller, G. A., Galanter, E., and Pribram, K. A. (1960). *Plans and the Structure of Behavior.* New York: Holt, Rinehart, and Winston.

21 **Students chose to create deadlines:** Ariely, D., and Wertenbroch, K. (2002). Procrastination, deadlines, and performance: Self-control by precommitment. *Psychological Science,* 13(3), 219–224.

22 **Set early deadlines to motivate themselves:** Zhang, Y., and Fishbach, A. (2010). Counteracting obstacles with optimistic predictions. *Journal of Experimental Psychology: General,* 139, 16–31.

23 **Energized when expecting a difficult but not impossible task:** Brehm, J. W., Wright, R. A., Solomon, S., Silka, L., and Greenberg, J. (1983). Perceived difficulty, energization, and the magnitude of goal valence. *Journal of Experimental Social Psychology,* 19(1), 21–48.

24 **As a side note for the curious:** https://www.livestrong.com/article/320124-how-many-calories-does-the-average-person-use-per-step/ https://www.mayoclinic.org/healthy-lifestyle/weight-loss/in-depth/calories/art-20048065.

25 **Jog for fifty minutes to burn off 250 extra calories:** Bleich, S. N., Herring, B. J., Flagg, D. D., and Gary-Webb, T. L. (2012). Reduction in purchases of sugar-sweetened beverages among low-income black adolescents after exposure to caloric information. *American Journal of Public Health,* 102(2), 329–335.

25 **An actionable food label:** Thorndike, A. N., Sonnenberg, L., Riis, J., Barraclough, S., and Levy, D. E. (2012). A 2-phase intervention to improve healthy food and beverage choices. *American Journal of Public Health,* 102(3), 527–533.

26 **"Psychological reactance":** Brehm, J. W. (1966). *A Theory of Psychological Reactance.* New York: Academic Press.

28 **Goal targets are also malicious:** Ordóñez, L. D., Schweitzer, M. E., Galinsky, A. D., and Bazerman, M. H. (2009). Goals gone

wild: The systematic side effects of overprescribing goal setting. *Academy of Management Perspectives*, 23(1), 6–16.

28 **Drivers often set a daily target:** Camerer, C., Babcock, L., Loewenstein, G., and Thaler, R. (1997). Labor supply of New York City cabdrivers: One day at a time. *Quarterly Journal of Economics*, 112(2), 407–441.

28 **An ambitious daily caloric target:** Uetake, K., and Yang, N. (2017). Success Breeds Success: Weight Loss Dynamics in the Presence of Short-Term and Long-Term Goals. *Working Papers 170002*, Canadian Centre for Health Economics (Toronto).

29 **"What the hell effect":** Cochran, W., and Tesser, A. (1996). The "what the hell" effect: Some effects of goal proximity and goal framing on performance. In L. L. Martin and A. Tesser (Eds.), *Striving and Feeling: Interactions Among Goals, Affect, and Self-Regulation* (99–120). Hillsdale, NJ: Lawrence Erlbaum Associates, Inc.

29 **"False-hope syndrome":** Polivy, J., and Herman, C. P. (2000). The false-hope syndrome: Unfulfilled expectations of self-change. *Current Directions in Psychological Science*, 9(4), 128–131.

29 **Fantasize instead of work to achieve the goal:** Oettingen, G., and Sevincer, A. T. (2018). Fantasy about the future as friend and foe. In G. Oettingen, A. T. Sevincer, and P. Gollwitzer (Eds.), *The Psychology of Thinking About the Future* (127–149). New York: Guilford Press.

CHAPTER 3

34 **Finding the right thing to reward:** Kerr, S. (1995). On the folly of rewarding A, while hoping for B. *Academy of Management Perspectives*, 9(1), 7–14.

36 In the play *Antigone*, Sophocles wrote around 440 BC: "For no man delights in the bearer of bad news."

37 "Overjustification effect": Lepper, M. R., Greene, D., and Nisbett, R. E. (1973). Undermining children's intrinsic interest with extrinsic reward: A test of the "overjustification" hypothesis. *Journal of Personality and Social Psychology*, 28(1), 129–137.

37 **Any added incentive, whether external or internal, can undermine the original one:** Higgins, E. T., Lee, J., Kwon, J., and Trope, Y. (1995). When combining intrinsic motivations undermines interest: A test of activity engagement theory. *Journal of Personality and Social Psychology*, 68(5), 749–767.

38 **A snack that serves multiple purposes:** Maimaran, M., and Fishbach, A. (2014). If it's useful and you know it, do you eat? Preschoolers refrain from instrumental food. *Journal of Consumer Research*, 41(3), 642–655.

39 **Advertising food as healthy can also make adults lose their appetite:** Turnwald, B. P., Bertoldo, J. D., Perry, M. A., Policastro, P., Timmons, M., Bosso, C., ... and Crum, A. J. (2019). Increasing vegetable intake by emphasizing tasty and enjoyable attributes: A randomized controlled multisite intervention for taste-focused labeling. *Psychological Science* 30(11), 1603–1615.

41 **Did not select the laser pen when signing their name:** Zhang, Y., Fishbach, A., and Kruglanski, A. W. (2007). The dilution model: How additional goals undermine the perceived instrumentality of a shared path. *Journal of Personality and Social Psychology*, 92(3), 389–401.

44 **Paying kids to play with blocks:** Kruglanski, A. W., Riter, A., Arazi, D., Agassi, R., Montegio, J., Peri, I., and Peretz, M. (1975). Effect of task-intrinsic rewards upon extrinsic and intrinsic motivation. *Journal of Personality and Social Psychology*, 31(4), 699–705.

48 **More people drank the water within the time limit when assigned an uncertain reward:** Shen, L., Fishbach, A., and Hsee, C. K. (2015). The motivating-uncertainty effect: Uncertainty increases resource investment in the process of reward pursuit. *Journal of Consumer Research*, 41(5), 1301–1315.

CHAPTER 4

51 **The number of hours firefighters work:** Grant, A. M. (2008). Does intrinsic motivation fuel the prosocial fire? Motivational synergy in predicting persistence, performance, and productivity. *Journal of Applied Psychology*, 93(1), 48.

51 **The creativity security officers display at work:** Grant, A. M., and Berry, J. W. (2011). The necessity of others is the mother of invention: Intrinsic and prosocial motivations, perspective taking, and creativity. *Academy of management journal*, 54(1), 73-96.

51 **New Year's resolutions:** Woolley, K., and Fishbach, A. (2017). Immediate rewards predict adherence to long-term goals. *Personality and Social Psychology Bulletin*, 43(2), 151–162.

54 **Innate and learned motives:** Ryan, R. M., and Deci, E. L. (2000). Self-determination theory and the facilitation of intrinsic motivation, social development, and well-being. *American Psychologist*, 55(1), 68–78.

58 **When it's served with a joke:** Woolley, K., and Fishbach, A. (2018). It's about time: Earlier rewards increase intrinsic motivation. *Journal of Personality and Social Psychology*, 114(6), 877–890.

59 **The game added 144 billion steps across the US:** Althoff, T., White, R. W., and Horvitz, E. (2016). Influence of Pokémon Go on physical activity: Study and implications. *Journal of Medical Internet Research*, 18(12), e315.

60 **"Temptation bundling":** Milkman, K. L., Minson, J. A., and Volpp, K. G. (2013). Holding the Hunger Games hostage at the gym: An evaluation of temptation bundling. *Management Science*, 60(2), 283–299.

60 **Gymgoers who chose a weight-lifting exercise they enjoyed:** Woolley, K., and Fishbach, A. (2016). For the fun of it: Harnessing immediate rewards to increase persistence on long-term goals. *Journal of Consumer Research*, 42(6), 952–966.

62 **Even convicted prisoners rated themselves as more moral:**

Sedikides, C., Meek, R., Alicke, M. D., and Taylor, S. (2014). Behind bars but above the bar: Prisoners consider themselves more prosocial than non-prisoners. *British Journal of Social Psychology,* 53(2), 396–403.

63 **Not realizing that others want to be intrinsically motivated:** Heath, C. (1999). On the social psychology of agency relationships: Lay theories of motivation overemphasize extrinsic incentives. *Organizational Behavior and Human Decision Processes,* 78, 25–62.

63 **Job candidates underemphasize intrinsic motivation:** Woolley, K., and Fishbach, A. (2018). Underestimating the importance of expressing intrinsic motivation in job interviews. *Organizational Behavior and Human Decision Processes,* 148, 1–11.

64 **Predicted they would care more about money than sound:** Woolley, K., and Fishbach, A. (2015). The experience matters more than you think: People value intrinsic incentives more inside than outside an activity. *Journal of Personality and Social Psychology,* 109(6), 968–982.

PART II

CHAPTER 5

71 **"Goal gradient effect":** Hull, C. L. (1932). The goal-gradient hypothesis and maze learning. *Psychological Review,* 39(1), 25–43.

72 **Consider college dropouts:** Shapiro, D., Dundar, A., Huie, F., Wakhungu, P. K., Bhimdiwala, A., and Wilson, S. E. (December 2018). Completing College: A National View of Student Completion Rates—Fall 2012 Cohort (Signature Report No. 16). Herndon, VA: National Student Clearinghouse Research Center.

73 **Partnered with a New York café to test the motivating effect of illusory progress:** Kivetz, R., Urminsky, O., and Zheng, Y.

(2006). The goal-gradient hypothesis resurrected: Purchase acceleration, illusionary goal progress, and customer retention. *Journal of Marketing Research*, 43(1), 39–58.

76 **"Sunk-cost fallacy":** Arkes, H. R., and Blumer, C. (1985). The psychology of sunk costs. *Organizational Behavior and Human Decision Processes*, 35, 124–140;

76 **Sunk-cost fallacy:** Thaler, R. H. (1999). Mental accounting matters. *Journal of Behavioral Decision Making*, 12, 183–206.

76 **Humans, rats, and mice:** Sweis, B. M., Abram, S. V., Schmidt, B. J., Seeland, K. D., MacDonald, A. W., Thomas, M. J., and Redish, A. D. (2018). Sensitivity to "sunk costs" in mice, rats, and humans. *Science*, 361(6398), 178–181.

78 **Cognitive dissonance theory:** Festinger, L. (1957). A *Theory of Cognitive Dissonance*. Palo Alto, CA: Stanford University Press.

78 **More men than women oppose abortion rights:** https://news.gallup.com/poll/244709/pro-choice-pro-life-2018-demographic-tables.aspx.

78 **Self-perception theory:** Bem, D. J. (1972). Self-perception theory. In *Advances in Experimental Social Psychology* (Vol. 6, 1–62). Cambridge, MA: Academic Press.

79 **"Foot-in-the-door":** Freedman, J. L., and Fraser, S. C. (1966). Compliance without pressure: The foot-in-the-door technique. *Journal of Personality and Social Psychology*, 4(2), 195–202.

80 **Those who realized they had already covered half of their study materials:** Koo, M., and Fishbach, A. (2008). Dynamics of self-regulation: How (un)accomplished goal actions affect motivation. *Journal of Personality and Social Psychology*, 94(2), 183–195.

81 **Cybernetic models:** Wiener, N. (1948). *Cybernetics: Control and Communication in the Animal and the Machine*. Cambridge, MA: MIT Press.

83 **Progress will inform the specific feelings:** Carver, C. S., and Scheier, M. F. (2012). Cybernetic control processes and the

self-regulation of behavior. In R. M. Ryan (Ed.), Oxford Library of Psychology. *The Oxford Handbook of Human Motivation* (28–42). New York: Oxford University Press.

84 **College students who were on a diet:** Louro, M. J., Pieters, R., and Zeelenberg, M. (2007). Dynamics of multiple-goal pursuit. *Journal of Personality and Social Psychology*, 93(2), 174.

84 **Memorize details such as the place of origin and the vintage of the wine from several wine labels:** Huang, S. C., and Zhang, Y. (2011). Motivational consequences of perceived velocity in consumer goal pursuit. *Journal of Marketing Research*, 48(6), 1045–1056.

CHAPTER 6

89 **Social organizations also vary by the dynamic they advise you to follow:** These examples are based on conversation with Drazen Prelec at MIT.

90 **Progress or merely looking back motivated people differently:** Koo, M., and Fishbach, A. (2010). A silver lining of standing in line: Queuing increases value of products. *Journal of Marketing Research*, 47, 713–724.

93 **Reflecting on what they would like to achieve in the future made people more ambitious:** Koo, M., and Fishbach, A. (2010). Climbing the goal ladder: How upcoming actions increase level of aspiration. *Journal of Personality and Social Psychology*, 99(1), 1–13.

97 **From assessing the goal to pushing forward:** Kruglanski, A. W., Thompson, E. P., Higgins, E. T., Atash, M. N., Pierro, A., Shah, J. Y., and Spiegel, S. (2000). To "do the right thing" or to "just do it": Locomotion and assessment as distinct self-regulatory imperatives. *Journal of Personality and Social Psychology*, 79(5), 793–815.

97 **From deliberating to implementing action plans:** Gollwitzer, P. M., Heckhausen, H., and Ratajczak, H. (1990). From weighing to willing: Approaching a change decision through pre- or

postdecisional mentation. *Organizational Behavior and Human Decision Processes*, 45(1), 41–65.

CHAPTER 7

103 **Naïve test makers hide the correct answer in the middle:** Bar-Hillel, M. (2015). Position effects in choice from simultaneous displays: A conundrum solved. *Perspectives on Psychological Science*, 10(4), 419–433.

103 **"Recency effect":** Greene, R. L. (1986). Sources of recency effects in free-recall. *Psychological Bulletin*, 99(2), 221–228.

104 **In the middle of pursuing a goal, people literally cut corners:** Touré-Tillery, M., and Fishbach, A. (2012). The end justifies the means, but only in the middle. *Journal of Experimental Psychology: General*, 141(3), 570–583.

107 **The small-area principle:** Koo, M., and Fishbach, A. (2012). The small-area hypothesis: Effects of progress monitoring on goal adherence. *Journal of Consumer Research*, 39(3), 493–509.

108 **"Fresh start effect":** Dai, H., Milkman, K. L., and Riis, J. (2014). The fresh start effect: Temporal landmarks motivate aspirational behavior. *Management Science*, 60(10), 2563–2582.

108 **People ate the healthiest food in January:** Cherchye, L., De Rock, B., Griffith, R., O'Connell, M., Smith, K., and Vermeulen, F. (2020). A new year, a new you? A two-selves model of within-individual variation in food purchases. *European Economic Review*, 127.

CHAPTER 8

111 **"Prospect theory":** Kahneman, D., and Tversky, A. (1979). Prospect Theory: An Analysis of Decision under Risk. *Econometrica*, 47(2), 263–291.

111 **Fewer people learned from the negative:** Eskreis-Winkler, L., and Fishbach, A. (2019). Not learning from failure—The greatest failure of all. *Psychological Science*, 30(12), 1733–1744.

112 **"History teaches, but it has no pupils"**: Gramsci, A. (1977). *Selections from political writings (1910–1920)* (Q. Hoare, Ed., J. Mathews, Trans.). London: Lawrence and Wishart.

113 **Learners learned more if they guessed the right answer**: Eskreis-Winkler, L., and Fishbach, A. (2019). Not learning from failure—The greatest failure of all. *Psychological Science*, 30(12), 1733–1744.

113 **This investor might build up false confidence**: Gervais, S., and Odean, T. (2001). Learning to be overconfident. *Review of Financial Studies*, 14(1), 1–27.

114 **"ostrich effect"**: Diamond, E. (1976). Ostrich effect. *Harper's*, 252, 105–106.

114 **Stick our heads in the sand**: Webb, T. L., Chang, B. P., and Benn, Y. (2013). "The Ostrich Problem": Motivated avoidance or rejection of information about goal progress. *Social and Personality Psychology Compass*, 7(11), 794–807.

114 **Investors avoid checking their accounts after market declines**: Sicherman, N., Loewenstein, G., Seppi, D. J., and Utkus, S. P. (2015). Financial attention. *Review of Financial Studies*, 29(4), 863–897.

116 **Assume you're selecting one of three boxes, each containing some unknown amount of money**: Eskreis-Winkler, L., and Fishbach, A. (2020). Hidden failures. *Organizational Behavior and Human Decision Processes*, 157, 57–67.

119 **Three groups of dogs**: Seligman, M. E., and Maier, S. F. (1967). Failure to escape traumatic shock. *Journal of Experimental Psychology*, 74(1), 1–9.

119 **Similar experiments with humans**: Hiroto, D. S., and Seligman, M. E. (1975). Generality of learned helplessness in man. *Journal of Personality and Social Psychology*, 31(2), 311–327.

121 **"Growth mind-set"**: Dweck, C. S. (2008). *Mindset: The New Psychology of Success*. Random House Digital, Inc.

122 **Experts and novices respond to feedback**: Finkelstein, S. R.,

and Fishbach, A. (2012). Tell me what I did wrong: Experts seek and respond to negative feedback. *Journal of Consumer Research,* 39, 22–38.

124 **How employees give feedback in the workplace:** Finkelstein, S. R., Fishbach, A., and Tu, Y. (2017). When friends exchange negative feedback. *Motivation and Emotion,* 41, 69–83.

126 **Helped ninth graders who had low GPAs get better grades:** Yeager et al. (2019). A national experiment reveals where a growth mindset improves achievement. *Nature,* 573, 364–369.

126 **The power of giving advice:** Eskreis-Winkler, L., Fishbach, A., and Duckworth, A. (2018). Dear Abby: Should I give advice or receive it? *Psychological Science,* 29(11), 1797–1806.

129 **Which information to share with another person:** Eskreis-Winkler, L., and Fishbach, A. (2020). Hidden failures. *Organizational Behavior and Human Decision Processes,* 157, 57–67.

130 **Negative information on failure is unique:** Koch, A., Alves, H., Krüger, T., and Unkelbach, C. (2016). A general valence asymmetry in similarity: Good is more alike than bad. *Journal of Experimental Psychology: Learning, Memory, and Cognition,* 42(8), 1171–1192.

132 **More words to describe negative emotions:** Rozin, P., and Royzman, E. B. (2001). Negativity bias, negativity dominance, and contagion. *Personality and Social Psychology Review,* 5(4), 296–320.

133 **Those who read negative reviews had an easier time identifying which restaurant was best:** Eskreis-Winkler, L., and Fishbach, A. (2020). Predicting success. Working paper.

PART III

135 **Half of Americans don't have enough time in the day:** https://news.gallup.com/poll/187982/americans-perceived-time-crunch-no-worse-past.aspx.

CHAPTER 9

142 **And those who listed their goals for the day identified even fewer acceptable lunch options:** Köpetz, C., Faber, T., Fishbach, A., and Kruglanski, A. W. (2011). The multifinality constraints effect: How goal multiplicity narrows the means set to a focal end. *Journal of Personality and Social Psychology,* 100(5), 810–826.

143 **When a new gym user learns about the variety of exercising options:** Etkin, J., and Ratner, R. K. (2012). The dynamic impact of variety among means on motivation. *Journal of Consumer Research,* 38(6), 1076–1092.

145 **Advertising ice cream as kosher reduced nonobservant consumers' interest in it:** Simonson, I., Nowlis, S. M., and Simonson, Y. (1993). The effect of irrelevant preference arguments on consumer choice. *Journal of Consumer Psychology,* 2(3), 287–306.

145 **A mouthwash that causes an unpleasant burning sensation is better:** Schumpe, B. M., Bélanger, J. J., Dugas, M., Erb, H. P., and Kruglanski, A. W. (2018). Counterfinality: On the increased perceived instrumentality of means to a goal. *Frontiers in Psychology,* 9, 1052.

147 **"licensing behavior":** Monin, B., and Miller, D. T. (2001). Moral credentials and the expression of prejudice. *Journal of Personality and Social Psychology,* 81(1), 33–43.

148 **Licensed to make ambiguously racist statements:** Effron, D. A., Cameron, J. S., and Monin, B. (2009). Endorsing Obama licenses favoring whites. *Journal of Experimental Social Psychology,* 45(3), 590–593.

150 **Compromising versus prioritizing in snack selections:** Shaddy, F., Fishbach, A., and Simonson, I. (2021). Trade-offs in choice. *Annual Review of Psychology,* 72, 181–206.

151 **"Taboo trade-offs":** Tetlock, P. E., Kristel, O. V., Elson, S. B., Green, M. C., and Lerner, J. S. (2000). The psychology of the unthinkable: Taboo trade-offs, forbidden base rates, and heretical

counterfactuals. *Journal of Personality and Social Psychology,* 78(5), 853–870.

CHAPTER 10

157 **Feel some desire about half the time you're awake:** Hofmann, W., Baumeister, R. F., Förster, G., and Vohs, K. D. (2012). Everyday temptations: An experience sampling study of desire, conflict, and self-control. *Journal of Personality and Social Psychology,* 102(6), 1318–1335.

158 **People who report having strong self-control:** de Ridder, D. T., Lensvelt-Mulders, G., Finkenauer, C., Stok, F. M., and Baumeister, R. F. (2012). Taking stock of self-control: A meta-analysis of how trait self-control relates to a wide range of behaviors. *Personality and Social Psychology Review,* 16(1), 76–99.

158 **The development of self-control:** Allemand, M., Job, V., and Mroczek, D. K. (2019). Self-control development in adolescence predicts love and work in adulthood. *Journal of Personality and Social Psychology,* 117(3), 621–634.

159 **Self-control gets easier as we grow older:** Casey, B. J., and Caudle, K. (2013). The teenage brain: Self control. *Current Directions in Psychological Science,* 22(2), 82–87.

162 **How likely they'd be to engage in various questionable work-related behaviors:** Sheldon, O. J., and Fishbach, A. (2015). Anticipating and resisting the temptation to behave unethically. *Personality and Social Psychology Bulletin,* 41(7), 962–975.

164 **Separate bowls indicated separate purposes:** Fishbach, A., and Zhang, Y. (2008). Together or apart: When goals and temptations complement versus compete. *Journal of Personality and Social Psychology,* 94(4), 547–559.

165 **Connected to your future self:** Parfit, D. (1984). *Reasons and Persons.* Oxford: Oxford University Press.

166 **Seniors who read that graduation would change them felt less**

connected: Bartels, D. M., and Urminsky, O. (2011). On inter-temporal selfishness: How the perceived instability of identity underlies impatient consumption. *Journal of Consumer Research*, 38(1), 182–198.

168 **Once binge-drinking is associated with an identity you don't hold:** Berger, J., and Rand, L. (2008). Shifting signals to help health: Using identity signaling to reduce risky health behaviors. *Journal of Consumer Research*, 35(3), 509–518.

168 **Relax their financial goal in the middle of the year:** Touré-Tillery, M., and Fishbach, A. (2015). It was(n't) me: Exercising restraint when choices appear self-diagnostic. *Journal of Personality and Social Psychology*, 109(6), 1117–1131.

169 **Identity fuels our motivation:** Oyserman, D., Fryberg, S. A., and Yoder, N. (2007). Identity-based motivation and health. *Journal of Personality and Social Psychology*, 93(6), 1011–1027.

171 **Those who expected to have a hard time planned to work harder:** Zhang, Y., and Fishbach, A. (2010). Counteracting obstacles with optimistic predictions. *Journal of Experimental Psychology: General*, 139(1), 16–31.

172 **Making compensation contingent on completing the exam:** Trope, Y., and Fishbach, A. (2000). Counteractive self-control in overcoming temptation. *Journal of Personality and Social Psychology*, 79(4), 493–506.

172 **Imposing penalties on yourself:** Giné, X., Karlan, D., and Zinman, J. (2010). Put your money where your butt is: A commitment contract for smoking cessation. *American Economic Journal: Applied Economics*, 2(4), 213–235.

175 **How much more appealing was the health bar compared to the chocolate bar?:** Myrseth, K. O., Fishbach, A., and Trope, Y. (2009). Counteractive self-control: When making temptation available makes temptation less tempting. *Psychological Science*, 20(2), 159–163.

176 **"Distanced self-talk":** Kross, E., Bruehlman-Senecal, E., Park,

J., Burson, A., Dougherty, A., Shablack, H., ... and Ayduk, O. (2014). Self-talk as a regulatory mechanism: How you do it matters. *Journal of Personality and Social Psychology*, 106(2), 304–324.

176 **How three-to-five-year-old children resist eating marshmallows:** Mischel, W., and Baker, N. (1975). Cognitive appraisals and transformations in delay behavior. *Journal of Personality and Social Psychology*, 31(2), 254.

177 **Thinking about temptation first:** Zhang, Y., and Fishbach, A. (2010). Counteracting obstacles with optimistic predictions. *Journal of Experimental Psychology: General*, 139(1), 16–31.

177 **"Ego depletion":** Baumeister, R. F., Tice, D. M., and Vohs, K. D. (2018). The strength model of self-regulation: Conclusions from the second decade of willpower research. *Perspectives on Psychological Science*, 13(2), 141–145.

177 **Skip mandatory hand-washing:** Dai, H., Milkman, K. L., Hofmann, D. A., and Staats, B. R. (2015). The impact of time at work and time off from work on rule compliance: The case of hand hygiene in healthcare. *Journal of Applied Psychology*, 100(3), 846–862.

177 **Prescribe unnecessary antibiotics:** Linder, J. A., Doctor, J. N., Friedberg, M. W., Nieva, H. R., Birks, C., Meeker, D., and Fox, C. R. (2014). Time of day and the decision to prescribe antibiotics. *JAMA Internal Medicine*, 174(12), 2029–2031.

179 **Faster to read their goal words after the temptation words were briefly flashed in the same location:** Fishbach, A., Friedman, R. S., and Kruglanski, A. W. (2003). Leading us not unto temptation: Momentary allurements elicit overriding goal activation. *Journal of Personality and Social Psychology*, 84(2), 296–309.

179 **Those with better self-control were able to draw straighter lines:** Stillman, P. E., Medvedev, D., and Ferguson, M. J. (2017). Resisting temptation: Tracking how self-control conflicts are successfully resolved in real time. *Psychological Science*, 28(9), 1240–1258.

180 **Once you've formed a habit, the context triggers your behavior directly:** Wood, W., and Neal, D. T. (2007). A new look at habits and the habit-goal interface. *Psychological Review*, 114(4), 843–863.

180 **A simple implementation plan can go a long way:** Gollwitzer, P. M. (1999). Implementation intentions: Strong effects of simple plans. *American Psychologist*, 54(7), 493-503.

CHAPTER 11

183 **Preschoolers who had been able to be patient in the face of a tempting marshmallow were doing better:** Mischel, W., Shoda, Y., and Rodriguez, M. L. (1989). Delay of gratification in children. *Science*, 244(4907), 933–938.

183 **These marshmallow test data have been analyzed several times:** Watts, T. W., Duncan, G. J., and Quan, H. (2018). Revisiting the marshmallow test: A conceptual replication investigating links between early delay of gratification and later outcomes. *Psychological Science*, 29(7), 1159–1177.

186 **Children's cognitive ability predicted the amount of time they could wait:** Duckworth, A. L., Tsukayama, E., and Kirby, T. A. (2013). Is it really self-control? Examining the predictive power of the delay of gratification task. *Personality and Social Psychology Bulletin*, 39(7), 843–855.

186 **A recent reanalysis Walter Mischel and his colleagues published after he passed:** Benjamin, D. J., Laibson, D., Mischel, W., Peake, P. K., Shoda, Y., Wellsjo, A. S., and Wilson, N. L. (2020). Predicting mid-life capital formation with pre-school delay of gratification and life-course measures of self-regulation. *Journal of Economic Behavior and Organization*, 179, 743–756.

187 **Trust that waiting will pay off:** McGuire, J. T., and Kable, J. W. (2013). Rational temporal predictions can underlie apparent failures to delay gratification. *Psychological Review*, 120(2), 395–410.

188 **How patient love (or even just liking something) can be:**

Roberts, A., Shaddy, F., and Fishbach, A. (2020). Love is patient: People are more willing to wait for things they like. *Journal of Experimental Psychology: General.*

189 **Desire for a consumer product changes over time:** Dai, X., and Fishbach, A. (2014). How non-consumption shapes desire. *Journal of Consumer Research*, 41(4), 936–952.

190 **People are also impatient to close debts:** Roberts, A., Imas, A., and Fishbach, A. Can't wait to lose: The desire for goal closure increases impatience to incur costs. Working paper.

193 **"Hyperbolic discounting":** Ainslie, G. (1975). Specious reward: a behavioral theory of impulsiveness and impulse control. *Psychological Bulletin*, 82(4), 463–496.

193 **The pigeons were impatient:** Rachlin, H., and Green, L. (1972). Commitment, choice and self-control. *Journal of the Experimental Analysis of Behavior*, 17(1), 15–22.

194 **Those who waited thirteen days before choosing were more likely to wait:** Dai, X., and Fishbach, A. (2013). When waiting to choose increases patience. *Organizational Behavior and Human Decision Processes*, 121, 256–266.

195 **Using virtual reality to generate an image of themselves at age seventy:** Hershfield, H. E., Goldstein, D. G., Sharpe, W. F., Fox, J., Yeykeelis, L., Carstensen, L. L., and Bailenson, J. N. (2011). Increasing saving behavior through age-progressed renderings of the future self. *Journal of Marketing Research*, 48, S23–S37.

195 **Writing a letter to their future self:** Rutchick, A. M., Slepian, M. L., Reyes, M. O., Pleskus, L. N., and Hershfield, H. E. (2018). Future self-continuity is associated with improved health and increases exercise behavior. *Journal of Experimental Psychology: Applied*, 24(1), 72–80.

196 **The children got the larger-later reward only if both independently decided to wait:** Koomen, R., Grueneisen, S., and Herrmann, E. (2020). Children delay gratification for cooperative ends. *Psychological Science*, 31(2), 139–148.

PART IV

201 **Solitary confinement has been identified as a major cause of mental illness:** Holt-Lunstad, J., Smith, T. B., Baker, M., Harris, T., and Stephenson, D. (2015). Loneliness and social isolation as risk factors for mortality: A meta-analytic review. *Perspectives on Psychological Science,* 10(2), 227–237.

CHAPTER 12

205 **Solomon Asch sought to bring conformity to the lab:** Asch, S. E. (1956). Studies of independence and conformity: I. A minority of one against a unanimous majority. *Psychological Monographs: General and Applied,* 70(9), 1–70.

207 **A tarantula crawls on someone's neck:** Keysers, C., Wicker, B., Gazzola, V., Anton, J. L., Fogassi, L., and Gallese, V. (2004). A touching sight: SII/PV activation during the observation and experience of touch. *Neuron,* 42(2), 335–346.

209 **Willing to hire a less-qualified white person over a more-qualified Black person:** Kouchaki, M. (2011). Vicarious moral licensing: The influence of others' past moral actions on moral behavior. *Journal of Personality and Social Psychology,* 101(4), 702–715.

210 **Compared conformity to others' stated goals to conformity to their taken actions:** Tu, Y., and Fishbach, A. (2015). Words speak louder: Conforming to preferences more than actions. *Journal of Personality and Social Psychology,* 109(2), 193–209.

212 **A group of friends at a restaurant will often order different dishes and drinks:** Ariely, D., and Levav, J. (2000). Sequential choice in group settings: Taking the road less traveled and less enjoyed. *Journal of Consumer Research,* 27(3), 279–290.

213 **Cyclists racing against each other are faster:** Triplett, N. (1898). The dynamogenic factors in pacemaking and competition. *American Journal of Psychology,* 9(4), 507–533.

214 **People believed that the amount of food they ate in public was**

larger than how much they ate alone: Steinmetz, J., Xu, Q., Fishbach. A., and Zhang, Y. (2016). Being Observed Magnifies Action. *Journal of Personality and Social Psychology*, 111(6), 852–865.

CHAPTER 13

216 **How hard people worked when others were helping:** Ringelmann, M. (1913). "Recherches sur les moteurs animés: Travail de l'homme" [Research on animate sources of power: The work of man], *Annales de l'Institut National Agronomique*, 2nd series, vol. 12, 1–40.

219 **Clap their hands and shout out loud in a group:** Latané, B., Williams, K., and Harkins, S. (1979). Many hands make light the work: The causes and consequences of social loafing. *Journal of Personality and Social Psychology*, 37(6), 822–832.

220 **Owning the pen made pen donation feel more meaningful:** Koo, M., and Fishbach, A. (2016). Giving the self: Increasing commitment and generosity through giving something that represents one's essence. *Social Psychological and Personality Science*, 7(4), 339–348.

222 **Teams made of true couples outperformed strangers:** Wegner, D. M., Erber, R., and Raymond, P. (1991). Transactive memory in close relationships. *Journal of Personality and Social Psychology*, 61(6), 923–929.

222 **They gain financial knowledge only if they're the ones in charge:** Ward, A. F., and Lynch, J. G. Jr. (2019). On a need-to-know basis: How the distribution of responsibility between couples shapes financial literacy and financial outcomes. *Journal of Consumer Research*, 45(5), 1013–1036.

225 **The closer people were to their friend, the more likely they were to opt for the self-benefiting package:** Tu, Y., Shaw., A., and Fishbach, A. (2016). The friendly taking effect: How interpersonal closeness leads to seemingly selfish yet jointly maximizing choice. *Journal of Consumer Research*, 42(5), 669–687.

228 **Donations to a charity designed to help orphans of the HIV epidemic:** Koo, M., and Fishbach, A. (2008). Dynamics of self-regulation: How (un)accomplished goal actions affect motivation. *Journal of Personality and Social Psychology,* 94(2), 183–195.

228 **Student groups generated marketing ideas for products like cell phones and protein bars:** Fishbach, A., Henderson, D. H., and Koo, M. (2011). Pursuing goals with others: Group identi-fication and motivation resulting from things done versus things left undone. *Journal of Experimental Psychology: General,* 140(3), 520–534.

CHAPTER 14

235 **Goal progress influences relationship strength:** Fitzsimons, G. M., and Fishbach, A. (2010). Shifting closeness: Interpersonal effects of personal goal progress. *Journal of Personality and Social Psychology,* 98(4), 535–549.

236 **A trivia game styled after *Who Wants to Be a Millionaire*:** Converse, B. A., and Fishbach, A. (2012). Instrumentality boosts appreciation: Helpers are more appreciated while they are useful. *Psychological Science,* 23(6), 560–566.

239 **A joint goal system:** Fitzsimons, G. M., Finkel, E. J., and Vandellen, M. R. (2015). Transactive goal dynamics. *Psychological Review,* 122(4), 648-673.

240 **College students who were reminded of their parents' support:** Fishbach, A., and Trope, Y. (2005). The substitutability of ex-ternal control and self-control. *Journal of Experimental Social Psychology,* 41(3), 256–270.

241 **Children rely on basic goals to create a social bond:** Fawcett, C. A., and Markson, L. (2010). Similarity predicts liking in 3-year-old children. *Journal of Experimental Child Psychology,* 105(4), 345–358.

241 **Strangers who ate similar foods trusted each other:** Woolley, K.,

and Fishbach, A. (2019). Shared plates, shared minds: Consuming from a shared plate promotes cooperation. *Psychological Science*, 30(4), 541–552.

241 **People who cannot share a meal:** Woolley, K., Fishbach, A., and Wang, M. (2020). Food restriction and the experience of social isolation. *Journal of Personality and Social Psychology*, 119(3), 657–671.

242 **Social isolation is comparable with smoking:** Holt-Lunstad, J., Smith, T. B., and Layton, J. B. (2010). Social relationships and mortality risk: a meta-analytic review. *PLOS Medicine*, 7(7), e1000316.

243 **Participants predicted their partner's answers:** Swann, W. B., and Gill, M. J. (1997). Confidence and accuracy in person perception: Do we know what we think we know about our relationship partners? *Journal of Personality and Social Psychology*, 73(4), 747–757.

243 **People overestimate how well others know them:** Kenny, D. A., and DePaulo, B. M. (1993). Do people know how others view them? An empirical and theoretical account. *Psychological Bulletin*, 114(1), 145.

244 **Feeling known and knowing someone:** Schroeder, J., and Fishbach, A. (2020). It's not you, it's me: Feeling known enhances relationship satisfaction more than knowing.

245 **Empty-vessel perceptions:** Schroeder, J., and Fishbach, A. (2015). The "empty vessel" physician: physicians' instrumentality makes them seem personally empty. *Social Psychological and Personality Science*, 6(8), 940–949.

246 **Women internalize the perspective of those who objectify them:** Fredrickson, B. L., and Roberts, T. A. (1997). Objectification theory: Toward understanding women's lived experiences and mental health risks. *Psychology of Women Quarterly*, 21(2), 173–206.

INDEX

ABOUT THE AUTHOR

Ayelet Fishbach is an award-winning psychologist at the University of Chicago Booth School of Business, and the past president of the Society for the Science of Motivation and the International Social Cognition Network (ISCON). She is an expert on motivation and decision making.

She has published over one hundred scientific articles in many psychology and business journals, including *Psychological Review*, *Psychological Science*, and the *Journal of Personality and Social Psychology*. Her research is regularly featured in the media, including the *Wall Street Journal*, CNN, the *Chicago Tribune*, and NPR, and was selected to be featured in the *New York Times's* annual Year in Ideas.

Fishbach's groundbreaking research on human motivation has won the Society of Experimental Social Psychology's Best Dissertation Award and Career Trajectory Award, and the Fulbright Educational Foundation Award. She received the Provost's Teaching Award from the University of Chicago. She earned a PhD in psychology from Tel Aviv University.